Practice*Planners*®

Arthur E. Jongsma, Jr., Series Editor

Helping therapists help their clients . . .

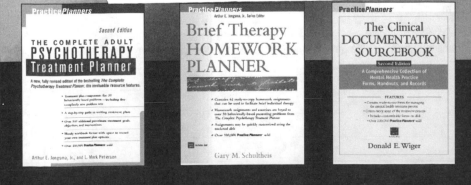

Practice*Planners*

Second Edition

THE COMPLETE ADULT
PSYCHOTHERAPY
Treatment Planner

A new, fully revised edition of the bestselling *The Complete Psychotherapy Treatment Planner*, this invaluable resource features:

- Treatment plan components for 35 behaviorally based problems—including five completely new problem sets
- A step-by-step guide to writing treatment plans
- Over 500 additional prewritten treatment goals, objectives, and instructions
- Handy workbook format with space to record your own treatment plan options
- Over 100,000 *Practice Planners* sold

Arthur E. Jongsma, Jr., and L. Mark Peterson

Practice*Planners* Arthur E. Jongsma, Jr., Series Editor

Brief Therapy
HOMEWORK
PLANNER

- Contains 62 ready-to-copy homework assignments that can be used to facilitate brief individual therapy
- Homework assignments and exercises are keyed to over 30 behaviorally-based presenting problems from *The Complete Psychotherapy Treatment Planner*
- Assignments may be quickly customized using the enclosed disk
- Over 100,000 *Practice Planners* sold

Gary M. Schultheis

Practice*Planners*

The Clinical
DOCUMENTATION
SOURCEBOOK

Second Edition

A Comprehensive Collection of
Mental Health Practice
Forms, Handouts, and Records

FEATURES

- Contains ready-to-use forms for managing the mental health treatment process
- Covers every stage of the treatment process
- Includes customizable forms on disk
- Over 100,000 *Practice Planners* sold

Donald E. Wiger

Practice*Planners* Arthur E. Jongsma, Jr., Series Editor

The Adult Psychotherapy
PROGRESS NOTES PLANNER

This time-saving resource:

- Contains 1,000s of prewritten progress notes
- Covers every major presenting problem, including the disorders and treatments covered in *The Complete Adult Psychotherapy Treatment Planner*, Second Edition
- Uses a 1,000s-of-jot-writer phrases, and quickly customizable
- Over 100,000 *Practice Planners* sold

Arthur E. Jongsma, Jr.

Over 250,000 Practice*Planners*® sold . . .   🔹 **WILEY**

Practice*Planners*®   Order Form

Treatment Planners cover all the necessary elements for developing formal treatment plans, including detailed problem definitions, long-term goals, short-term objectives, therapeutic interventions, and DSM-IV™ diagnoses.

❑ **The Complete Adult Psychotherapy Treatment Planner,** Second Edition
    0-471-31924-4 / $44.95

❑ **The Child Psychotherapy Treatment Planner,** Second Edition
    0-471-34764-7 / $44.95

❑ **The Adolescent Psychotherapy Treatment Planner,** Second Edition
    0-471-34766-3 / $44.95

❑ **The Addiction Treatment Planner,** Second Edition
    0 471 41814 5 / $44.95

❑ **The Couples Psychotherapy Treatment Planner**
    0-471-24711-1 / $44.95

❑ **The Group Therapy Treatment Planner**
    0-471-37449-0 / $44.95

❑ **The Family Therapy Treatment Planner**
    0 471 34768-X / $44.95

❑ **The Older Adult Psychotherapy Treatment Planner**
    0-471-29574-4 / $44.95

❑ **The Employee Assistance (EAP) Treatment Planner**
    0-471-24709-X / $44.95

❑ **The Gay and Lesbian Psychotherapy Treatment Planner**
    0-471-35080-X / $44.95

❑ **The Crisis Counseling and Traumatic Events Treatment Planner**
    0-471-39587-0 / $44.95

❑ **The Social Work and Human Services Treatment Planner**
    0-471-37741-4 / $44.95

❑ **The Continuum of Care Treatment Planner**
    0-471-19568-5 / $44.95

❑ **The Behavioral Medicine Treatment Planner**
    0-471-31923-6 / $44.95

❑ **The Mental Retardation and Developmental Disability Treatment Planner**
    0-471-38253-1 / $44.95

❑ **The Special Education Treatment Planner**
    0-471-38872-6 / $44.95

❑ **The Severe and Persistent Mental Illness Treatment Planner**
    0-471-35945-9 / $44.95

❑ **The Personality Disorders Treatment Planner**
    0-471-39403-3 / $44.95

❑ **The Rehabilitation Psychology Treatment Planner**
    0-471-35178-4 / $44.95

❑ **The Pastoral Counseling Treatment Planner**
    0-471-25416-9 / $44.95

❑ **The Juvenile Justice Treatment Planner**
    0-471-43320-9 / $44.95

❑ **The Psychiatric Evaluation & Psychopharmacology Treatment Planner**
    0-471-43322-5 / $44.95 (available 2/02)

❑ **The Adult Corrections Treatment Planner**
    0-471-20244-4 / $44.95 (available 6/02)

❑ **The School Counseling and School Social Work Treatment Planner**
    0-471-08496-4 / $44.95 (available 8/02)

Progress Notes Planners contain complete prewritten progress notes for each presenting problem in the companion Treatment Planners.

❑ **The Adult Psychotherapy Progress Notes Planner**
    0-471-34763-9 / $44.95

❑ **The Adolescent Psychotherapy Progress Notes Planner**
    0-471-38104-7 / $44.95

❑ **The Child Psychotherapy Progress Notes Planner**
    0-471-38102-0 / $44.95

- -

Name_____

Affiliation_____

Address_____

City/State/Zip_____

Phone/Fax_____

E-mail_____

To order, call 1-800-225-5945
(Please refer to promo #1-4019 when ordering.)
Or send this page with payment* to:
John Wiley & Sons, Inc., Attn: J. Knott
605 Third Avenue, New York, NY 10158-0012

❑ Check enclosed   ❑ Visa   ❑ MasterCard   ❑ American Express
Card #_____

Expiration Date_____

Signature_____

On the web: practiceplanners.wiley.com   *Please add your local sales tax to all orders.

The
Special Education
Treatment Planner

PRACTICE*PLANNERS*® SERIES

Treatment *Planners*

The Continuum of Care Treatment Planner
The Couples Psychotherapy Treatment Planner
The Employee Assistance Treatment Planner
The Pastoral Counseling Treatment Planner
The Older Adult Psychotherapy Treatment Planner
The Complete Adult Psychotherapy Treatment Planner, 2e
The Behavioral Medicine Treatment Planner
The Group Therapy Treatment Planner
The Gay and Lesbian Psychotherapy Treatment Planner
The Child Psychotherapy Treatment Planner, 2e
The Adolescent Psychotherapy Treatment Planner, 2e
The Family Therapy Treatment Planner
The Severe and Persistent Mental Illness Treatment Planner
The Mental Retardation and Developmental Disability Treatment Planner
The Social Work and Human Services Treatment Planner
The Crisis Counseling and Traumatic Events Treatment Planner
The Personality Disorders Treatment Planner
The Rehabilitation Psychology Treatment Planner
The Addiction Treatment Planner, 2e
The Special Education Treatment Planner

Progress Notes *Planners*

The Child Psychotherapy Progress Notes Planner
The Adolescent Psychotherapy Progress Notes Planner
The Adult Psychotherapy Progress Notes Planner

Homework *Planners*

Brief Therapy Homework Planner
Brief Couples Therapy Homework Planner
Chemical Dependence Treatment Homework Planner
Brief Child Therapy Homework Planner
Brief Adolescent Therapy Homework Planner
Brief Employee Assistance Homework Planner
Brief Family Therapy Homework Planner

Documentation *Sourcebooks*

The Clinical Documentation Sourcebook
The Forensic Documentation Sourcebook
The Psychotherapy Documentation Primer
The Chemical Dependence Treatment Documentation Sourcebook
The Clinical Child Documentation Sourcebook
The Couple and Family Clinical Documentation Sourcebook
The Clinical Documentation Sourcebook, 2e
The Continuum of Care Clinical Documentation Sourcebook

PracticePlanners®
Arthur E. Jongsma, Jr., Series Editor

The Special Education Treatment Planner

Julie A. Winkelstern

Arthur E. Jongsma, Jr.

JOHN WILEY & SONS, INC.
New York • Chichester • Weinheim • Brisbane • Singapore • Toronto

This book is printed on acid-free paper. ♾

Published by John Wiley & Sons, Inc.

Published simultaneously in Canada.

This publication is designed to provide accurate and authoritative information in regard to the subject matter covered. It is sold with the understanding that the publisher is not engaged in rendering professional services. If legal, accounting, medical, psychological or any other expert assistance is required, the services of a competent professional person should be sought.

Designations used by companies to distinguish their products are often claimed as trademarks. In all instances where John Wiley & Sons, Inc. is aware of a claim, the product names appear in initial capital or all capital letters. Readers, however, should contact the appropriate companies for more complete information regarding trademarks and registration.

Library of Congress Cataloging-in-Publication Data:

Winkelstern, Julie A.
  The special education treatment planner / Julie A. Winkelstern, Arthur E. Jongsma, Jr.
    p.   cm. — (Practice planners series)
  ISBN 0-471-38872-6 (pbk. : alk. paper)
    1. Handicapped children—Education—United States—Handbooks, manuals, etc.   2. Disability evaluation—Handbooks, manuals, etc.   3. Special education—United States—Handbooks, manuals, etc.   I. Jongsma, Arthur E., 1943–   II. Title.   III. Practice planners.

LC4031 .W55   2001
371.9—dc21
                                                                                    2001026072

Printed in the United States of America.

10 9 8 7 6 5 4 3 2 1

To my lifelong, deeply respected, and beloved friend, Dr. Garrett Boersma, a very special educator of special educators.

Art Jongsma

To my supportive husband, David, and talented son, Ian, for their unwavering support of this endeavor, and to the many students who have taught me about the challenges of living with a disability.

Julie Winkelstern

CONTENTS

SERIES PREFACE

The practice of psychotherapy has a dimension that did not exist 30, 20, or even 15 years ago—accountability. Treatment programs, public agencies, clinics, and even group and solo practitioners must now justify the treatment of patients to outside review entities that control the payment of fees. This development has resulted in an explosion of paperwork.

Clinicians must now document what has been done in treatment, what is planned for the future, and what the anticipated outcomes of the interventions are. The books and software in this Practice Planner series are designed to help practitioners fulfill these documentation requirements efficiently and professionally.

The Practice Planner series is growing rapidly. It now includes not only the original *Complete Psychotherapy Treatment Planner* and the *Child and Adolescent Psychotherapy Treatment Planner,* but also Treatment Planners targeted to specialty areas of practice, including: chemical dependency, the continuum of care, couples therapy, employee assistance, behavioral medicine, therapy with older adults, pastoral counseling, family therapy, group therapy, neuropsychology, therapy with gays and lesbians, and more.

In addition to the Treatment Planners, the series also includes *TheraScribe®,* the latest version of the popular treatment planning, patient record-keeping software, as well as adjunctive books, such as the *Brief, Chemical Dependence, Couple, Child,* and *Adolescent Therapy Homework Planners, The Psychotherapy Documentation Primer,* and *Clinical, Forensic, Child, Couples and Family, Continuum of Care,* and *Chemical Dependence Documentation Sourcebooks*—containing forms and resources to aid in mental health practice management. The goal of the series is to provide practitioners with the resources they need in order to provide high-quality care in the era of accountability—or, to put it simply, we seek to help you spend more time on patients, and less time on paperwork.

ARTHUR E. JONGSMA, JR.
Grand Rapids, Michigan

ACKNOWLEDGMENTS

My indebtedness is to the many, many students and their families I have had the privilege of knowing and working with over the course of 26 years. Their courage and determination in facing the challenges of living with a disability has been a true and valuable education for me. I am indebted to the professional staff of outstanding special education teachers, teacher consultants, speech and language clinicians, school psychologists, school social workers, occupational therapists, and physical therapists with whom I have the honor of working every day. I am grateful for the dedication they bring, diligently serving in the school setting, the positive changes they bring to lives of children and adolescents with disabilities, and the many lessons they have taught me about best practices in providing quality interventions to students. My direct supervisor, Fred Wisniewski, from whom I learn every day a new focus or a new way to problem solve, has provided me with ongoing encouragement throughout the longevity of this project, for which I am most grateful. The kind words of enthusiasm from the office staff at my day job cannot be overlooked. Thank you to Gayle Sims, Glenna Bird, and Lisa Clemence for your interest in and frequent verbal support of this endeavor.

My most sincere thanks to Art Jongsma for giving me the opportunity to participate in this project. I am most appreciative for his patience, support, creativity, and vision in making this text a reality. I wish to thank William McInnis for suggesting to Art that I might be a viable candidate as a coauthor for this topic. My special thanks to Jennifer Bryne, whose endless dedication in competently, if not magically, making an organized script out of a sometimes tangled weave of writing, has been simply outstanding. I would like to thank the staff of Wiley, especially Kelly Franklin and Peggy Alexander, the editors of this work, for their valuable support. Finally, I recognize my family and extended family including, my mother Rena Buchholz, my aunt Virginia Howard, and my in-laws Phil and Bette Winkelstern for their ongoing enthusiasm, encouragement, patience, support and sacrifice throughout the duration of this project.

The
Special Education
Treatment Planner

INTRODUCTION

PLANNER FOCUS

The Special Education Treatment Planner is designed for all professionals working in the school setting who provide instruction, therapy, and support to students with special needs. It incorporates all special education categories recognized in the federal mandate, as well as other conditions and disorders frequently recognized among children and adolescents. The most common challenges for the student with a disability, for the parents, and for the school professionals are targeted within each chapter. These include issues presenting in the physical, cognitive, affective, behavioral, social, and neurological domains.

Interventions have been designed to offer the educational specialist a variety of workable, constructive, and meaningful strategies to improve the quality of the student's educational experience in a collaborative model involving the student, parents, and other school professionals. Emphasis is always on furthering the independence and personal competency of the student, regardless of the type or intensity of the disability. While many interventions focus on the student's functioning in the classroom, others expand the instruction into the community for opportunities in reality-based learning, whether it be for social skill development, attainment of daily living skills, or prevocational training.

The writing of quality educational treatment plans for students with disabilities based on specific, targeted areas of need can offer the school professional an essential tool in identifying meaningful and effective interventions. Further, it is our belief that in creating and following an individualized educational treatment plan, this process can enhance, and in many situations increase, the educational functioning and performance of the student.

HISTORY AND BACKGROUND

The inception and passage of the Education for All Handicapped Children Act (PL-142) in 1975 began a new era for students with disabilities in public schools in the United States. This federal law mandated the states to provide a free, appropriate public education for all children with disabilities beginning at age five, transforming the educational access and experiences of those with special needs. An amendment to the Education for All Handicapped Children Act in 1986 (PL-99-457) extended special education to all eligible children ages three to five years. The name of the law was changed to the Individuals with Disabilities Education Act (IDEA) in 1990 with another amendment by Congress (PL101-476). Most recently, the Individuals with Disabilities Education Act was reauthorized by Congress (PL105-17) in 1997, known as IDEA 97, outlining, again, for the states the requirements to provide a free, appropriate public education for all children with disabilities, ages three to 22 years of age. One of the major provisions identified in IDEA 97 mandates that children with disabilities are to be educated with their typically developing peers "to the maximum extent appropriate." Another major provision requires that the evaluation process, when determining if the child is a child with a disability, include "a variety of assessment tools and strategies" when gathering functional and developmental data, and must include information as provided by the parent. IDEA 97 specifies that each child with a disability has an Individualized Education Plan (IEP), which identifies his/her goals and objectives and outlines programs and/or services (interventions) to meet the unique educational and learning needs of the student. Through the entire evaluation and IEP team process, emphasis is placed on parent involvement. Specifically, the mandate of IDEA 97 advocates that parents should be involved in all decisions regarding their child's eligibility, placement, and services.

A focus of this book, as noted in all chapters, is the parent participation requirement. In keeping with the emphasis of IDEA 97, meaningful parent involvement is a potential element of all the educational treatment plans for all disabilities in this text throughout the referral process, the multidisciplinary evaluation team process, the IEP team process, the implementation of programs, services, accommodations/modifications, and the general day-to-day communication between home and school. In effectively working with any student, establishing and maintaining a positive relationship of trust with both the student and the parents is imperative.

Additionally, the IEP team's mandate under IDEA 97 is to create a plan for the child that addresses deficit areas and plans for his/her unique educational needs. Throughout the text, numerous, varied, and research-based interventions are identified that can offer the educational specialist developing a treatment plan viable options to assist in meeting those unique educational needs of the student. The therapeutic interventions are suggestions for consideration by the reader and are subject to required professional judgment, as each student and learning situation warrants in-person, individualized consideration and attention.

As most chapters begin with evaluation, it is our assumption that the pre-referral intervention process, as initially identified in the 1990 version of the IDEA, has been rigorously implemented in a thorough and comprehensive manner. The pre-referral process requires an effective consultative/collaborative model where specialists in the school (e.g., counselor, special education teacher, school psychologist, school social worker, speech and language pathologist, occupational therapist, physical therapist) work with the general education teacher(s) and parents to suggest, coordinate, and/or plan for interventions to improve the functioning of the targeted student in the general education setting. The assumption is that the referral for a special education evaluation is sought only after all quality pre-referral interventions have been exhausted. Of course, there can be exceptional circumstances warranting a swift move to comprehensive evaluation, such as when a student is exhibiting dangerous behavior toward self or others. Our purpose in writing this book is to support and assist the educational specialist in clarifying and simplifying plans of intervention based on student needs once an evaluation appears imminent.

TREATMENT PLAN UTILITY

Detailed, written educational treatment plans can benefit not only the student, the teacher(s), the support team of related service providers and paraprofessionals, but also the parents, the school, and the greater community. The student is served by a written plan because it stipulates the issues that are the focus of the treatment process. The focus of how to best serve the student in meeting his/her goals from the IEP, or needs as identified on a Section 504 Plan, can be lost in the day-to-day logistics of the hectic and frequently interrupted school day. The treatment plan is a guide that structures the focus of the instructional and therapeutic interventions that are essential for the student to progress. Since issues can change as the student's circumstances or needs change, the educational treatment plan must be viewed as a dynamic document that can, and must, be updated to reflect any major change of problem, definition, goal, objective, or intervention.

The student and the school providers for that student benefit from the educational treatment plan, which forces all to think carefully and directly about the desired educational outcomes. Behaviorally stated, measurable objectives clearly focus the educational endeavor. The student and parents no longer have to wonder what is trying to be accomplished instructionally. Clear objectives also allow the student to channel effort into specific changes that will lead to the long-term goal of problem resolution and/or improved functioning. Both student and instructional or therapy support staff are concentrating on specifically stated objectives using specific interventions.

School staff are aided by educational treatment plans because they are forced to think analytically and critically about the most sound instructional and therapeutic interventions that are best suited for objective attainment for the student. The providers to the student must give advance attention to the technique, approach, or assignment that will form the basis for an intervention.

A well-crafted treatment plan that clearly stipulates presenting educational problems, learning deficits, and intervention strategies facilitates the educational treatment process carried out by school team members in the special education classroom, in the general education classroom, at community-based instructional settings, and at vocational training sites. Good communication among the school staff team members about what approaches are being implemented and who is responsible for which intervention is important. A thorough educational treatment plan stipulates in *writing* the details of the established objectives and the varied interventions and can identify who will implement them.

Use of the educational treatment plan process as described in this text takes the educational professional a step further past the writing of goals for the IEP. It can assist the professional in identifying the chosen interventions to be used and then communicating to others the specific method, means, format, sequential process, and/or creative experience by which the student will be assisted in eventually attaining the IEP goals.

HOW TO DEVELOP A TREATMENT PLAN

The process of developing a treatment plan involves a logical series of steps that build on each other much like constructing a house. The foundation of any effective treatment plan is the data gathered in a comprehensive multidisciplinary evaluation. As part of the process prior to developing the treatment plan, school professionals must sensitively listen to and understand what the student struggles with in terms of learning deficits, emotional status, current stressors, social network, physical health and physical challenges, coping skills, self-esteem, family issues, and so on. It is imperative that assessment data be drawn from a variety of sources, which could include developmental and social history, physical exam, clinical interview, psychoeducational testing, psychiatric evaluation/consultation, and evaluation in the therapy areas of occupational, physical, and language, with considerable attention to parent input throughout the evaluation process. The integration of the data by the multidisciplinary evaluation team is critical for understanding the student and his/her needs. We have identified five specific steps for developing an effective treatment plan based on assessment data.

Step One: Problem Selection

Although the student (or parents) may discuss a variety of issues during the assessment, the members of the multidisciplinary evaluation team must ferret out the most significant problems on which to focus the educational treatment process. Usually a primary problem will surface, and secondary problems may also be evident. Some other problems may have to be set aside as not urgent enough to require treatment at this time. An effective treatment plan can only deal with a few selected problems, or treatment will lose its direction. A variety of problems is presented as chapter titles representing a specific disability within *The Special Education Treatment Planner*. The school professional may select those that most accurately represent the student's current needs.

As the problems to be selected become clear to the educational specialist or the student's team of providers, it is important to consider opinions from the student (as appropriate, dependent upon the student's age and mental status) and the parents as to the prioritization of school issues or learning struggles. The student's motivation to participate in and cooperate with the treatment process depends, to some extent, on the degree to which educational treatment addresses his/her greatest needs, particularly in circumstances with secondary students who may have strong feelings as to what should be emphasized.

Step Two: Problem Definition

Each student presents with unique nuances as to how a problem or learning deficit behaviorally reveals itself in his/her life. Therefore, each problem that is selected for treatment focus requires a specific definition about how it is evidenced in the particular student. Turn to the chapter that best describes the identified or suspected disability of the student. Select from the behavioral definitions listed at the beginning of the chapter the statements that appear most descriptive of the student's needs or challenges or appear to be interfering the most with the educational process for the student.

Step Three: Goal Development

The next step in treatment plan development is that of setting broad goals for the resolution of the target educational problem. These statements need not be crafted in measurable terms but can be global, long-term goals that indicate a desired positive outcome to the treatment procedures. The Planner suggests several possible goal statements for each problem, but one statement is all that is required in a treatment plan.

Step Four: Objective Construction

In contrast to long-term goals, educational objectives must be stated in behaviorally measurable language. It must be clear when the student has achieved the objectives; therefore, vague, subjective objectives are not acceptable. Various alternatives are presented to allow construction of a variety of educational treatment plan possibilities for the same presenting problem. The educational specialist must exercise professional judgment as to which objectives are most appropriate for a given student.

Each objective should be developed as a step toward attaining the broad instructional goal. In essence, objectives can be thought of as a series of steps that, when completed, will result in the achievement of the long-term goal. There should be at least two objectives for each problem, but the school professional may construct as many as are necessary for goal achievement. Target attainment dates may be listed for each objective. New objectives should be added to the plan as the student's treatment progresses. When all the necessary objectives have been achieved, the student should have resolved the target educational problem successfully.

Step Five: Intervention Creation

Interventions are the instructional and/or therapeutic actions of the school professional designed to help the student complete the objectives. There should be at least one intervention for every objective. If the student does not accomplish the objective after the initial intervention has been implemented, new interventions should be added to the plan.

Interventions should be selected on the basis of the student's needs and the educational specialist's full instructional and/or therapeutic repertoire. *The Special Education Treatment Planner* contains interventions from a broad range of approaches including cognitive, behavioral, academic, motoric, medical, and family-based. Other interventions may be written by the provider to reflect his/her own training and experience. The addition of new problems, definitions, goals, objectives, and interventions to those found in the Planner is encouraged because doing so adds to the database for future reference and use.

Some suggested interventions listed in the Planner refer to specific books or journals where specific methodologies can be located for the educational specialist to look for a more lengthy explanation or discussion of the intervention. Appendix B contains a full bibliographic reference for the professional organized by disability or disorder. Appendix A offers a bibliographic reference for parents, suggesting reading material that may be helpful to families, referenced by disability or disorder.

HOW TO USE THIS PLANNER

The Special Education Treatment Planner was developed as a tool to aid school professionals in writing an educational treatment plan in a rapid manner that is clear, specific, and highly individualized according to the following progression:

1. Choose one presenting problem/disability (Step One) you have identified through your assessment process. Locate the corresponding page number for that problem/disability in the Planner's table of contents.
2. Select two or three of the listed behavioral definitions (Step Two) and record them in the appropriate section on your treatment plan form. Feel free to add your own defining statement if you determine that your student's behavioral manifestation of the identified problem is not listed.
3. Select one or more long-term goals (Step Three) and again write the selection, exactly as it is written in the Planner or in some appropriately modified form, in the corresponding area of your own form.
4. Review the listed objectives for this problem and select the ones that you judge to be clinically indicated for your student (Step

Four). Remember, it is recommended that you select at least two objectives for each problem. Add a target date allocated for the attainment of each objective, if necessary.

5. Choose relevant interventions (Step Five). The Planner offers suggested interventions related to each objective in the parentheses following the objective statement. But do not limit yourself to those interventions. Just as with definitions, goals, and objectives, there is space allowed for you to enter your own interventions into the Planner. This allows you to refer to these entries when you create a plan around this problem in the future. You may have to assign responsibility to a specific person for implementation of each intervention if the treatment is being carried out by a multidisciplinary team.

Congratulations! You should now have a complete, individualized, educational treatment plan that is ready for immediate implementation for your student. It should resemble the format of the sample plan presented on the next page.

A FINAL NOTE

One important aspect of effective educational treatment planning is that each plan should be tailored to the individual student's disability, problems, deficit areas, and/or needs. The student's strengths and weaknesses, unique stressors, social network, family circumstances, and symptom patterns *must* be considered in developing a treatment strategy. Drawing upon our own years of educational and clinical experience, we have put together a variety of treatment choices. These statements can be combined in thousands of permutations to develop detailed treatment plans. Relying on their own good judgment, school professionals can easily select the statements that are appropriate for the students on their caseload. In addition, we encourage readers to add their own definitions, goals, objectives, and interventions to the existing samples. It is our hope that *The Special Education Treatment Planner* will promote effective, creative educational treatment planning—a process that will ultimately benefit the student, the team working with that student, the parents, and the greater school community.

SAMPLE TREATMENT PLAN

PROBLEM: READING COMPREHENSION

Definitions: General reading achievement is significantly below
learning potential.
Reading comprehension is substantially reduced and
impairs the ability to succeed across subject areas.

Goals: Improve reading comprehension abilities to obtain skills
necessary to assimilate grade level material or to be
commensurate with learning potential.

Objectives

1. Participate in a comprehensive reading or psychoeducational evaluation.

2. Parents participate in an interpretive meeting to hear test results.

3. Parents take part in an IEP team meeting or general planning meeting and agree to implementation of a reading improvement plan.

4. Demonstrate increased accuracy in reading comprehension.

Interventions

1. Refer the student for a psychoeducational evaluation.

1. School evaluation clinician(s) meets with the parents to discuss assessment results.

1. Conduct an IEP team meeting or general planning meeting with the parents present to determine the student's eligibility for special education and/or ascertain general education reading services.

1. Provide instruction for the elementary student in identifying and developing the story's main strategy where the main idea of a story is placed in the center and extensions are drawn that contain other main ideas, con-

cepts, events, and characters to break down the selection into meaningful visual information (see "Story Maps Improve Comprehension" by Reutzel in *The Reading Teacher* [1985, 38: 400–405]).

2. Assist the student in organizing the meaning of a selection by using story grammar, which is a system to consistently describe text features such as setting, responses by characters, goals and consequences (see *Stories, Scripts and Scenes: Aspects of a Schema Theory* [Mandler]).

5. Identify the main characters and their actions in a literary piece or text.

1. Have the student compare a main character in the readings to someone in his/her family or to a well-known actor to help create visualization of the character (e.g., personality, physical attributes), (i.e., Who would Anne Frank have looked like that you know?).

2. Have the student describe personality and physical traits, create significant quotes from the character, and identify with whom the character associates in the readings.

6. Identify the main idea and subtopics of the literary piece or text.

   1. Assign the student to create a new cover for the book or article, or to make a poster of what the text would be as a movie or video.

   2. Have the student categorize the setting, characters, conflict(s), and outcome with assistance from marginal glosses, which are notes written by the teacher in the margin of the readings to the student, giving prompts such as vocabulary highlights, clarification of points, and interpretation of events.

7. Parents demonstrate a more accepting attitude and understanding of their child's reading deficit.

   1. Communicate with the parents frequently to keep them well-informed of their child's learning needs and progress.

   2. Assist the parents with seeking out information and support on reading disabilities from such organizations as the International Reading Association and Council for Exceptional Children—Division for Learning Disabilities.

Note: The numbers in parentheses accompanying the short-term objectives in each chapter correspond to the list of suggested therapeutic interventions in that chapter. Each objective has specific interventions that have been designed to assist the student in attaining that objective. Clinical judgment should determine the exact intervention to be used, including any outside of those suggested.

ASPERGER'S DISORDER

BEHAVIORAL DEFINITIONS

1. Acquisition of language within reasonable age-appropriate time line.
2. Cognitive development, self-help skills, and adaptive behavior are present within a reasonable developmental time frame.
3. Limited social skill development with significant egocentricity and without reciprocal interactions.
4. Nonverbal communication cues including eye contact, facial expression, and body posture are restricted or nonexistent.
5. Affective interaction with others is limited or absent (e.g., failure to seek or give comfort to others in moments of distress, or an inability to express enjoyment or pleasure as a function of good fortune for self or others).
6. Limited repertoire of behaviors, interests, and activities and an emphasis on nonfunctional routines and rituals.
7. Difficulties with transition and change in the environment including an overfocus on small, nonfunctional details or specific topics.
8. Unusual voice intonation with speech production (e.g., monotone, lacks appropriate pauses, etc.).

—. _____
   _____
—. _____
   _____
—. _____
   _____

LONG-TERM GOALS

1. Develop improved interpersonal interactions including the use of verbal and nonverbal cues with adults and peers.
2. Master the use of pragmatic language in social situations.
3. Achieve prevocational and/or vocational goals.
4. Expand the variety of interests and activities to more age-appropriate development.
5. Reduce ritualistic and compulsive behaviors, and show more even functioning with change and transition.
6. Attain achievement in academic areas to the level of potential.
7. School staff and family develop an understanding and acceptance of the student's strengths and deficit areas as ongoing lifetime issues.

—. _____

_____

—. _____

_____

—. _____

_____

SHORT-TERM OBJECTIVES	THERAPEUTIC INTERVENTIONS
1. Parents complete preliminary screening devices rating their son/daughter on characteristics of Asperger's Disorder. (1)	1. A mental health professional administers or assigns an autism screening device (e.g., the Autism Spectrum Screening Questionnaire [Ehlers, Gillberg, and Wing]) to obtain rating responses from the parents and the classroom teacher.
2. Participate in a psychoeducational evaluation. (2)	2. Based on results of the screening instrument, conduct a psychoeducational evaluation to examine the student's cognitive, academic, social, behavioral, and adaptive functioning.
3. Participate in a speech and language evaluation. (3)	
4. Cooperate with an occupational and/or physical therapy evaluation. (4)	
5. Cooperate with a psychiatric evaluation. (5)	3. Arrange for a speech and language evaluation, at-
6. Parents participate in the multidisciplinary evaluation and the Individual Ed-	

ucational Planning (IEP) team meeting and/or a Section 504 planning meeting and agree to implementation of a plan and recommendations. (6)

7. Increase the amount of focused productive attention as a result of environmental changes in the classroom. (7, 8, 9)

8. Complete assigned tasks utilizing visual cues for direction. (10, 11, 12)

9. Increase the percentage of correct academic responses to 80 percent or greater. (13, 14, 15)

10. Demonstrate progress in the use of pragmatic language. (16, 17, 18)

11. Verbalize a clear and accurate understanding of directions and social cues. (11, 13, 18, 19)

12. Implement communication skills within areas of interest. (20)

13. Demonstrate a decrease in anxiety as evidenced by focused attention, reduced restlessness and irritability. (21, 22, 23)

14. Reduce the frequency and severity of disruptive, dysfunctional behaviors. (24, 25)

15. Implement problem-solving skills within social situations. (26, 27, 28)

tending specifically to the student's pragmatic communication needs.

4. Conduct or arrange for a motor evaluation of the student to ascertain needs in fine and gross motor areas.

5. Refer the student for a psychiatric consultation to assist with differential diagnosis.

6. Conduct a multidisciplinary evaluation and IEP team meeting and/or Section 504 planning meeting to ascertain the student's eligibility for programming, support services, and/or accommodations.

7. Organize the classroom to provide a calm, structured work environment where distraction can be kept as minimal as possible.

8. Modify the student's assignments/tasks so that expectations are clear and the amount of work requested is directly correlated to the student's attention span and ability.

9. Implement self-monitoring techniques with the student, allowing him/her to mark a chart or retain a visual reward for task completion.

10. Emphasize visual cues to provide information to the student (e.g., use of pictures or comic strip drawings to portray routine schedules).

11. Highlight the beginning and end of a task clearly

16. Develop meaningful friend-ships with peers. (26, 29, 30)

17. Practice motor skills and show improvement in deficit areas. (31)

18. Increase the quantity and quality of self-care and adaptive skills. (32)

19. Participate in a prevoca-tional/vocational assess-ment to ascertain interests and skills. (33, 34)

20. List and demonstrate the responsible behavior associ-ated with being employed. (34, 35, 36)

21. Verbalize interests academ-ically and/or vocationally to pursue after high school. (34, 37)

22. Parents report satisfaction with progress and educa-tional planning for the stu-dent. (38, 39, 40)

___. _____

_____

___. _____

_____

___. _____

_____

and provide a list of visual prompts (e.g., cards, pic-tures) identifying the steps to completion of the task.

12. Provide a picture or model depicting the final product of the task to ensure expec-tations are clear.

13. Give academic instructions at the student's level, using individual and small group configurations whenever possible.

14. Grade academic tasks at the child's level, slowly in-creasing the difficulty of the requirements.

15. Provide prompt feedback to the student regarding in-structional successes and model desired changes for the student to make on fu-ture tasks.

16. Organize language use in the classroom to be struc-tured and clear in content.

17. Teach the pragmatic pieces of both verbal and nonver-bal interaction (see *The So-cial Use of Language* [Rinaldi]).

18. Simplify language used with the student, if needed, to lower anxiety.

19. Assist the student with in-terpreting situations (e.g., explain more obvious non-verbal cues in the situation to the student, clarify any misunderstood verbage to the student [example: "sub" means submarine, not a turkey sub/sandwich], write

out or model the directions)
and teach peers to assist
the student as well.

20. Build language skills by
    using the student's
    strengths, interests, and
    skill areas.

21. Provide a space in the class-
    room where the student can
    move to when group activi-
    ties create high anxiety.

22. Offer periods of physical
    activity to reduce stress
    and anxiety.

23. Teach relaxation techniques
    to the student and provide
    prompts as to when he/she
    should implement these
    strategies.

24. At a point of escalating dis-
    ruptive or dysfunctional be-
    havior, approach the student
    in a calm and emotionally
    benign manner to negotiate
    a favorable outcome.

25. Use behavior therapy prin-
    ciples to develop a positive
    behavior support plan, tar
    geting the most seriously
    inappropriate behaviors im-
    pacting the student's school
    functioning.

26. Place the student in a small
    social skills group run by a
    school mental health profes-
    sional with emphasis on
    problem solving, role play-
    ing, and modeling of appro-
    priate social interaction,
    social communication, and a
    more flexible thinking style.

27. Use the creation of social
    stories to assist the student

in problem solving with difficult social, emotional, and transitional issues (see *High Functioning Adolescents and Young Adults with Autism* [Fullerton, Stratton, Coyne, and Gray]).

28. Teach problem solving and decision making in the classroom by introducing choices slowly and presenting viable options to the student.

29. Match the student with mature peers who can act as buddies during different activities in the school day.

30. With parental permission, talk with the class(es) about Asperger's Disorder, answering questions the student's peers may have.

31. Follow recommendations from the motoric evaluations as to implementation of activities that will most greatly benefit the student's fine and gross motor skills.

32. Create opportunities for the student to work on self-care skills as needed (e.g., brushing teeth, hair, etc.) and activities of daily living (ADLs) (e.g., answering the phone, shopping, asking for directions in the community, etc.).

33. Conduct an evaluation of the student's abilities and interests related to future vocational experience.

34. Organize visits for the student and parents to voca-

tional training sites that match the student's skills and interests.

35. Establish functional prevocational experiences in the classroom and school to teach the responsibilities of maintaining a job.

36. Teach social skills directly related to those necessary in the workplace (e.g., attitude, responsibility, initiative, motivation).

37. Provide guidance to the student and parents as to viable higher education options if the student wants to pursue college.

38. Conduct periodic communication meetings as needed with the family and school staff to examine the student's progress and any outstanding concerns.

39. Designate a case manager to take a leadership role in communicating to all parties when crucial issues arise.

40. Communicate closely with the parents and school team members, monitoring progress and evaluating and altering strategies.

___. _____

_____

___. _____

_____

___. _____

_____

ATTENTION-DEFICIT/HYPERACTIVITY DISORDER—ADOLESCENT

BEHAVIORAL DEFINITIONS

1. Less than age-appropriate attention span.
2. Difficulty with attending to details, often making careless mistakes.
3. Poor organizational skills (e.g., not having materials ready for classroom tasks and activities).
4. Does not follow verbal directions consistently.
5. Does not consistently complete assigned work at home and school.
6. Easily distracted by extraneous stimuli.
7. A high activity level, sometimes participating in reckless or even dangerous activities.
8. Impulsiveness that leads to making quick, self-defeating decisions or blurting out responses in an inappropriate manner.
9. Aggressive, disruptive, or engages in attention-seeking through negative means.
10. Low self-esteem and poor social skills.
11. Tendency to not accept responsibility for behavior.
12. Obvious impairment in academic and/or social functioning.
13. Engages in daydreaming or is internally preoccupied.

—. _____
  _____

—. _____
  _____

—. _____
  _____

LONG-TERM GOALS

1. Increase focus, attention, and concentration gradually for longer periods of time that are closer to age-appropriate expectations.
2. Demonstrate increasingly higher percentages of completion of schoolwork and home tasks.
3. Exhibit improved quality and accuracy of work and more effective organization of materials and assignments.
4. Present with greater self-management by demonstrating decreased impulsiveness and significantly fewer disruptive behaviors.
5. Show more appropriate social skills and higher self-esteem as identified by increased numbers of peer interactions and positive participation in school activities.
6. Take medication and be able to identify the benefits of using pharmacological methods.
7. Bring curriculum achievement up to levels of potential.
8. Identify and plan for vocational interests and goals.
9. Family and school staff recognize how Attention-Deficit/ Hyperactivity Disorder (ADHD) relates to the student's difficulties at school and home, and work together to sustain communication and improve the student's quality of life.

—. _____
    _____
—. _____
    _____
—. _____
    _____

SHORT-TERM OBJECTIVES

1. Parents, teacher, and student cooperate with a school mental health professional who will gather data on the student. (1)
2. Participate in a psychoeducational evaluation. (2, 3, 4)
3. Follow the directions given by the teacher in the classroom. (4, 5)

THERAPEUTIC INTERVENTIONS

1. A school mental health professional gathers from the teacher, student, and parents salient information about the student's school functioning to include developmental history, a school record review, systematic classroom observation, completion of rating

4. Reduce disruptive behavior during unstructured periods of the school day. (6)

5. Utilize opportunities for moving about the classroom at times specifically designated. (7)

6. Demonstrate the ability to make changes from one task to another without distraction. (8)

7. Report success at utilizing cognitive strategies to focus attention. (9, 10)

8. Respond favorably to environmental interventions designed to increase on-task attention and reduce distractibility. (10, 11, 12, 13)

9. Utilize devices to cover ears in order to reduce auditory distractions. (14)

10. Highlight important information to help focus attention. (15)

11. Demonstrate an increase in the amount of time spent focused on a task. (10, 16)

12. Significantly reduce the frequency of aggressive behavior and impulsive breaking of rules. (17, 18, 19)

13. Utilize self-talk strategies to increase rule-governed behavior. (20)

14. Participate in small group social skills, problem solving, and anger management training. (21)

15. Increase involvement in extracurricular social activities. (22)

scales/checklists by the teacher and parents, and interview of the student.

2. Based on the compilation of the student's data, arrange for a psychoeducational evaluation.

3. Conduct a multidisciplinary evaluation team meeting and an Individualized Education Planning (IEP) team meeting or a Section 504 meeting to design an education plan for the student.

4. Develop an individual plan of appropriate interventions with input from the parents and student based on a process of defining specific target behaviors, brainstorming potential solutions, implementing the strategies, and evaluating results.

5. Implement classroom didactic interventions to assist the student with following directions (e.g., present directions in a brief, concise, and more global manner, use visual prompts, have the student repeat directions back, provide written directions, select a positive peer to repeat directions to the student, check to ensure the student has correctly begun the task).

6. Take steps to reduce the student's impulsive social disruption that occurs during unstructured times in the school schedule (e.g.,

16. Identify the negative consequences of immature, impulsive, unkind social interaction. (23)

17. Exhibit more frequent prosocial behavior with peers and adults. (22, 23, 24)

18. Organize study material (notes, assignments, handouts, etc.) in a notebook. (25)

19. Implement a system of keeping and organizing assignments that will facilitate their on-time completion. (26, 27, 28, 29)

20. Implement study skills designed to increase frequency of assignment completion and mastery of material. (29, 30, 31)

21. Work on assignments in short time periods that allow for breaks and a return to on-task behavior until completion. (32, 33, 34)

22. Verbalize a plan or contract for studying. (34, 35, 36)

23. Participate constructively in small groups or with a partner to complete assignments. (37)

24. Parents utilize structured techniques to assist the student in organization of study time and assignment completion. (38)

25. Reduce the frequency of errors in assignments completed. (39, 40, 41, 42)

26. Increase the frequency of positive statements made

strategically locating his/her locker in a lesser traffic area, providing supervision in the hallways as students move from class to class, have a staff member strategically near the student in assemblies, pep rallies, lunchroom, etc.).

7. Provide opportunities for structured movement in the classroom by allowing intermittent work breaks and permitting the student to move around the room at designated times.

8. Structure the school day to organize the majority of academics in the morning, establish a routine and predictable school day, give information to the student prior to transition or changes, and provide a daily written schedule of the day's events in each class.

9. Instruct the student in metacognitive strategies in which the individual learns to use his/her inner voice to monitor attention and behavior.

10. Promptly reinforce the student for on-task behavior.

11. Seat the student away from distractions such as noisy heaters and high traffic areas, but close to calm students who display attentive behaviors.

12. Provide a study carrel or "office space" to reduce extraneous stimuli where the

about himself/herself.
(43, 44, 45)

27. Verbalize a more complete understanding of the nature and treatment of ADHD. (46)

28. Attend individual or group counseling to build self-esteem and overcome depression. (47, 48)

29. Demonstrate assertiveness in advocating for own learning needs. (49)

30. Parents verbalize a more tolerant, accepting attitude toward their child and his/her attention, behavioral, and academic issues. (50, 51)

31. Parents implement positive parenting techniques with their child with ADHD. (52)

32. Take medication as prescribed and verbalize an understanding of the benefits of doing so. (53, 54, 55)

33. Identify vocational interests and goals and pursue training for those goals.
(56, 57, 58)

34. Parents report their satisfaction with their child's overall school experience and progress. (59, 60)

__. _____
   _____

__. _____
   _____

__. _____
   _____

student may work independently.

13. Create a larger personal space for the student such as an extra desktop area or more space between desks.

14. Permit the wearing of earplugs or headphones during intense work times such as test taking.

15. Teach the student to highlight with color essential words, concepts, and so on to increase attention to salient information.

16. Plan for within-task novelty in some lessons to stimulate interest and increase attention and motivation.

17. Develop a positive behavior support plan targeting the impulsive and aggressive behaviors of the student to include a strong incentive reinforcement system for controlled behavior, a hierarchy of consequences for negative behavior, and use of time-out procedures (e.g., cool down/respite area and in-school suspension).

18. Review classroom rules regularly and keep them posted in a very visible place.

19. Anticipate situations in which the student will incur difficulty in maintaining decorum (e.g., passing in halls, lunchroom) and engage in proactive planning for those times (e.g., allowing the student to travel to

his/her next class before or after other students have passed between classes, assign a lunchroom seat for the student near positive peer models).

20. Teach the student the use of self-talk to maintain rule-governed behaviors (see *Attention-Deficit Hyperactivity Disorder: A Handbook for Diagnosis and Treatment* [Barkley]).

21. Provide small group social skills training and consider including instruction in initiation of social interaction, conversation skills, conflict resolution and problem-solving strategies, and anger management (see *Understanding ADHD: A Practical Guide for Teachers and Parents* [Bender]).

22. Enlist parental participation in expanding the student's involvement in extracurricular or outside-of-school events to increase peer interaction opportunities.

23. In the classroom, use reading materials that emphasize positive people traits and that depict negative outcomes when individuals are insolent, nasty, and self-centered (see *Understanding ADHD: A Practical Guide for Teachers and Parents* [Bender]).

24. Engage the entire school in instructional themes involving positive social skill de-

velopment such as the AS-SIST program (see *Teaching Friendship Skills, An Intermediate Version* [Huggins, Manion, and Moen] or *Helping Kids Handle Anger* [Huggins and Huggins]).

25. Provide direction to the student in organizing his/her notebook, assignments, and materials using dividers and folders coordinated by subject and schedule.

26. Instruct the student in the use of an agenda for recording both short- and long-term assignments.

27. Teach the student to color coordinate assignments by using the same color folders, dividers, and highlighter pens for the same subject, including recording assignments in the agenda with a same colored pen for a specific subject.

28. Visually display assignments and due dates in a predictable place in the classroom every day.

29. Offer periodical checks of the student's notebook and agenda and reinforce positive progress of organization and of handing work in.

30. Instruct the student in previewing material, searching for and highlighting salient aspects of the material, and self-evaluation techniques of comprehension/acquisition of the material.

31. Teach the student different study methods so that he/she may match his/her learning style with one or more options (i.e., mapping, outlining, charting, self-questioning, visual imagery, pneumonic memory techniques).

32. Break assignments into smaller, more workable segments, or shorten tasks as needed.

33. Have the student establish reasonable start/stop times for a specified task and monitor his/her own completion of the task.

34. Instruct the student regarding how long, when, and where to work on an assignment for the best quality and greatest efficiency.

35. Teach the student to plan for an assignment (e.g., gather materials, how to break the task into segments, how to estimate and plan for the length of the task).

36. Develop a contract with the student specifying the amount of work, quality of work required, and date expected.

37. On some tasks, allow students to work with partners or in small groups.

38. Teach the parents ways that they can help their son/daughter organize a positive homework routine (e.g., establish a set time

for homework, organize a place in the home conducive for doing homework, make homework a priority before enjoyable evening activities) and, if needed, encourage them to create incentives for work completion.

39. If legible handwriting is difficult for the student to achieve, allow word processing for completion of assignments, access to a peer's lecture notes, and accept tape-recorded assignments.

40. Integrate technological assistance to include visually responsive software, recorded books, an electronic speller, spell check/grammar check programs on the computer, word-processing access, and Dictaphone and calculator use.

41. Teach the student how to proofread his/her work to eliminate errors.

42. Provide the student with prompt feedback so he/she may experience success, learn from errors, and self-correct mistakes made.

43. Provide frequent positive reinforcement to the student, being especially alert to give reinforcement to positive self-descriptive statements made by the student.

44. Work diligently to build a trusting relationship with the student through communicating unconditional

positive regard, warm acceptance, and affirmation of self-worth.

45. Emphasize the student's interests and strengths when presenting material to be learned.

46. Counsel the student with materials about ADHD to help him/her understand more about the disorder.

47. Engage the student in individual or small group counseling by a school mental health professional for self-concept improvement.

48. Refer the family to a private therapist should affective issues appear paramount within the student.

49. Teach the student self-advocacy skills in relation to his/her learning needs.

50. Teach the parents about the ramifications of the child's ADHD and refer them to materials that clearly explain ADHD; respond to questions/concerns they may have.

51. Encourage the parents to seek out a support group for families with children who have been diagnosed with attention disorders.

52. Refer to a school mental health professional or meet with the parents to discuss ways they can parent more positively and assist their son/daughter.

53. At the parents' request, arrange for a teacher and/or school mental health provider to talk with the student about ADHD medication and its expected benefits as one intervention that is part of a more complete plan to treat ADHD.

54. The school nurse consults with school staff/parents/physician on salient issues regarding the ADHD medication dosage, side effects, and so on.

55. Gather data on the student regarding his/her change in school functioning on medication and report this to the prescribing physician.

56. Arrange for the student to complete a vocational inventory and/or assessment.

57. Refer the student and parents to meet with a high school counselor to determine a course of study for the student that is in alignment with his/her vocational/career interests.

58. Facilitate the student and parents' visitation of vocational training sites.

59. Keep in contact with the parents to maintain open communication between home and school and to continue positive gains made by the student.

60. Gather information on the strategies and supports that have been most effective for

the student and arrange for this information to be shared with the teaching staff in the new school year.

—. _____

_____

—. _____

_____

—. _____

_____

ATTENTION-DEFICIT/HYPERACTIVITY DISORDER—CHILD

BEHAVIORAL DEFINITIONS

1. Less than age-appropriate attention span.
2. Difficulty with attending to details, often making careless mistakes.
3. Poor organizational skills (e.g., not having materials ready for classroom tasks and activities).
4. Does not follow verbal directions consistently.
5. Does not consistently complete assigned work at home and school.
6. Easily distracted by extraneous stimuli.
7. A high activity level, sometimes participating in reckless or even dangerous activities.
8. Impulsiveness that leads to making quick, self-defeating decisions or blurting out responses in an inappropriate manner.
9. Aggressive, disruptive, or engages in attention-seeking through negative means.
10. Low self-esteem and poor social skills.
11. Tendency to not accept responsibility for behavior.
12. Obvious impairment in academic and/or social functioning.
13. Engages in daydreaming or is internally preoccupied.

—. _____
_____

—. _____
_____

—. _____
_____

LONG-TERM GOALS

1. Increase focus, attention, and concentration gradually for longer periods of time that are closer to age-appropriate expectations.
2. Demonstrate increasingly higher percentages of completion of schoolwork and home tasks.
3. Exhibit improved quality and accuracy of work and more effective organization of materials and assignments.
4. Present with greater self-management by demonstrating decreased impulsiveness and significantly fewer disruptive behaviors.
5. Show more appropriate social skills and higher self-esteem as identified by increased numbers of peer interactions and positive participation in school activities.
6. Take medication and be able to identify the benefits of using pharmacological methods.
7. Bring curriculum achievement up to levels of potential.
8. Family and school staff recognize how Attention-Deficit/Hyperactivity Disorder (ADHD) relates to the student's difficulties at school and home, and work together to sustain communication and improve the student's quality of life.

—. _____
_____
_____
—. _____
_____
—. _____
_____

SHORT-TERM OBJECTIVES

1. Parents, the teacher, and student cooperate with a school mental health professional who will gather data on the student. (1)
2. Participate in a psychoeducational evaluation. (2)
3. Parents meet with school staff to discuss evaluation data and to develop an edu-

THERAPEUTIC INTERVENTIONS

1. A school mental health professional works with the teacher and parents to gather salient information about the student's school functioning that includes a developmental history, a school record review, systematic classroom observation, completion of rating scales/checklists by the

cational plan for the student. (3)

4. Reduce disruptive behavior during unstructured periods of the school day. (4)

5. Demonstrate greater self-management, responding to structure of the school day. (5, 6, 7)

6. Decrease aggressive and overt behaviors in the school setting. (8, 9, 10, 11)

7. Use self-talk to monitor aggressiveness and inattentiveness. (12, 13)

8. Increase attention in the classroom to the task at hand. (14, 15, 16)

9. Show greater attention to the salient aspects of instruction. (17, 18)

10. Demonstrate improved social interaction with peers and adults. (19, 20, 21)

11. Increase completion of daily classroom work to 90 percent. (22, 23, 24, 25)

12. Demonstrate competency with organization of materials. (26, 27, 28)

13. Effectively use a daily assignment sheet or assignment book. (29, 30)

14. Exhibit enhanced academic performance as a result of curricular adjustments. (31, 32, 33)

15. Integrate technology into daily work habits to improve the quantity and quality of work produced. (34)

teacher and parents, and interview of the student.

2. Based on the compilation of the student's data, arrange for a psychoeducational evaluation.

3. Conduct a multidisciplinary evaluation team meeting and an Individual Education Planning (IEP) meeting or a Section 504 meeting to design an education plan for the student.

4. Implement classroom didactic interventions to assist the student with following directions (e.g., present directions in a brief, concise, and more global manner, use visual prompts, have the student repeat directions back, provide written directions, select a positive peer to repeat directions to the student, check to ensure the student has correctly begun the task).

5. Provide support for the student during the day: offer indoor recess with a friend, provide structured games at recess time, pair with a socially appropriate friend for lunch, maintain a buddy system in physical education, allow the student to avoid standing in line if this proves to be difficult, organize a plan in advance for assemblies and other out-of-the-routine activities.

6. Provide limited opportunities for movement within the

16. Complete homework tasks in a successful manner at least 90 percent of the time. (35, 36, 37, 38)

17. Increase the frequency of positive statements made about himself/herself to at least three times per week. (39, 40, 41, 42)

18. Parents verbalize a more tolerant, accepting attitude toward their child and his/her attention, behavioral, and academic issues. (43, 44)

19. Parents report greater success with managing their child at home resulting in less family disruption. (45, 46)

20. Take medication and recognize the benefits of doing so. (47, 48, 49)

21. Parents report satisfaction with their child's overall school experience and progress. (50)

__. _____
    _____

__. _____
    _____

__. _____
    _____

structure of the classroom by allowing intermittent work breaks, doing stretching activities with the class, giving the student errands, and providing two seats to the student where he/she can move between them.

7. Structure the school day to organize the majority of the student's academics in the morning, establish a routine and predictable school day, give information to the student prior to transition or changes, and provide a daily pictorial or written schedule.

8. Develop a positive behavior support plan targeting the impulsive and aggressive behaviors of the student to include a strong incentive reinforcement system for controlled behavior, a hierarchy of consequences for negative behavior, and use of time-out procedures (e.g., cool down/respite area, in-school suspension).

9. Develop a communication plan with the parents and the student whereby target behaviors are rated by the student and teacher as to the student's success in acquiring those behaviors for the school day; this information is sent home and reinforcers for success are provided by the parents.

10. Provide the student with opportunities to use correspondence training, which

rewards the student for following through on verbal commitments (see "Clinical Effects of Correspondence Training in the Management of Hyperactive Children" by Paniagua, Morrison, and Black in *Behavioral and Residential Treatment* [1988, 3: 19–40].

11. Use physical proximity to the student to decrease inappropriate behaviors (e.g., standing close to the student, lightly touching his/her shoulder).

12. Teach the student self-talk strategies (e.g., utilize the program from *Think Aloud* [Camp and Bash]), assisting the student in monitoring his/her actions or performance.

13. Instruct the student in cognitive self-monitoring behaviors (e.g., using tapes that intermittently signal to the student to ask, "Am I paying attention?" or "Am I keeping my feet and hands to myself?").

14. Institute seating changes for the student away from distractions and provide a study carrel ("office") to reduce extraneous stimuli during work periods.

15. Create an incentive system to promptly reinforce the student for on-task classroom behavior.

16. Use a subtle signal with the student that redirects

him/her back to the task or lesson at hand.

17. Highlight with color essential words, pictures, concepts, and so on, to increase the student's attention to salient information.

18. Provide within-task novelty in a lesson or activity that is congruent with the student's interests to increase attention and motivation.

19. Have the student participate in a structured social skills group with emphasis on modeling, role playing, and generalizations to real situations (e.g., *The Prepare Curriculum: Teaching Prosocial Competencies* [Goldstein]).

20. Use incidental teaching moments to assist the student, when making marked social fouls with peers or adults, to identify what he/she could do more appropriately in a similar situation the next time.

21. Enlist parental participation in expanding the student's involvement in extracurricular or outside-of-school events to increase peer interaction opportunities.

22. Break assignments into smaller, more workable segments, or shorten tasks as needed.

23. Assist the student in setting a start and stop time for independent tasks and

monitor his/her adherence to this structure.

24. Use a timer to establish with the student the length of time given to a task.

25. Provide incentives or positive reinforcement for tasks completed within the time limits.

26. Teach the student to organize his/her desk, cubby, locker, or personal space on a weekly basis.

27. Develop a checklist (or picture list) of needed materials for use at school and home to prevent forgetting items for schoolwork and homework.

28. Enlist the parents to provide organizational aids for the student (e.g., a pencil case, notebook dividers, folders for each subject, and a school bag with compartments to organize small items such as keys and money).

29. Organize a daily assignment book to be filled out at school and reviewed and signed by a parent at home.

30. Create a checklist of daily assignments for the student to check off and self-monitor as each task is completed.

31. Adapt curricular needs by extending the time required for task completion for learning a skill or concept or for test taking.

32. Intensify the amount of assistance the student receives (e.g., increasing student/teacher contact time, student/teacher assistant contact time, assigning a peer tutor or a cross-age tutor) to provide greater support with academic tasks.

33. Intensify instruction in deficit areas with shorter lessons and direction instruction formats offering the student frequent opportunities to respond and experience success and receive immediate feedback.

34. Integrate technological assistance into the instructional formats for the student (e.g., visually responsive software, headphones for taped presentations, recorded books, an electronic speller, spell check/grammar check programs on the computer, keyboarding skills/word-processing access for upper elementary students, calculator use, voice-activated software, and Dictaphone access for writing tasks) as appropriate.

35. Enlist parental support in establishing a consistent and best time in the home for homework completion every day.

36. Assist the parents with strategies to help their child study (e.g., show them word

analysis techniques, alternative math methods, send home examples/ models of how to complete certain tasks as they are taught in the classroom).

37. Alter homework assignments by reducing the length of the tasks, the time allotted for the tasks, or adapt how the student may approach the task (e.g., dictating written answers, using a calculator to complete math problems).

38. For middle and upper elementary students, encourage parental support for their child to participate in after-school study support.

39. Work diligently to build a relationship of trust with the student, providing frequent positive reinforcement for both academic and nonacademic successes.

40. Emphasize the student's interests and strengths in the classroom, providing opportunities for the student to shine.

41. Engage the student in individual or small group counseling by a school mental health professional with emphasis on building self-concept.

42. Refer the family to a private therapist should affective issues become paramount within the student.

43. Refer the parents to materials that clearly explain

ADHD and respond to questions/concerns they may be asking of school personnel.

44. Encourage the parents to seek out local support for families with children who have attention disorders (e.g., Children with Attention-Deficit Disorder (CH.A.D.D.)].

45. Organize a collaborative meeting between a school mental health professional and the parents to discuss ways they can manage and assist their child at home.

46. Arrange for systematic parenting skills training by a school mental health professional dealing with typical parent-child conflict areas (e.g., compliance, positive reinforcement, setting parameters in advance) (see *Defiant Children: A Clinician's Manual for Parent Training* [Barkley]).

47. At parent request, arrange for the teacher and/or school mental health professional to speak with the student about medication as one intervention to support him/her.

48. Arrange for the school nurse to consult with the staff/parents/physician on salient issues regarding medication dosage, side effects, and so on.

49. Assist the school staff in gathering for the physician

school-based data on the student regarding his/her performance on medication.

50. A case manager gathers information on the strategies and supports that are most effective for the student to share with the teacher(s) prior to the new school year.

__. _____

_____

__. _____

_____

__. _____

_____

AUTISM

BEHAVIORAL DEFINITIONS

1. Delayed and limited spoken language.
2. Prominence of echolalia.
3. No spoken language.
4. An inability to maintain a conversation with others.
5. Significant difficulty with social interactions including deficits in the use of nonverbal behaviors such as eye contact and facial expression.
6. An inability to initiate or establish peer relationships, demonstrating no interest or excitement about events that would seem important to self or others.
7. Delay in or no acquisition of play beyond self-involvement.
8. Lack of interpersonal social reciprocity.
9. Restricted emotional expression.
10. Minimal repertoire of interests and activities in conjunction with strong perseverations on unusual objects or parts of objects.
11. Consistent and extreme involvement with rituals or routines, an emphasis on sameness, and a difficulty with change or transitions.
12. Motor movements of a repetitive nature such as hand flapping, or, in some instances, self-injurious behaviors.
13. Varying levels of cognitive and intellectual functioning.
14. Extremely superior cognitive capabilities in very limited areas such as memory or basic arithmetic.

__. _____

_____

__. _____

_____

__. _____

_____

LONG-TERM GOALS

1. Demonstrate basic language and communication skills.
2. Develop interpersonal interactions including verbal and nonverbal cues with adults and peers to the level of potential.
3. Extinguish or reduce self-stimulating behaviors and extinguish all self-injurious acts.
4. School staff and family develop an understanding and acceptance of the student's strengths and deficit areas and of autism as a life-long disability.
5. Achieve prevocational and/or vocational skills.
6. Obtain basic academic and functional skills.

—. _____
   _____

—. _____
   _____

—. _____
   _____

SHORT-TERM OBJECTIVES

1. Participate in a psychoeducational evaluation. (1)
2. Participate in a speech and language evaluation. (2)
3. Cooperate with an occupational therapy evaluation. (3)
4. Cooperate with a psychiatric evaluation. (4)
5. Parents participate in the multidisciplinary evaluation process. (5)
6. Parents participate in an Individualized Educational Planning (IEP) team meeting and agree to the implementation of the plan and

THERAPEUTIC INTERVENTIONS

1. Examine the student's cognitive, academic, behavioral, and adaptive functioning through a complete psychoeducational evaluation.
2. Arrange for a thorough evaluation of the student's communication needs by a speech and language therapist.
3. Refer the student for an occupational therapy evaluation to assess sensory, fine motor, and self-care needs.
4. Facilitate a referral of the student for a psychiatric consultation to assist with

recommendations therein. (6)

7. Adjust to new classroom programming in a peaceful, calm, receptive manner. (7, 8, 9)

8. Utilize learning tools as provided in the educational environment. (7, 8, 10)

9. Parents provide positive support to the student who is making a transition to a new program or new material. (6, 11, 12, 13)

10. Parents follow a plan for home/school communication by reading the notes written by school staff and providing information back to the school staff as to events at home impacting the student. (11, 12, 13, 14)

11. Decrease the frequency and severity of self-injurious behaviors. (15, 16, 17, 18)

12. Exhibit fewer tantrums and more tempered behavioral functioning. (15, 16, 18, 19)

13. Parents implement the behavioral intervention plan within the home that has been developed and instituted by the school staff. (11, 12, 17, 19, 20)

14. Demonstrate the skills necessary for instrumental activities of daily living (ADLs). (21, 22, 23, 24)

15. Participate in individual or small group learning sessions focused on increasing

differential diagnosis and placement decisions.

5. A member of the multidisciplinary evaluation team interviews the parents regarding the student's strengths, learning capabilities and deficits, education needs, and special education eligibility.

6. Conduct an IEP team meeting to determine the student's special education eligibility, programming, and/or appropriate support services.

7. Implement a structured and physically well-organized learning environment individualized for the student's needs that includes identifying areas of the classroom for certain purposes (i.e., reading area, cooking area) and labeling salient objects in the room.

8. Develop visual (as opposed to verbal) strategies appropriate for the student's functioning level such as a daily and monthly schedule of events both routine and special, a depiction of choices for the student involving both work and leisure activities, visual cues for classroom rules and direction following, and visually sequenced organization of tasks.

9. Implement sensory input for the student that is con-

basic math and language skills. (25, 26, 27)

16. Demonstrate an increase in the number of appropriate social interactions with peers and adults. (23, 28, 29, 30)

17. Cooperate with speech exercises focused on airstream supply. (31)

18. Terminate the incidence of echolalia. (32, 33)

19. Utilize nonverbal means of communication. (34)

20. Increase the frequency of responsive and initiated communication. (35, 36)

21. Produce an increase in the quality of fine motor tasks. (37, 38, 39)

22. Increase the frequency of self-care skills. (40)

23. Participate in community interaction activities. (41, 42)

24. Participate meaningfully in general education classroom activities. (43)

25. Participate in prevocational/vocational assessment to ascertain interests and skills. (44, 45)

26. Demonstrate prevocational skills within the classroom setting. (46, 47)

27. Identify and implement a plan for working within the community setting. (48, 49)

28. Parents verbalize an increased understanding of

gruent with the occupational therapy evaluation recommendations as calming techniques (e.g., music, sitting on a beanbag chair, swinging, spinning).

10. Utilize social, verbal, and/or nutritional rewards to reinforce the student's small behavioral steps indicative or using the learning tools provided in the educational environment.

11. Organize a communication system (daily if needed) between home and school (e.g., a log in which the primary teacher documents to the family both routine and special events of the day and any issues confronted by the student).

12. Acquaint the parents with the student's daily schedule and routine, encouraging them to reinforce what is accomplished at school.

13. Provide a weekly or monthly calendar of events to the parents so they may assist in preparing their son/daughter for change.

14. Develop with the parents a method and process of consistent written communication from them to the school staff regarding home events that may impact the student's mood, attitude, and behavior.

15. Complete a functional behavioral analysis of the stu-

autism and its management. (50)

29. Parents report satisfaction with progress and/or planning for the student. (51)

—. _____
   _____

—. _____
   _____

—. _____
   _____

dent's self-injurious (e.g., head banging) and self-defeating (e.g., tantruming, lack of attention, etc.) behaviors by describing the setting, the identification of antecedent events preceding the target behaviors, and the consequent conditions after the problem occurs.

16. Include the student, when possible, in the selection of reinforcers from a menu of acceptable choices.

17. Using the functional behavioral assessment data, develop a behavior intervention plan that is reinforcement-rich and specifically targets the elimination of self-abusive behavior as the primary objective.

18. Use prevention strategies by manipulating the environment (e.g., changing the setting, changing the activity, changing the participants) to assist the student in not acting or reacting in a negative manner to a stimulus situation.

19. Alter the behavior intervention plan to address the student's secondary self-defeating behaviors (e.g., tantruming, interpersonal conflict, and attention span).

20. Incorporate parental ideas and concerns into the behavioral intervention plan to ensure consensus and

carryover at school and at home; monitor and reinforce parental follow-through with the plan at home.

21. Organize the student's curriculum to emphasize functional academics (e.g., following recipes, interpreting survival signs, and using money).

22. Utilize a learning approach that involves response opportunities for the student and engage him/her as an active learner (e.g., direct instruction, choral responding, response cards, and choice making) (see "Instructional Strategies to Facilitate Successful Learning Outcomes for Students with Autism" by Earles, Carlson, and Bock in *Educating Children and Youth with Autism* [Simpson and Smith Myles, eds.]).

23. Create a peer tutorial program by developing an environment whereby general education students assist the autistic student in learning such things as self-care, basic academic skills, and socialization skills under teacher supervision and monitoring.

24. Instruct the student at his/her functioning level in skills such as food preparation, laundry chores, and household cleaning procedures.

25. Offer instructional sessions in small group or individual

settings (e.g., three or fewer students) to more effectively optimize the student's attention.

26. Develop instructional plans for language arts using holistic methodologies (e.g., language experiences and thematic units).

27. Teach basic math skills with visual cues and prompts (e.g., hands-on materials) and with functional activities (e.g., sorting coins or counting money from the school soda machine).

28. Develop social stories (see *The New Social Stories: Illustrated Edition* [Gray]) with and/or for the student to teach desired responses to specific interpersonal situations (i.e., eating in the lunchroom, riding the bus, behavior in the mainstream classroom).

29. Organize a small social skills training group in which the student will have exposure to modeling, role playing, and rehearsal of positive social interactions.

30. When the student appears especially interested, use spontaneous teaching moments throughout the school day to assist him/her with generalizing appropriate social responses to new and different situations.

31. Provide the student with oral motor exercises to include emphasis on air sup-

ply and voiced airstream for speech production, and production of different phonemes (see *The Source for Autism* [Richard]).

32. Present opportunities for use of repetitive language to change the student's echolalia to meaningful responses (see *The Source for Autism* [Richard]).

33. Reinforce the student's responsive speech, which is free of echolalia.

34. If speaking is not an option for the student as a means of communication, consider sign language, pictorial communication boards, and/or assistive technology.

35. Teach the student pragmatics and social perceptions of language as appropriate for his/her developmental age.

36. Create a consistent plan to increase the student's communication skills that can be reinforced by the speech and language therapist, the classroom teacher, and the family; reinforce responsive and initiated communication.

37. Assign the student fine motor tasks at his/her developmental level.

38. Use adaptations to promote handwriting as a less frustrating experience for the student (i.e., providing a slant board, using a white board with markers, intro-

ducing the program *Hand-writing Without Tears* [Olsen]).

39. Vary opportunities for the student to work on developmentally appropriate fine motor skills that may include cutting, stringing beads, squeezing putty or clay, manipulating small pieces of a puzzle or game.

40. Develop a behavioral reinforcement program focused on the student's acquisition of self-care skills at his/her functioning level (e.g., hair grooming, appropriate dress for different weather and activities, toileting, hand washing, and tooth brushing).

41. Plan for and conduct a variety of community-based outings with the student that emphasize pragmatic language skills and intact behavior.

42. Break down community integration activities prior to going on the excursion and allow the student to discuss and role-play each piece of the situation (e.g., studying a restaurant menu, practicing ordering, and organizing money to pay the check).

43. Provide meaningful opportunities for the student in the general education setting per IEP team recommendations.

44. Conduct an evaluation of the student's abilities and

interests related to future vocational experiences.

45. Organize visits for the student and parents to vocational training sites that match the student's skills and interests.

46. Establish functional prevocational experiences in the classroom and school (e.g., picking up attendance slips, performing errands, etc.) to develop the responsibility piece of the student maintaining a job.

47. Seek out jobs from the school and community that can be completed by the student in the classroom (e.g., stapling mailings for the school office staff, folding menus for a local restaurant, sorting and counting money from the school vending machines).

48. Contact agencies in the community that provide vocational resources applicable to the student's interests and abilities.

49. By age 16, arrange a transition planning meeting to identify student transition (school to work) goals and the resources necessary to obtain those goals.

50. Create a support system for the parents that could include providing salient information on autism in the form of literature, parent support groups, and/or speakers in the community.

51. Conduct periodic communi-
    cation meetings with the
    family and school staff to ex-
    amine the student's progress
    and any outstanding issues.

___.   _____

        _____

___.   _____

        _____

___.   _____

        _____

BASIC READING SKILLS

BEHAVIORAL DEFINITIONS

1. General reading achievement is significantly below learning potential.
2. Substantial difficulty in developing an awareness that language is composed of small units of speech (phonemes).
3. Needs tailored instruction to acquire phonemic awareness to promote progress in early reading and math achievement.
4. Limited sight word vocabulary in contrast to grade level.
5. Inadequate recognition of basic words necessary for daily functioning within the community (e.g., stop, exit, restroom, etc.).
6. Difficulty with using context clues to identify unknown words.
7. Reading rate is slow and/or halting showing omissions, additions, and repetitions in oral reading; exhibits general dysfluency.
8. Reading deficits interfere with general academic functioning and/or daily living skills.

__. _____
   _____

__. _____
   _____

__. _____
   _____

LONG-TERM GOALS

1. Increase reading achievement to a level commensurate with learning potential.
2. Use reading to effectively carry out daily living needs including acquisition of vocational training.

3. Respond to tailored instruction showing substantial gains in the acquisition of phonemic awareness.
4. As a result of progress with phonemic awareness, demonstrate mastery of pre-literacy and early reading skills.
5. Increase reading rate and accuracy of reading comprehension.
6. Increase sight word vocabulary to grade level or to learning potential.
7. Parents accept the student's achievement deficits and provide supports to improve remedial areas.

—. _____
   _____
   _____
—. _____
   _____
   _____
—. _____
   _____

SHORT-TERM OBJECTIVES

1. Cooperate with hearing, vision, and/or medical examination. (1, 2)
2. Participate in a comprehensive reading or psychoeducational evaluation. (3)
3. Parents participate in an interpretive meeting to hear test results. (4)
4. Parents take part in an Individualized Education Planning (IEP) team meeting or general planning meeting and agree to implementation of a reading improvement plan. (5)
5. Demonstrate the ability to rhyme simple words at 90 percent accuracy. (6, 7, 8)

THERAPEUTIC INTERVENTIONS

1. Refer the student for hearing, vision, and/or medical examinations to rule out any physical impairment that could be the cause of his/her deficit achievement in the reading area.
2. Explore with the family any sensory modality reasons for their child's reading difficulties (i.e., vision, hearing).
3. Refer the student for evaluation.
4. School evaluation clinician(s) meets with the parents to discuss assessment results.
5. Conduct an IEP team meeting or general planning meeting with the parents

6. Recognize individual syllables in words 90 percent of the time. (9)

7. Identify initial and final sounds in words at 90 percent accuracy. (10)

8. Show the ability to separate sounds (analysis) of words at 90 percent accuracy. (11)

9. Demonstrate the ability to put sounds together to make words (synthesis) at 90 percent accuracy. (12)

10. Exhibit skill with analyzing and synthesizing words that follow the consonant/vowel/consonant (CVC) pattern. (13)

11. Recognize the sounds and letters in consonant blends at 90 percent accuracy. (14)

12. Demonstrate increased accuracy in word recognition through the use of visual strategies.
(15, 16, 17, 18, 19)

13. Demonstrate increased accuracy in word recognition through the use of auditory strategies. (20, 21, 22, 23)

14. Demonstrate increased accuracy in word recognition as a result of multisensory instructional approaches. (24, 25, 26, 27, 28)

15. Master the basic words necessary for functioning within the community as part of a sight word vocabulary. (29)

16. Use structural analysis

present to determine the student's eligibility for special education and/or ascertain general education reading services.

6. Using a rhyming book, read the book aloud, stopping after rhyming words and asking the child what words they heard that rhyme (see *Phonemic Awareness in Young Children—A Classroom Curriculum* [Adams, Foorman, Lundberg, and Beeler] and *Sound Practice: Phonological Awareness in the Classroom* [Layton, Deeny, and Upton]).

7. Play a word rhyming game with the student in which he/she is given a clue word (e.g., car) and then must identify a word that rhymes with the clue word (e.g., bar, far, star) (see *Phonemic Awareness in Young Children—A Classroom Curriculum* [Adams, Foorman, Lundberg, and Beeler] and *Sound Practice: Phonological Awareness in the Classroom* [Layton, Deeny, and Upton]).

8. Play a game using rhyming phrases in which the student must identify a rhyming word to complete the phrase (e.g., A bee in a hive in a [tree]) (see *Phonemic Awareness in Young Children—A Classroom Curriculum* [Adams, Foorman, Lundberg, and Beeler] and *Sound Practice: Phono-*

skills effectively to decode unknown words. (30, 31)

17. Successfully incorporate the use of context clues to identify unknown words. (32, 33)

18. Increase vocabulary acquisition through the use of grouping words by their meaning. (34, 35, 36)

19. Implement a word bank to build word recognition and word meaning. (37)

20. Demonstrate appropriate use of dictionary skills to enhance vocabulary and comprehension. (38)

21. Increase the amount of time spent weekly on leisure reading. (39, 40, 41, 42, 43)

22. Parents demonstrate a more accepting attitude and understanding of their child's reading deficit. (44, 45)

23. Parents report satisfaction with their child's overall school experience and progress. (46)

—. _____
_____
—. _____
_____
—. _____
_____

logical Awareness in the Classroom [Layton, Deeny, and Upton]).

9. Ask the student to clap the syllables of various words and to count how many syllables are heard in each word.

10. Using picture cards for each phoneme to be learned, have the student select a card and say the name of the picture, model saying the name of the picture, emphasizing and exaggerating the initial or final sound of the word. Have the student identify all pictures that begin with the same sound and that end with the same sound (see *Phonemic Awareness in Young Children—A Classroom Curriculum* [Adams, Foorman, Lundberg, and Beeler]).

11. Identify a list of words to use with the student such that when an initial sound is removed, an entirely different word is made; model for the student removing the initial sound of a word and have the student also participate (e.g., s-s-s-eat eat; t-t-t-all all) (see *Phonemic Awareness in Young Children—A Classroom Curriculum* [Adams, Foorman, Lundberg, and Beeler]).

12. Identify a list of words to use with the student such that when an initial sound

is added, a new word is made; model for the student adding an initial sound to a word and have the student also participate (e.g., arm-f-f-f-arm = farm) (see *Phonemic Awareness in Young Children—A Classroom Curriculum* [Adams, Foorman, Lundberg, and Beeler]).

13. Model the process and then give blocks to the student for him/her to carry out these steps: Each block (of a different color) represents a sound in a word (e.g., in the word *name,* one color block stands for *n,* a second block stands for *a* and a third block stands for the *m* sound; the student arranges blocks together to represent a three-sound word, which he/she eventually recognizes as they synthesize the sounds together repeatedly (see *Phonemic Awareness in Young Children—A Classroom Curriculum* [Adams, Foorman, Lundberg, and Beeler]).

14. Using a rhyming strategy, introduce a three-letter word and add a word beginning with a consonant blend that rhymes with the initial three-letter word (e.g., row = grow, may = stay); continue building words with the student in this manner (see *Phonemic Awareness in Young Children—A Class-*

room Curriculum [Adams, Foorman, Lundberg, and Beeler]).

15. Teach the student whole word configuration strategies where each word is outlined and memorized per its shape.

16. Provide instruction in the compare/contrast method in which the student systematically compares and identifies words by examining the beginning, middle, and ending of words that are very similar in appearance.

17. Use modeling in which a word is introduced verbally, but then exhibited in written form again and again, repeatedly show the student the initial, medial, and final letters of the word.

18. Develop word bank cards upon which the student learns to readily identify words in simple games with peers or the teacher.

19. Structure word identification activities such as word bingo in which the student is repeatedly requested to read selected words.

20. Teach the elementary student auditory discrimination skills using a phonemic awareness program that involves teaching spoken sounds, using the ear, eye, and mouth in producing the sounds and integrating them into the processes of

reading, spelling, and speaking (see *The Lindamood Auditory Discrimination In-Depth Program* [Lindamood and Lindamood]).

21. Instruct the secondary student in a phonemic awareness program with an emphasis on sequencing sounds and matching them to written symbols and processing written language through auditory channels (see *Reading From Scratch / RFS* [Honert]).

22. Teach implicit phonetic skills by introducing the student to a number of words that are similar in their makeup (e.g., seat, treat, heat), and then assist the student, using inductive reasoning to identify the phonic rules and generalizations in the words.

23. Use a phonetic approach in which the student learns consonant and vowel sounds in isolation and in words as he/she is taught 1,500 of the most frequently used reading/spelling words (see *The Writing Road to Reading* [Spaulding and Spaulding]).

24. Provide instruction in a visual, auditory, kinesthetic, and tactile approach in which the student sees the word, hears the word said aloud, traces the word, and feels the word as it is traced (see *Remedial Techniques in*

Basic School Subjects [Fernald]).

25. Offer a visual, auditory, and kinesthetic phonics method in which the sounds of letters are learned in level one; blending sounds and analyzing words into sounds is level two; level three involves writing sentences and stories using words that can be identified phonetically; and level four addresses phonetically irregular words, dictionary usage, and prefixes/suffixes/root words (see *Remedial Training For Children With Specific Disability in Reading, Spelling and Penmanship* [Gillingham and Stillman]).

26. Follow a visual/auditory format in which the teacher acts as an analyzer of words into sounds for the student in an intensive one-on-one approach (see *The Early Detection of Reading Difficulties* [Clay]).

27. Provide instruction for the elementary student in a structured visual, auditory, and kinesthetic rote approach, requiring auditory and visual perceptual tasks (e.g., identifying auditorily the position of a vowel and visually identifying words on a word list), discrimination tasks (e.g., working with different letter/sound combinations), and sequenc-

ing tasks (e.g., learning to write letters and connecting them in a cursive format) (see *A Multi-Sensory Approach to Language Arts for Specific Language Disability Children: A Guide for Primary Teachers* [Slingerland]).

28. Introduce a word chunking system to teach the student visually and auditorily to break a word into familiar, workable parts (e.g., *Glass Analysis for Decoding Only* [Glass and Glass]).

29. Teach sight recognition of words necessary for adaptation to the community (e.g., gender identification for restrooms, traffic signs, exit signs, etc.).

30. Give the student opportunities to learn to pronounce major prefixes (initial syllables) and major suffixes (word endings).

31. Organize lessons that assist the student in identifying the root word when a prefix and/or suffix is present.

32. Model for the student, when faced with an unidentified word in a sentence or paragraph, the use of the meaning of the nearby text coupled with word analysis skills to ascertain the unknown word.

33. Teach the student the SCANR process in which a *Substitute* word is used for

the unknown word; he/she
is to *Check* to see if the substitute word is reasonable
in the context; then *Ask* if
the word actually does fit;
and finally adjust if a new
word is *Needed* and *Revise*
as necessary (see "Two Approaches to Vocabulary Instruction: The Teaching of
Individual Word Meanings
and Practice in Deriving
Word Meaning from Con-
text" by Jenkins, Matlock,
and Slocum in *Reading Research Quarterly* [1989, 24:
215–235]).

34. Introduce the student to the
keyword strategy whereby a
new vocabulary word is
linked to an already known
word through pneumonic
memory methods (e.g., *bril-
liant* is linked to a picture
of a twinkling star; *melancholy* is linked to a sad
melody the student knows)
(see *Literacy Disorders:
Holistic Diagnosis and Remediation* [Manzo and
Manzo]).

35. Organize vocabulary into
categorical formats for the
student (e.g., placing words
that are alike in their
meaning into vocabulary
circles) (see *Dyslexia: Research and Resource Guide*
[Spafford and Grosser]).

36. Use the List-Group-Label
strategy when teaching
technical vocabulary
whereby the student lists

essential words from a lesson and groups the words into lists by main topic and subtopics (see *Teacher's Handbook for Elementary Social Studies* [Taba]).

37. Preview vocabulary with the student for a particular reading selection by using a vocabulary splash method where keywords are listed from the selection, then the student records the words, their meanings, and synonyms to develop a word bank (see *Strategies For Success* [Meltzer, Roditi, Haynes, Biddle, Paster, and Taber]).

38. Teach dictionary skills, including alphabetical order, using guide words, and interpreting multiple definitions.

39. Organize daily reading activities in a positive classroom climate with praise and encouragement for reading accomplishments and progress.

40. Create a visual chart to display the increased reading time of the student and/or offer extrinsic rewards for reading goals attained.

41. Seek out recreational reading materials that are at the student's independent reading level and that match his/her interests.

42. Encourage parents to create a family reading time and

activities that promote practice for the student's reading skills and reading for enjoyment.

43. Encourage the student to participate in after-school activities that value reading such as poetry club, drama club, school newspaper, and/or a book club.

44. Communicate with the parents frequently to keep them well-informed about their child's learning needs and progress.

45. Assist the parents with seeking out information and support on reading disabilities from such organizations as the International Reading Association and the Council for Exceptional Children—Division for Learning Disabilities.

46. A case manager (reading specialist, resource teacher) gathers information on the strategies and supports that are most effective for the student to share with the teacher(s) prior to the new school year.

___. _____

_____

___. _____

_____

___. _____

_____

BEHAVIORALLY/EMOTIONALLY IMPAIRED—ADOLESCENT

BEHAVIORAL DEFINITIONS

1. An emotional/behavioral dysfunction that interferes with academic, social, personal, and vocational functioning in the school setting and negatively affects functioning in the home and community.
2. Behavioral or emotional response far different from age-appropriate norms, considering cultural or ethnic background.
3. Deficit is primarily noted within the affective domain and may be the result of a serious mental illness (e.g., schizophrenia, bipolar disorder, etc.).
4. Exhibits aggressive behavior toward self or others.
5. Anxious, depressed mood with potential to act against self and exhibits withdrawn, isolating behavior.
6. Difficulty with initiating and/or maintaining relationships with peers or adults.
7. Unexplainable, unusual, or unpredictable behavior and/or feelings that occur under normal circumstances.
8. Physical symptoms or fears related to health issues for which there appears to be no rational or organic basis.
9. Exhibits low frustration tolerance and poor anger control.

—. _____
   _____

—. _____
   _____

—. _____
   _____

LONG-TERM GOALS

1. Attain the goals and short-term objectives that are identified on the Individualized Education Plan (IEP) and that seek to replace maladaptive behavior or emotions with behavior/emotions more adaptive to the school setting.
2. Eliminate all aggressive behavior toward self or others.
3. Increase prosocial behavior in daily functioning while reducing the severity, frequency, and duration of disruptive, acting-out behavior.
4. Increase prosocial behavior in daily functioning while reducing the severity, frequency, and duration of anxious, fearful, or withdrawn behavior.
5. Demonstrate self-management and employability skills in the community and vocational training settings.
6. Maintain good attendance in school and employment settings, eliminating truant or school refusal behaviors.
7. Parents learn to understand their son's/daughter's challenges, seek out supportive resources for their adolescent and for the family, and work closely with the school in developing and following through with a meaningful, effective treatment plan.

__. _____
_____
_____
__. _____
_____
_____
__. _____
_____

SHORT-TERM OBJECTIVES

1. Cooperate with a psychoeducational evaluation. (1, 2, 3)
2. Participate willingly in a psychiatric evaluation. (4)
3. Parents participate in the multidisciplinary evaluation team meeting process, collaborate on and agree to a positive behavior intervention support plan. (5)

THERAPEUTIC INTERVENTIONS

1. Refer the student for a psychoeducational evaluation to include an assessment of social/emotional, academic, intellectual, and adaptive functioning.
2. Complete a functional behavioral assessment of the student's dysfunctional behaviors, examining the situational antecedents, the

4. Parents, and the student as appropriate, participate in the IEP team meeting and accept identified recommendations. (6)

5. Assimilate all components of the positive behavior intervention support plan and agree to its implementation. (7)

6. Parents consult with a physician on potential medication for the student and share school-related recommendations with selected school staff. (8)

7. Agree to a behavior contract identifying a specific target behavior to work toward changing and select contingent reinforcers as incentives that are parent- and teacher-approved. (9)

8. Increase the frequency of targeted positive behaviors as a result of systematic monitoring and an extrinsic reward system. (10)

9. Utilize the Situation/ Options/Consequences/ Solutions (SOCS) problem-solving method as a means of coping with frustrating, anger- or anxiety-provoking situations. (11)

10. Report experiencing markedly less anxiety and/or fear as a result of desensitization experiences. (12, 13)

11. Show steady improvement in decreasing the frequency

nature of the negative behaviors, and the consequences of the negative behaviors.

3. Organize the data from the functional behavioral assessment, along with input from the student, parents, and school staff, resulting in a report that describes the behavior(s), predicts when the behavior(s) may occur, hypothesizes reasons for the behavior(s), and proposes interventions that lead to resolution of the problem(s) (see *Positive Behavior Support for ALL Michigan Students: Creating Environments That Assure Learning* [Michigan Department of Education—Office of Special Education and Early Intervention Services]).

4. Refer the student for a psychiatric consultation/evaluation.

5. Meet with the parents to obtain their input into the multidisciplinary evaluation team process, interpret evaluation results to them, and collaborate on the development of a positive behavior intervention support plan.

6. Collaborate with the family at the IEP team meeting to determine the student's eligibility for special education, establish goals and short-term objectives in deficit areas, identify appropriate programs and/or services, decide upon needed

of negative behaviors using self-management skills. (14)

12. Increase prosocial interactions through participation in social skills training. (15, 16)

13. Reduce the frequency of disruptive behaviors by participating in a cuing procedure. (17)

14. Participate in coping skills training and implement positive responses in stressful situations. (18)

15. Verbalize positive self-descriptive statements, making at least one positive statement about self per week regarding his/her actions or accomplishments. (19)

16. Meet with a mental health professional to address emotional/behavioral issues that are negatively impacting social and academic functioning in the school. (20, 21)

17. Exhibit significant improvement in school attendance. (22, 23, 24)

18. Demonstrate measurable academic gains in the general education curriculum commensurate with learning potential. (25, 26)

19. Demonstrate 80 percent mastery of academic material in a class schedule tailored to own needs, strengths, and interests. (27)

accommodations and modifications, and finalize a positive behavior intervention support plan.

7. Review and discuss with the student and family all aspects of the positive behavior intervention support plan and have them sign an agreement that includes target behaviors, a hierarchy of reinforcers, and a hierarchy of consequences (e.g., in-school suspension, home/school reporting).

8. Refer the parents to a physician to evaluate the student as to the need for psychotropic medication; discuss with the parents any implications for the school setting from their medical consultation.

9. Develop from the functional behavioral assessment a specific behavior contract to implement with the student that targets one of the most maladaptive behaviors to extinguish using a contingency of reinforcers as selected by the student (see *Toward Positive Classroom Discipline* [Clarizio] and *On Our Best Behavior: Positive Behavior-Management Strategies for the Classroom* [Zimmerman]).

10. Implement a behavioral system whereby the student's target positive behaviors are identified and his/her performance in exhibiting those behaviors are routinely

20. Routinely use study skill strategies to increase comprehension and mastery of content. (28, 29, 30)

21. Effectively use technology to improve academic performance. (31)

22. Exhibit an assignment completion rate above 85 percent using organizational strategies. (32)

23. Demonstrate prosocial behaviors needed for employment. (33)

24. Identify postsecondary academic and/or vocational goals. (34, 35, 36)

25. Parents seek out and identify strategies to assist them with parenting their child. (37, 38)

26. Parents express satisfaction with their child's progress in the behavioral and affective domain, as well as with his/her overall school program. (39, 40)

—. _____
   _____

—. _____
   _____

—. _____
   _____

evaluated in a point system or a token system; discuss outcomes with the student and give rewards from a reinforcement menu on a predetermined schedule.

11. In the classroom and in small group counseling sessions, incorporate the student as a participant in the SOCS model of problem solving: Identify what the problem *situation* is and the feelings generated by it; identify solution *options;* outline what the *consequences* might be; select the best *solution* and implement it (see *Emotional Intelligence* [Goleman]).

12. Create a hierarchy of desensitization experiences for the student as steps to overcoming academic fear and/or anxiety (e.g., steps for overcoming the fear of participating in class could be: The teacher designates a question in advance for the student to answer the following day; the student writes out the answer to the question the evening before; the student practices answering the question alone in front of a mirror at home; the student practices answering the question with note cards in front of a family member; the student creates a positive visual image of answering the question in a confident, competent manner; the teacher calls

on the student in the classroom allowing him/her to
answer using note cards as
a backup prompt).

13. In a gradual approach over
the course of time, expose
the student to a threatening
stimulus paired with a fa-
vorable or desired item or
experience (e.g., stage fright
matched with favorite
music being played while
the student is on stage; test
taking matched with previously learned relaxation
techniques (see *Toward Positive Classroom Discipline*
[Clarizio]).

14. Train the student in self-
management strategies at
his/her developmental level
including: self-assessment
(observe own behavior and
decide if the responses meet
an established criteria);
self-recording (record the
frequency of responses that
meet the criteria); self-
determination of reinforcement (decide on the type
and amount of consequences
based on own performance);
and self-administration of
reinforcement (access the
reinforcers and take what is
appropriate based on performance). For students with
more seriously maladaptive
behavior, self-management
mastery determines the
level of freedom and privileges the student has in the
special education classroom
(see *Assessment and Treat-*

ment of Emotional or Behavioral Disorders [Ninness, Glenn, and Ellis]).

15. Refer the student to a social skill training group in which instruction, modeling, practice, rehearsal (role playing), feedback, and generalization will be used to assist him/her in replacing maladaptive social responses with more adaptive choices (see *Skillstreaming the Adolescent: New Strategies and Perspectives for Teaching Prosocial Skills* [Goldstein and McGinnis]).

16. Implement a peer tutoring program matching the student with a same-age peer for both academic and social intervention; ask the peer tutor to offer problem-solving strategies and verbal feedback to the student as to his/her prosocial choices (see "Using a Peer Confrontation System in a Group Setting" by Salend, Jantzen, and Giek in *Behavior Disorders* [1992, 17: 211–218]).

17. Within a small group instructional setting, use the stimulus cuing procedure in which the teacher provides a neutral, unemotional cue to the student when the student has engaged in a disruptive behavior, giving the student the opportunity to replace the negative behavior with an appropriate one; a positive replacement response can be linked to a

contingent reinforcer (see "A Simple Stimulus Cue for Controlling Disruptive Classroom Behavior" by Lobitz in *Journal of Abnormal Child Psychology* [1974, 2: 143–152]).

18. In individual or small group counseling sessions, teach the student stress-management strategies (e.g., relaxation techniques, guided imagery, positive self-talk, problem-solving strategies, etc.) to implement in the place of anxious or aggressive responses (see *Cognitive-Behavior Modification* [Meichenbaum]).

19. Establish a time each week when the student is asked to identify a positive social, behavioral, or academic accomplishment about himself/herself.

20. Engage the student in individual counseling with a school mental health professional emphasizing improved self-concept and prosocial behavior.

21. Should issues of anxiety, conduct, anger control, depression, or tendencies toward suicide become severe, refer the family and student to a therapist outside the school setting or to a community mental health clinic for more intensive intervention; talk with the parents and the student about a more restrictive

school placement if appropriate.

22. Explore with the family any reasons (e.g., a chronic medical condition) why the student is frequently absent from school, and if appropriate, institute homebound services.

23. Establish a contract providing incentives, rewards, and/or recognition as negotiated with the student for consistent school attendance; hold a weekly conference to review with the student his/her attendance record for the week as well as academic and social/behavioral progress.

24. Seek out resources from the community that can assist or require family enforcement of school attendance by the adolescent (e.g., day care services on a sliding scale so that the student is no longer required by parents to stay with younger siblings; a visit by a truancy officer to enforce the legal mandate of school attendance).

25. Assist the student with working in the general education curriculum, providing support only as needed.

26. Adapt the general education curriculum in deficit areas or areas of need, considering the methods that apply most successfully for the student as defined through the IEP

team meeting (e.g., reduce the number of items to learn or to complete; increase the amount of time for learning, task completion, or testing; increase the amount of assistance [e.g., using a peer tutor, a teacher assistant, using the coteaching model]; alter the instructional format in terms of how information is delivered to the student [e.g., using hands-on activities, providing models, organizing the student in a cooperative learning group]; and change how the student may respond [e.g., answering questions verbally instead of in written form, completing a project instead of a research paper]).

27. Work with the student and parents to develop a schedule of core academic courses and electives that match the instructional needs and interests of the student (e.g., taking advanced algebra instead of a pre-algebra course).

28. Instruct the student in an organized approach to studying (e.g., SQ3R: Survey, Question, Read, Recite, Review) (see Steps in the SQ3R Method in *Effective Study* [Robinson]).

29. Teach the Cornell Study Skill Method of note taking to improve both the student's comprehension and writing abilities whereby

the student and/or teacher may make notes in the margins of the material to be mastered pertaining to very specific, salient content that must be learned (see *How to Study in College* [Pauk]).

30. Create study guides or assist the student with developing study guides that outline salient information to be covered on a given test.

31. Integrate technological assistance into the academic regimen for the student (e.g., an electronic speller, spell check/grammar programs, how-to word-processing programs, Dictaphone, tape recorder, calculator, and use of specially designed software matching the academic needs of the student).

32. Instruct the student in logistical organizational skills to improve the rate and quality of assignment completion (e.g., keeping a daily agenda of assignments both short- and long-term, using a weekly/monthly calendar on which are identified dates for projects and tests, keeping materials and school supplies readily available).

33. Teach social skills that are specifically necessary for success in the workplace to include positive interpersonal initiative and response skills, community access skills, and dealing with conflict scenarios in

the workplace; provide job shadowing and prevocational experiences in the community to practice these skills.

34. Set up opportunities for the student and family to visit potential vocational training sites that coincide with the student's strengths and interests.

35. Provide information to the student and family regarding higher education institutions that address the scholastic strengths, weaknesses, expectations, and interests of the student.

36. Collaborate with the student and parents in conducting an individualized transition plan meeting in which the student identifies future goals and steps to obtain those goals in areas such as independent living, higher education or vocational training, community involvement; include agency representatives who can contribute to this planning.

37. Have the parents read *Parents and Adolescents Living Together* (Forgatch and Patterson) or *Surviving Your Adolescents: How to Manage and Let Go Of Your 13 to 18 Year Olds* (Phelan); meet with the parents to counsel them on ways to improve their parenting skills.

38. Assist the parents with finding local and/or national re-

sources that provide support to families with adolescents maintaining emotional difficulties such as the National Alliance for the Mentally Ill and the Federation of Families for Children's Mental Health.

39. Maintain close communication with the parents for joint problem solving, reporting successes of their adolescent and building a trusting relationship with them.

40. Designate the student to have a case manager in the school setting (e.g., special education teacher, school mental health professional) to maintain a positive focus on the student and his/her ongoing needs over the long term, act as an advocate in times of adversity or crisis, maintain an ongoing positive relationship with the family, take a leadership role in problem solving, and act as a liaison to outside clinicians and/or agencies involved with the student.

__. _____
   _____

__. _____
   _____

__. _____
   _____

BEHAVIORALLY/EMOTIONALLY IMPAIRED—CHILD

BEHAVIORAL DEFINITIONS

1. An emotional/behavioral dysfunction that interferes with academic and social functioning in the school setting and impacts functioning in the home and community.
2. Behavioral or emotional response far different from age-appropriate norms, considering cultural or ethnic background.
3. Deficit is primarily noted within the affective domain and may be the result of a serious mental illness (e.g., schizophrenia, bipolar disorder, etc.).
4. Exhibits aggressive behavior toward self or others.
5. Anxious, depressed mood with potential to act against self and exhibits withdrawn, isolating behavior.
6. Difficulty with initiating and/or maintaining relationships with peers or adults.
7. Unexplainable, unusual, or unpredictable behavior and/or feelings that occur under normal circumstances.
8. Physical symptoms or fears related to health issues for which there appears to be no rational or organic basis.
9. Exhibits low frustration tolerance and poor anger control.

LONG-TERM GOALS

1. Attain the goals and short-term objectives that are identified on the Individualized Education Plan (IEP) and that seek to replace maladaptive behavior or emotions with behavior/emotions more adaptive to the school setting.
2. Control behavior and emotions sufficiently to socially interact appropriately and academically achieve to level of potential.
3. Eliminate all aggressive behavior toward self or others.
4. Increase prosocial behavior in daily functioning while reducing the severity, frequency, and duration of disruptive, acting-out behavior.
5. Increase prosocial behavior in daily functioning while reducing the severity, frequency, and duration of anxious, fearful, or withdrawn behavior.
6. Parents understand their child's challenges, seek out supportive resources for their child and family, and work closely with the school in developing and following a meaningful, effective treatment plan.

—. _____

_____

—. _____

_____

—. _____

_____

SHORT-TERM OBJECTIVES	THERAPEUTIC INTERVENTIONS
1. Cooperate with a psychoeducational evaluation. (1, 2, 3)	1. Refer the student for a psychoeducational evaluation to include an assessment of social/emotional, academic, intellectual, and adaptive functioning.
2. Participate willingly in a psychiatric evaluation. (4)	
3. Parents participate in the multidisciplinary evaluation team process, collaborate on and agree to a positive behavior intervention support plan. (5)	2. Complete a functional behavioral assessment of the student's dysfunctional behaviors, examining the situational antecedents, the nature of the negative behaviors, and the conse-
4. Parents, and the student as appropriate, participate in	

the IEP team meeting and accept identified recommendations. (6)

5. Assimilate all components of the positive behavior intervention support plan and agree to its implementation. (7)

6. Parents consult with a physician on potential medication for the student and share school-related recommendations with selected school staff. (8)

7. Agree to a behavior contract identifying a specific target behavior to work toward changing, and select contingent reinforcers as incentives that are parent- and teacher-approved. (9)

8. Demonstrate a reduction in negative behavior as a result of a group contingency plan. (10)

9. Increase the frequency of targeted positive behaviors as a result of systematic monitoring and an extrinsic reward system. (11)

10. Increase positive reactions to stressful situations through the experience of psychodrama or role playing. (12)

11. Use music effectively as a positive outlet for anger or frustration. (13)

12. Increase prosocial interactions through participation in social skills training. (14, 15, 16)

quences of the negative behaviors.

3. Organize the data from the functional behavioral assessment, along with input from the student, parents, and school staff, resulting in a report that describes the behavior(s), predicts when the behavior(s) may occur, hypothesizes reasons for the behavior(s), and proposes interventions that lead to resolution of the problem(s) (see *Positive Behavior Support for ALL Michigan Students: Creating Environments That Assure Learning* [Michigan Department of Education—Office of Special Education and Early Intervention Services]).

4. Refer the student for a psychiatric consultation/evaluation.

5. Meet with the parents to obtain their input into the multidisciplinary evaluation team process, interpret evaluation results to them, and collaborate on the development of a positive behavior intervention support plan.

6. Collaborate with the family at the IEP team meeting to determine the student's eligibility for special education, establish goals and short-term objectives, identify appropriate programs and/or services, decide on needed accommodations and modifications, and fi-

13. Demonstrate more frequent prosocial actions by learning empathy. (17)

14. Show steady improvement with self-management skills. (18)

15. Verbalize positive self-descriptive statements, making at least one positive statement about self two times per week. (19)

16. Meet with a mental health professional to address emotional/behavioral issues that are negatively impacting social and academic functioning in the school. (20, 21)

17. Exhibit significant improvement in school attendance. (22, 23, 24, 25)

18. Demonstrate measurable academic gains in the general education curriculum commensurate with learning potential. (26, 27)

19. Demonstrate 80 percent mastery of academic material in a curriculum tailored to own needs and strengths. (28)

20. Divide tasks into meaningful segments and work toward completion with accuracy. (29)

21. Utilize study skill strategies to increase comprehension and mastery of content. (30)

22. Stay focused 80 percent of the time on difficult tasks without displaying a low

nalize a positive behavior intervention support plan.

7. Review and discuss with the student and family all aspects of the positive behavior intervention support plan and have them sign an agreement that includes target behaviors, a hierarchy of reinforcers, and a hierarchy of consequences (e.g., time-out, home/school reporting).

8. Refer the parents to a physician to evaluate the student as to the need for psychotropic medication; discuss with the parents any implications for the school setting from their medical consultation.

9. Develop from the functional behavioral assessment a specific behavior contract to implement with the student that targets one of the most maladaptive behaviors to extinguish using a contingency of reinforcers as selected by the student (see *Toward Positive Classroom Discipline* [Clarizio] and *On Our Best Behavior: Positive Behavior-Management Strategies for the Classroom* [Zimmerman]).

10. Develop a group contingency plan to reduce a targeted negative behavior of the behaviorally troubled student in which his/her positive performance earns contingent reinforcement for self *and* classmates (see "Pro-

frustration tolerance or quitting. (31, 32, 33)

23. Utilize checklists to enhance the organization of materials and assignments. (34, 35, 36)

24. Implement a system for keeping an organized desk and/or locker. (37, 38)

25. Parents participate in a parent training course to improve child management at home. (39)

26. Parents identify new child behavior management techniques they will try. (39, 40, 41)

27. Parents verbalize acceptance of their child's emotional status, seek out supports and resources to meet their child's needs, and work collaboratively with school personnel to develop an effective treatment plan for him/her. (4, 5, 42, 43)

28. Parents express satisfaction with their child's progress in the behavioral and affective domain, as well as with his/her overall school program. (44)

—. _____
   _____
—. _____
   _____
—. _____
   _____

gramming Generalization and Maintenance of Treatment Effects Across Time and Across Settings" by Walker and Buckley in *Journal of Applied Behavior Analysis* [1972, 5: 209–224]).

11. Implement a behavioral system whereby the student's target positive behaviors are identified, and his/her performance in exhibiting those behaviors are routinely evaluated in a point system or a token system; discuss outcomes with the student and give rewards from a reinforcement menu on a predetermined schedule.

12. Use role play or psychodrama with classmates to assist the student in solving an individual social or emotional concern, targeting a common problem that same-age peers may be experiencing, and developing more cohesiveness with classmates (see *Understanding and Teaching Emotionally Disturbed Children* [Newcomer]).

13. Organize frequent vocal and/or instrumental musical activities to provide a positive expressive outlet for the student's feelings, allow the opportunity for the student to be successful, use music as a reward, and create a relaxed, calm atmosphere (see *Understanding and Teaching Emotionally*

Disturbed Children [Newcomer]).

14. Refer the student to a social skills training group with same-age peers to replace maladaptive social responses with more adaptive choices through the use of instruction, modeling, practice, rehearsal (role playing), feedback, and generalizations (see *Think Aloud* [Camp and Bash]).

15. Provide the student classroom instruction in a social skills curriculum where the classroom teacher serves as a cotherapist with a school mental health professional in implementing the instruction, covering areas of interpersonal problem solving, anger control, stress management, cooperation, and situation perception (see *The Prepare Curriculum: Teaching Prosocial Competencies* [Goldstein]).

16. Pair the student with a same-age or older peer who can assist the student in social problem solving and can provide verbal feedback to him/her as to what are positive choices (see "Using a Peer Confrontation System in a Group Setting" by Salend, Jantzen, and Giek in *Behavior Disorders* [1992, 17: 211–218] and *Changing Behaviour: Teaching Children with Emotional and Behavioral Difficulties in Primary and*

Secondary Classrooms [McNamara and Moreton]).

17. Create a classroom environment in which kindness, responsibility, and self-control are reinforced, and where help-giving behavior (e.g., showing kindness and understanding) is modeled by all classroom staff and is an expectation for students (see *Interventions for Students with Emotional Disorders* [Morgan and Reinhart]).

18. Train the student in self-management strategies at his/her developmental level including: self-instruction (give self verbal instruction and repeat the instruction as a prompt when completing a task); self-assessment (observe own behavior and decide if the responses meet an established criteria); self-recording (record the frequency of responses that meet the criteria); self-determination of reinforcement (decide on the type and amount of consequences based on own performance); and self-administration of reinforcement (access the reinforcers and take what is appropriate based on performance) (see *Assessment and Treatment of Emotional or Behavioral Disorders* [Ninness, Glenn, and Ellis]).

19. Establish a specified time on two occasions per week when the student meets

with the teacher to verbalize a positive statement about self (e.g., recognizing academic or social accomplishments during the week).

20. Engage the student in individual counseling with a school mental health professional emphasizing improved self-concept and prosocial behavior.

21. Should issues of anxiety, conduct, anger control, depression, or tendencies toward suicide become severe, refer the family and student to a private therapist outside of the school setting or to a community mental health clinic for more intensive intervention; talk with the parents about a more restrictive school placement if appropriate.

22. Explore with the family any reasons (e.g., a chronic medical condition) why the student is frequently absent from school.

23. Establish an incentive program with the student that offers positive reinforcement for every day the student is in school.

24. Develop a caring, nurturing relationship with the student and the parents to build trust between home and school to help parents enforce their child's school attendance.

25. Make a home visit to assess reasons why the student

may be remaining at home and contact community service agencies that may be supportive of the family's needs.

26. Assist the student with working in the general education curriculum, providing support only as needed.

27. Adapt the general education curriculum implementing methods that will apply most successfully for the student (e.g., reduce the number of items to learn or complete; increase the amount of time for learning, task completion, or testing; increase the amount of assistance [e.g., using a buddy system, a cross-age tutor, a teacher assistant, the coteaching model]; alter the instructional format in terms of how information is delivered to the student [e.g., using hands-on activities, providing models or concrete samples]; adjust the level of difficulty [e.g., simplify directions, allow a calculator to complete the math portion of a science experiment]; and change how the student may respond [e.g., answering questions verbally instead of in written form, completing a hands-on project instead of a written report]).

28. Consider the student's learning needs, current level of achievement, and

parental expectations when determining a curriculum (e.g., consider a general education curriculum at a lower grade level or a highly individualized curriculum designed to match the strengths and areas of deficit of the student).

29. Teach the student task analyzing skills by instructing him/her to break a difficult task into smaller, easier to understand pieces.

30. Instruct the student in an organized approach to studying (e.g., SQ3R: Survey, Question, Read, Recite, Review) (see Steps in the SQ3R Method in *Effective Study* [Robinson]).

31. Assist the student in identifying a list of rewards and then develop a positive reinforcement plan targeting the extension of time the student works at a more difficult task.

32. Assist the student with setting goals for tackling more difficult tasks and creating meaningful plans to do so.

33. Engage the student in attribution retraining in which the student moves away from negative self-talk and does not allow himself/herself excuses for not learning or taking responsibility (see "An Attribution Training Program with Learning Disabled Children" by Shelton, Anastopoulous, and

Linden in *Journal of Learning Disabilities* [1985, 18(5): 261–265]).

34. Create a checklist with the student that identifies the items needed for him/her to perform academic tasks at school each day.

35. Develop a checklist or assignment notebook wherein the student keeps track of assignments in progress, assignments completed, and due dates.

36. Assist the student in learning to prioritize work by creating a list of tasks in order of importance.

37. Instruct the student in a system for organizing his/her desk and/or locker (e.g., using plastic boxes, zippered pencil cases, file folders, and specifying areas of the desk or locker for textbooks and personal items); solicit the parent's physical and financial support.

38. Show the student the benefit of color coding materials by subject with parent support for the purchase of needed items.

39. Offer effective parenting technique training to assist the parents in learning to deal with issues of compliance, rewards, time-out, and general child management (see *Your Defiant Child: 8 Steps to Better Behavior* [Barkley and Ben-

ton] and *Defiant Children:
A Clinician's Manual for
Parent Training* [Barkley]
or *Skills Training for Chil-
dren with Behavior Disor-
ders: A Parent and
Therapist Guidebook*
[Bloomquist]).

40. Have the parents read the
appropriate chapters in
The Challenging Child
(Greenspan) or *When Your
Child is Afraid* (McCauley
and Schachter) and then
meet with them to discuss
the techniques most useful
with their child.

41. Use the book and video
*1-2-3 Magic: Training Your
Preschoolers and Preteens to
Do What You Want* (Phelan)
to teach child management
techniques to the parents;
meet with them to discuss
the strategies most useful
with their child.

42. Provide the parents with
frequent, routine communication on their child's
progress, needs, and suc-
cesses, and work diligently
with them to problem solve
concerns.

43. Assist the parents with locating supportive information involving local and
national resources (e.g.,
Federation of Families for
Children's Mental Health).

44. Designate the student to
have a case manager in the
school setting (e.g., special
education teacher, school

mental health professional) to maintain a positive focus on the student and his/her ongoing needs over the long term, act as an advocate in times of adversity or crisis, maintain an ongoing positive relationship with the family, take a leadership role in problem solving, and act as a liaison to outside clinicians and/or agencies involved with the student.

—. _____

_____

—. _____

_____

—. _____

_____

CHRONICALLY HEALTH IMPAIRED

BEHAVIORAL DEFINITIONS

1. A chronic illness that compromises health continuously or by acute episodes (e.g., diabetes mellitus, cancer, sickle-cell anemia, asthma, recurrent headaches, HIV/AIDS, juvenile arthritis, seizure disorders).
2. The illness compromises cognitive, physical, and/or affective functioning.
3. School attendance is interrupted due to hospitalization or more extensive stays at home, resulting in a need for homebound services.
4. Lower academic achievement, below learning potential, due to absences and/or weakened tolerance to daily activities including school tasks.
5. Essential medical needs require environmental changes in the classroom.

___. _____

_____

___. _____

_____

___. _____

_____

LONG-TERM GOALS

1. Maintain the greatest degree of normalcy in the school setting.
2. Keep academic functioning commensurate with learning potential across the curriculum.
3. Student and parents understand the medical condition and advocate for health accommodations needed in school.

4. Accept responsibility for performing medical interventions that can be done in the school setting.
5. Parents work closely with school personnel to establish a quality educational program and health care plan for their son/daughter.

—. _____
_____
—. _____
_____
—. _____
_____

SHORT-TERM OBJECTIVES

1. Parents provide initial information to school personnel regarding the student's medical condition and give permission for access to the child's medical records and treating personnel. (1)
2. Parents meet with school personnel to assist with specific health-related plans for the student at school. (2, 3)
3. Cooperate with a psychoeducational or neuropsychological evaluation. (4)
4. Participate in a speech and language assessment. (5)
5. Cooperate with physical/occupational therapy assessment. (6)
6. Parents meet with school personnel to discuss evaluation outcomes. (7)
7. Parents agree to recommendations of the Individualized Educational Planning

THERAPEUTIC INTERVENTIONS

1. Arrange for a consultation with the family and obtain a release of information from them for medical personnel to give pertinent health information on the student.
2. Organize a school-based team of pertinent members including a school nurse to review health issues of the student as they relate to the educational setting.
3. The school nurse meets with the family and medical personnel to create any protocols that are needed for daily health care issues of the student and/or a crisis response plan.
4. Conduct or refer the student for psychoeducation or neuropsychological evaluation.
5. Refer the student for a speech/language evaluation.

(IEP) team and/or Section 504 team meeting. (8, 9)

8. Master and perform the routine self-care health needs as independently as possible. (10, 11, 12, 13)

9. Allow for peers to obtain information regarding the medical condition. (14, 15, 16, 17)

10. Use self-advocacy skills to get medical, emotional, and academic needs met. (18, 19, 20, 21)

11. Exhibit coping skills during times of a health crisis. (22, 23, 24, 25)

12. Demonstrate steady progress with academic achievement. (26, 27, 28, 29)

13. Cooperate with periodic curriculum-based assessment. (30)

14. Cooperate with caregiving staff in having all health needs met. (31, 32)

15. Parents take an active role in clearly communicating needs of the student (e.g., placing in writing requests for medical care at school, reporting changes in the student's condition, reporting new information regarding the student's medical interventions). (33)

16. Parents express satisfaction with their son's/daughter's academic status and care plan in the school environment. (34, 35)

6. Refer the student for physical/occupational therapy assessment.

7. Multidisciplinary evaluation team meets with the parents to review evaluation findings.

8. Conduct an IEP team meeting and/or Section 504 planning meeting to determine the student's eligibility for programs and/or services and needed classroom and school accommodations.

9. Through meetings with the family and in-service, assist all need-to-know school personnel in acquiring insight and knowledge of the pertinent health issues of the student; also encourage strict adherence to matters of confidentiality.

10. Provide appropriate prompts to the student to perform self-care of his/her health needs per the established plan as needed (e.g., encouraging a student with diabetes mellitus to remember to make appropriate dietary selections at lunch).

11. Organize the classroom curriculum and school into a healthful learning environment to meet the student's medical needs (e.g., offer only low-impact physical education activities such as swimming or volleyball in place of more strenuous sports if the student's condition of juvenile

—.   _____

_____

—.   _____

_____

—.   _____

_____

arthritis warrants such intervention).

12. Encourage the student's independence as appropriate while making sure that the individualized medical intervention plan is closely followed.

13. Communicate closely with the parents on an ongoing basis to ensure that the student's health needs are being met at school using a weekly phone call or communication notebook, making a written record of all such contact time and content.

14. In collaboration with the family and the school nurse, familiarize other students with appropriate visible aspects of the student's condition and needs that they might witness (e.g., should the student have a seizure disorder, provide information as to what a seizure is, how it is not a contagious condition, how the student's safety is most important during a seizure, and how they can be understanding to their friend afterward) (see *Managing Chronic Illness in the Classroom* [Wishnietsky and Wishnietsky]).

15. Working with the parents and the student, organize an education session about the student's illness for his/her class with the affected stu-

dent having the option to be at the center of the class discussion answering questions or opting not to be present (e.g., discussing symptoms of asthma, causes, and showing the way in which an inhaler is used).

16. Create a classroom climate where acknowledgment, respect, and acceptance of individual differences are applauded.

17. Using the Circle of Friends concept, develop a closer bonded set of established peers who openly include the student in activities both in and out of school (see *Circle of Friends* [Perske and Perske]).

18. Encourage the student to verbalize his/her needs in an assertive manner.

19. Establish a subtle type of communication with the student should he/she indicate a need for assistance with a private concern (e.g., a need for medication for pain; an incident of minor external bleeding).

20. As a classroom teacher or service provider, offer an opportunity for the student to periodically privately share current personal health issues and fears.

21. Role-play activities in which the student can practice scenarios such as explaining his/her condition,

requesting assistance from an adult or peer, letting others know he/she is in an emergency situation and requires immediate response, and showing that he/she can perform certain medical self-care functions without assistance.

22. Provide emotional support for the student through an ongoing relationship with a school mental health professional who focuses on self-esteem, stress, and other affective issues pertinent to the student, his/her condition, and the school setting.

23. Maintain communication (with parent permission) with mental health clinicians outside the school setting to coordinate counseling approaches with school interventions for the student (e.g., a private psychologist develops an affective treatment plan for the student who has cancer that is supported by school personnel).

24. If the student is still able to be in attendance at school, organize the classroom with the normal routine, yet individualize it for the special health needs of the student.

25. Teach the student methods of coping such as talking through feelings of fear and sadness, identifying triggers that ignite positive feelings of comfort, hope, and strength, and under-

standing what medical steps will be forthcoming in his/her treatment.

26. During periods of better health, provide remedial interventions that match the student's individualized instructional needs.

27. During periods of stress and/or health deterioration, adjust the student's educational plan to incorporate modified academic expectations such as shortened or eliminated assignments, extended time to complete tasks, and being read to as opposed to reading material himself/herself.

28. Develop a program for delivering academics in the home or hospital when the student is too ill to attend school, focusing on select skills that are related to overall development and quality of life (e.g., working on elements of applied math versus medieval history).

29. Select and introduce technology that will facilitate the student's learning needs (e.g., dictating into a tape recorder instead of writing assignments, having the student use CD-ROM materials such as talking books, reinforcing skills with computer-assisted instructional software for use at school and home, etc.).

30. Use frequent curriculum-based/criterion-referenced evaluation periodically to

examine specifically what skills and objectives in the curriculum the student has mastered and where he/she needs further instructional development.

31. Should the condition of the student warrant serious monitoring and attention, consider the addition of a health care assistant to meet these chronic and on-going medical needs.

32. Provide supportive medical training to the assistant and to the team involved with the student to assure quality care.

33. Cooperate with the parents fully in communicating the student's needs, if necessary, reporting the daily condition of the student or contacting the parents when emergencies arise.

34. The school nurse remains a medical liaison to the family and medical personnel treating the student.

35. The academic supports and care plan, with special attention to the successes for the student, are conveyed to the new teacher(s)/staff prior to the new school year.

___. _____

_____

___. _____

_____

___. _____

_____

GENERAL LEARNING DISABILITIES—ADOLESCENT

BEHAVIORAL DEFINITIONS

1. Experiences a significant discrepant level of functioning relative to potential in areas of academic achievement.
2. Lower academic achievement is the suspected result of perceptual disabilities, brain injury or dysfunction, dyslexia, or developmental aphasia.
3. Academic deficits below learning potential have been apparent throughout much of school history.
4. The learning disability substantially interferes with academic performance or with basic daily living skills requiring reading, math, and/or written language.
5. Low motivation with school tasks as a result of long-term academic frustration and failure.
6. Low self-esteem, anxiety, and/or depression as a result of the frustration caused by learning deficits in school.

—. _____

—. _____

   _____

—. _____

   _____

LONG-TERM GOALS

1. Substantially improve academic functioning over the long term in deficit areas.

2. Attain annual goals and objectives as identified on the Individual-ized Education Plan (IEP).

3. Learn coping techniques that allow for improved achievement in spite of learning disability.

4. Exhibit higher self-esteem and improved motivation in relation to academic tasks.

5. Demonstrate an understanding and acceptance of the learning dis-ability.

6. Parents implement strategies at home to assist the student with successfully completing academic tasks.

7. Parents exhibit an acceptance of their son's/daughter's learning deficits and develop reasonable expectations for his/her progress.

8. Establish vocational and/or postsecondary goals and begin on a school-to-work transition plan.

—. _____

_____

—. _____

_____

—. _____

_____

SHORT-TERM OBJECTIVES

1. Cooperate with a hearing, vision, and/or medical ex-amination. (1, 2)

2. Participate in a comprehen-sive psychoeducational evaluation. (3)

3. Parents participate in the multidisciplinary evalua-tion process. (4)

4. Parents take part in an IEP team meeting and agree to the implementation of the plan. (5)

5. Verbalize an understanding of the changes in academic

THERAPEUTIC INTERVENTIONS

1. Refer the student for hear-ing, vision, and/or medical examinations to rule out any physical impairment that could be the cause of his/her underachievement.

2. Explore with the family any sensory modality reasons for their child's academic difficulties (i.e., vision, hearing).

3. Refer the student for a psy-choeducational evaluation.

4. The multidisciplinary eval-uation team meets with the parents to discuss and iden-

programming that will be made. (6)

6. Verbalize renewed motivation to achieve due to individualized teaching methods being utilized. (7, 8, 9)

7. Divide tasks into meaningful segments and work toward completion and accuracy. (10)

8. Utilize cognitive strategies to acquire new skills. (11, 12)

9. Use guided practice and multiple instructional approaches to learn new material. (13, 14)

10. Routinely use study skills strategies to increase comprehension and mastery of content. (15, 16, 17, 18)

11. Demonstrate proficiency with the graphic representation of text to organize new material. (19)

12. Utilize memorization strategies to more efficiently learn new material. (20, 21)

13. Effectively use technology to improve academic skills. (22)

14. Demonstrate improved performance on tests. (23, 24, 25, 26, 27)

15. Show greater accuracy on completion of assignments. (28, 29)

16. Effectively work in the general education curriculum with adaptations to the

tify the student's strengths, learning capabilities and deficits, educational needs, and special education eligibility.

5. Conduct an IEP team meeting with the parents present to determine the student's special education eligibility, programming, and/or appropriate support services.

6. Provide the student with ample information and explanation regarding changes in his/her daily academic programming.

7. Match individual instructional formats with the learning style of the student, being careful to account for his/her strengths and weaknesses.

8. Introduce new techniques so that novel approaches, methods, and materials motivate the student and alter his/her former negative feelings regarding learning.

9. Help the student plan for small increments of change, using modeling, prompting, and shaping to teach new material; provide for practice, review, and generalization, give feedback and reinforcement, and then evaluate the effectiveness of the instruction (see *Teaching Learning Strategies to Adolescents and Adults with Learning Disabilities* [Lenz]).

teaching methods.
(29, 30, 31, 32, 33)

17. Complete homework tasks within the individualized time frames and with good accuracy. (34, 35, 36)

18. Express at least one positive statement per day about school experiences and confidence in the ability to succeed academically. (37, 38, 39)

19. Demonstrate assertiveness and self-determination in advocating for own learning needs. (40)

20. Exhibit prosocial behavior needed for employment. (41)

21. Establish postsecondary academic and vocational goals. (42, 43, 44)

22. Parents verbalize a more accepting attitude toward their son/daughter and express an understanding of learning disabilities. (45, 46)

23. Parents report satisfaction with their son's/daughter's overall school experience and progress. (47, 48)

___. _____
    _____
___. _____
    _____
___. _____
    _____

10. Teach the student task-analysis skills by instructing him/her to break a difficult task into smaller, easier to understand pieces.

11. Incorporate direct instruction methods including teacher-developed scripts for the cognitive strategies to be taught to the student, providing modeling by the teacher and practice for the student (see *Strategy Assessment and Instruction for Students with Learning Disabilities* [Meltzer]).

12. Use procedural steps of cognitive behavior modification to teach new skills following these steps: (a) The adult models/performs the task by thinking aloud; (b) the student performs the same task with external guidance from the adult; (c) the student performs the task, instructing himself/herself aloud while doing so; (d) the student performs the task while whispering instructions to self; and (e) the student performs the task using private, inner speech (see "Teaching Thinking: A Cognitive-Behavioral Perspective" by Meichenbaum in *Thinking and Learning Skills: Vol. 2: Research and Open Questions* [Chipman, Segal, and Glaser, eds.).

13. Provide sufficient, meaningful practice with material to be mastered that includes

ample examples and guided practice.

14. Use flexibility with the rate and the approaches the student requires in obtaining mastery of the material.

15. Implement the strategies intervention model, or parts thereof, to assist the student with applying salient learning and study strategies in the general education setting (e.g., for specific reading needs, the student could work on strategies such as visual imagery, paraphrasing, and interpreting visual aids) (see *SIM Training Library: The Strategies Instructional Approach* [Lenz, Clark, Deshler, Schumaker, and Rademacher]).

16. Instruct the student in an organized approach to studying (e.g., Steps in the SQ3R Method in *Effective Study* [Robinson]).

17. Teach the Cornell Study Skill Method of note taking, whereby the student and/or teacher may make notes in the margins of the material to be mastered pertaining to very specific, salient content, which must be learned to improve both the student's comprehension and writing skill abilities (see *How to Study in College* [Pauk]).

18. Instruct the student in logistical study skill techniques (e.g., keeping an agenda of major assignment events [both short- and long-term],

setting up a study area at home for that purpose only, keeping materials and supplies readily available, taking periodic breaks in study sessions, and using five-minute blocks of free time to review notes).

19. Instruct the student in using graphic representation diagrams to organize his/her comprehension and writing skills (e.g., visually depicting cause and effect, descriptive or enumerative, sequential, compare and contrast, or problem and solution) (see "Improving Comprehension: Causal Relations Instruction for Learning Handicapped Learners" by Varnhagen and Goldman in *The Reading Teacher* [1986, 39: 896–904]).

20. Provide instruction in pneumonic memory strategies that include having the student group together similar concepts, develop labels for items, use rhythm, music, or jingles to retain material, or rehearse material frequently.

21. Utilize questioning techniques (e.g., presenting completion-type questions and providing feedback, questioning before and after a lesson, and embedding questions in the text or material to alert students to important information) to enhance memorization of material.

22. Integrate technological assistance into the academic regimen for the student that includes recorded books, an electronic speller, spell check/grammar programs, how-to word-processing programs, Dictaphone, tape recorder, calculator, and use of specially designed software for the learning disabled population in the areas of reading, math, and written language as appropriate for the student.

23. Create study guides or assist the student with developing study guides that outline the salient information to be covered on a given test.

24. Provide the student general test wise strategies (e.g., reading directions to the test carefully, underlining important words in the directions, beginning with questions that are the easiest, and being alert to information in some questions that can help answer other questions).

25. Teach strategies for objective tests to include underlining key words in an item, skipping unknown items and returning to them later, eliminating choices and selecting among the remaining choices, paraphrasing the question and recalling some example to stimulate memory, reading the question separately with each alternative answer.

26. Teach strategies for essay tests to include highlighting direction words in the questions, numbering the part of a question to ensure all parts are answered, outlining answers before beginning to write, allocating sufficient time to get to all questions.

27. Provide to the student as needed extended time lines for test completion, allow for dictated responses from the student on essay questions, read the test items to the student, or create an alternative type of assessment to best meet the learner's mode of output.

28. Incorporate proofing skills into daily instruction whereby the student takes time to check over tests and papers, routinely reviews the models and visions he/she is to follow, and frequently reviews criteria to be used on a given assignment or project.

29. Individualize the expectations for assignment completion by reducing the number of items to be learned or answered.

30. Adapt the time allotted for learning or for task completion.

31. Increase the amount of personal assistance the student receives (e.g., assign a peer tutor, a teacher assistant, or organizing a coop-

erative/consensus learning group for a lesson or task).

32. Change how the student may respond (e.g., allowing a verbal, instead of a written, response).

33. Alter the level of difficulty to meet the student's learning needs (e.g., adapting the skill level required for a task, the problem type, or the approach the student may use).

34. Assist the student and parents in improving homework assignments by scheduling a routine homework time and place, setting high but reasonable expectations for assignment accuracy, praising the student for good work and effort, and, if needed, providing extrinsic rewards as reinforcement.

35. Encourage the student to use a planner or agenda to identify assignments and projects for which he/she receives credit or extra credit for proper use.

36. Develop some homework tasks that favor the student's more prominent learning style to allow the student to appreciate his/her learning strengths.

37. Create a plan with the student in which he/she is to make at least one positive self-statement per day about school and his/her

ability to be successful with academic tasks.

38. Engage the student in individual or small group counseling by a school mental health professional for self-concept improvement.

39. Refer the family to a private therapist should affective issues become paramount.

40. Teach the student self-advocacy skills (e.g., stating a particular need to the teacher such as using the resource room for test taking, knowing his/her learning style and stating this information to an uninformed teacher, simply requesting assistance and ensuring that his/her question is answered) in relation to his/her learning needs.

41. Teach social skills that are necessary for achieving success in employment settings to include interpersonal initiative and response skills, community skills, and dealing with specific scenarios in the workplace.

42. Assist the student and family with developing goals to transition the student from high school to an acceptable postsecondary experience (see *Transition and Students with Learning Disabilities* [Patton and Blalock]).

43. Set up opportunities for the student and family to visit

potential vocational training sites.

44. Provide information to the student and family regarding higher education institutions that address the needs of the learning disabled population.

45. Give the parents materials explaining learning disabilities; respond to questions/concerns they may have.

46. Encourage the parents to seek out organizations that work with families of children with learning disabilities (e.g., Learning Disabilities Association of America and the National Center for Learning Disabilities).

47. Keep in contact with the parents to maintain open communication between home and school and to continue positive gains made by the student.

48. Gather information on the strategies and supports that have been most effective for the student and arrange for this information to be shared with the teaching staff in the new school year.

__. _____
   _____

__. _____
   _____

__. _____
   _____

GENERAL LEARNING DISABILITIES—CHILD

BEHAVIORAL DEFINITIONS

1. Experiences a significant discrepant level of functioning relative to potential in areas of academic achievement.
2. Lower academic achievement is the suspected result of perceptual disabilities, brain injury or dysfunction, dyslexia, or developmental aphasia.
3. Academic deficits below learning potential have been apparent throughout much of school history.
4. The learning disability substantially interferes with academic performance or with basic daily living skills requiring reading, math, and/or written language.
5. Low motivation with school tasks as a result of long-term academic frustration and failure.
6. Low self-esteem, anxiety, and/or depression as a result of the frustration caused by learning deficits in school.

—. _____
   _____
—. _____
   _____
—. _____
   _____

LONG-TERM GOALS

1. Substantially improve academic functioning over the long term in the deficit areas.

2. Attain annual goals and objectives as identified on the Individualized Education Plan (IEP).
3. Learn coping techniques that allow for improved achievement in spite of learning disability.
4. Exhibit higher self-esteem and improved motivation in relation to academic tasks.
5. Demonstrate an understanding and acceptance of the learning disability.
6. Parents implement strategies at home to assist the student with successfully completing academic work.
7. Parents exhibit an acceptance of their son's/daughter's learning deficits and develop reasonable expectations for their child's progress.

__. _____
_____
__. _____
_____
__. _____
_____

SHORT-TERM OBJECTIVES

1. Cooperate with a hearing, vision, and/or medical examination. (1, 2)

2. Participate in a comprehensive psychoeducational evaluation. (3)

3. Parents participate in the multidisciplinary evaluation process. (4)

4. Parents take part in an IEP team meeting and agree to the implementation of the plan. (5)

5. Verbalize an understanding of the changes in academic programming that will be made. (6)

THERAPEUTIC INTERVENTIONS

1. Refer the student for hearing, vision, and/or medical examinations to rule out any physical impairment that could be the cause of his/her underachievement.

2. Explore with the family any sensory modality reasons for their student's academic difficulties (i.e., vision, hearing).

3. Refer the student for a psychoeducational evaluation.

4. The multidisciplinary evaluation team meets with the parents regarding the student's strengths, learning capabilities and deficits, ed-

6. Verbalize renewed motivation to achieve due to individualized teaching methods being utilized. (7, 8, 9)

7. Divide tasks into meaningful segments and work toward completion with accuracy. (10)

8. Show academic progress through group learning techniques. (11)

9. Utilize cognitive strategies to acquire new skills. (12)

10. Utilize guided practice and multiple instructional approaches to learn new material. (13, 14)

11. Utilize study skill strategies to increase comprehension and mastery of content. (15)

12. Demonstrate proficiency with graphic representation of text to organize new material. (16)

13. Utilize memorization strategies to more efficiently learn new material. (17, 18, 19)

14. Demonstrate improved long-term memory retention of material. (19)

15. Show the ability to effectively work in the general education curriculum with adaptations to the teaching methods. (20, 21, 22, 23, 24)

16. Demonstrate success with alternative materials. (25)

17. Stay focused on difficult tasks without displaying learned helplessness or quitting. (26, 27, 28)

ucational needs, and special education eligibility.

5. Conduct an IEP team meeting with the parents present to determine the student's special education eligibility, programming, and/or appropriate support services.

6. Provide the student with ample information and explanation regarding changes in his/her daily academic programming.

7. Match individualized instructional formats to match the learning style of the student, being careful to account for his/her strengths and weaknesses.

8. Introduce new techniques so that novel approaches, methods, and materials motivate the student and alter his/her former negative feelings regarding learning.

9. Help the student plan for small increments of change, using modeling, prompting, and shaping to teach new material; provide for practice, review, and generalization, give feedback and reinforcement, and then evaluate the effectiveness of the instruction (see *Metacognition and Learning Disabilities* [Wong]).

10. Teach the student task-analysis skills by instructing him/her to break a difficult task into smaller, easier to understand pieces.

18. Cooperate with behavior modification and cognitive retraining methods to increase time and effort spent on challenging tasks. (26, 28)

19. Utilize checklists to enhance the organization of materials and assignments. (29, 30, 31)

20. Implement a system for keeping an organized desk. (32, 33)

21. Complete homework tasks within the individualized time frames and with good accuracy. (34, 35, 36)

22. Make at least one positive statement per day about school experiences and confidence in the ability to succeed academically. (37, 38, 39)

23. Attend individual or group counseling to build self-esteem and overcome depression, anger, or low self-esteem. (38, 39)

24. Parents verbalize a more accepting attitude toward their child and express an understanding of learning disabilities. (40, 41)

25. Parents report their satisfaction with their child's overall school experience and progress. (42, 43)

___. _____

_____

11. Use cooperative learning techniques in which students work in small groups in a problem-solving format; use the reciprocal teaching method in which the teacher and students take turns reading, formulating questions, and switching roles as the material is covered (see "Reciprocal Teaching of Comprehension-Fostering and Comprehension-Monitoring Activities" by Palinscar and Brown in *Cognition and Instruction* [1984, 1: 117–175]).

12. Incorporate the direct explanation methodology whereby the teacher talks aloud about the mental processes required to attain a specific skill (see *Two Styles of Direct Instruction in Teaching Second-Grade Reading and Language Arts* [Duffy, Roehler, and Reinsmoen]).

13. Provide sufficient, meaningful practice with material to be mastered that includes ample examples and guided practice.

14. Use flexibility with the rate and the approaches the student requires in obtaining mastery of the material.

15. Instruct the student in an organized approach to studying (e.g., Steps in the SQ3R Method in *Effective Study* [Robinson]).

16. Teach the student different visual methods (e.g., the Star Strategy), identifying

—. _____
    _____
—. _____
    _____

the main idea and answering who, what, where, and why questions in organizing material for comprehension and/or writing tasks (see *Strategies For Success* [Meltzer, Roditi, Haynes, Biddle, Paster, and Taber]).

17. Provide instruction in pneumonic strategies that include having the student group together similar concepts, develop labels for items, use rhythm, music, or jingles to retain material, or rehearse material frequently.

18. Utilize questioning techniques to enhance memorization of material (e.g., ask questions of the student before and after a lesson, and embed questions in the text or material to alert students to important information).

19. Enhance long-term memory skills of the student by presenting information at a slower rate (an average of three pieces of information at one time), review frequently (every two or three days), and cover only small amounts of material at a time.

20. Reduce the number of items given to the student, or individualize a time line for completing work.

21. Adapt the manner in which the student curriculum is delivered (e.g., using many visual aids, giving many

concrete examples), providing hands-on activities.

22. Alter the skill level, the problem type, or how the student approaches the work (e.g., the student uses a calculator, task directions are simplified).

23. Change how the student may respond (e.g., allowing a verbal response instead of writing).

24. Provide individualized expectations for a lesson or unit (e.g., expecting the student to locate the states while others also identify the capitals).

25. While others are working in a specific math curriculum, ask the student with a learning disability in math to work in a curriculum that requires less abstract thinking and offers more concrete, functional math opportunities.

26. Assist the student in identifying a list of rewards and then develop a positive reinforcement plan targeting the extension of the time the student works at a more difficult task.

27. Assist the student with setting goals for tackling more difficult tasks and creating meaningful plans to do so.

28. Engage the student in attribution retraining in which the student moves away from negative self-talk and does not allow ex-

cuses for not learning or taking responsibility (see "An Attribution Training Program with Learning Disabled Children" by Shelton, Anastopoulous, and Linden in *Journal of Learning Disabilities* [1985, 18(5): 261–265]).

29. Create with the student a checklist that identifies the items needed to perform academic tasks at school each day.

30. Develop a checklist or assignment notebook wherein the student keeps track of assignments in progress, assignments completed, and due dates.

31. Assist the student in learning to prioritize work by creating a list of tasks in order of importance.

32. Instruct the student in a system for organizing his/her desk (e.g., using plastic boxes, zippered folders, and specifying areas of the desk for textbooks) with the parents' physical and financial support.

33. Show the student the benefit of color coding materials by subject with parent support for purchases of needed items.

34. Teach the parents how to assist their son/daughter with homework assignments by scheduling a routine homework time and place, setting high but reasonable expecta-

tions for assignment accuracy, and praising the child for good work and effort.

35. Establish a communication system (e.g., a planner or agenda between home and school in which homework tasks are clearly delineated and in which notes between school staff and the parents can be exchanged on an as-needed basis).

36. Develop some homework tasks that favor the student's more prominent learning style to allow parents to appreciate their child's learning strengths.

37. Create a plan with the student in which he/she is to make one positive self-statement per day about school and his/her ability to be successful in school.

38. Engage the student in individual or small group counseling by a school mental health professional for self-concept improvement.

39. Refer the family to a private therapist should affective issues become paramount.

40. Provide the parents with materials explaining learning disabilities; respond to questions/concerns they may have.

41. Encourage the parents to seek out organizations that work with families of children who have learning disabilities (e.g., Learning

Disabilities Association of America or the National Center for Learning Disabilities).

42. Keep in contact with the parents to maintain open communication between home and school and to continue positive gains made by the student.

43. Gather information on the strategies and supports that have been most effective for the student and arrange for this information to be shared with the teaching staff in the new school year.

__. _____
   _____

__. _____
   _____

__. _____
   _____

HEARING IMPAIRED AND DEAF

BEHAVIORAL DEFINITIONS

1. A mild (under 40 dB) to profound (over 91 dB) hearing loss that interferes with communication.
2. A severe or profound hearing loss that mandates that the auditory channel is not the primary means of speech and language development for the student.
3. The hearing loss or deafness is due to genetics, in utero infection, postbirth disease, trauma, or some unknown cause.
4. Conductive hearing loss that results in interference of the sound transmission to the inner ear due to difficulties in the outer ear canal or middle ear and can be improved by medical or surgical intervention.
5. A sensorineural hearing loss that results in impaired functioning of the cochlear or auditory nerve and can be improved with modern hearing aid devices but not through surgical means.
6. Management of the hearing impairment through amplification (e.g., hearing aids, vibrotactile aids, artificial cochlear, etc.).
7. Management of the hearing impairment through various communication modes including auditory-verbal, cued speech, oral/aural, total or simultaneous communication, or signed communication.

__. _____

_____

__. _____

_____

__. _____

_____

LONG-TERM GOALS

1. Attain the goals and objectives for coping with hearing loss in the educational setting as identified through the Individualized Education Planning (IEP) team process.
2. Achieve academic functioning to the level of potential, considering hearing impairment.
3. Develop communication skills commensurate with learning potential to be used at home, in school, and in the community.
4. Decrease overt, acting-out behaviors that occur as a result of frustration related to hearing impairment.
5. Demonstrate increased feelings of competence and self-esteem.
6. Parents understand and accept their child's hearing deficits, establish realistic expectations, and seek out resources to support their child's needs.

—. _____
   _____
—. _____
   _____
—. _____
   _____

SHORT-TERM OBJECTIVES

1. Cooperate with an audiological and medical exam. (1)
2. Participate cooperatively in a psychoeducational evaluation. (2)
3. Cooperate with a speech and language evaluation. (3)
4. Parents participate in the multidisciplinary evaluation team process. (4)
5. Parents, and the student as appropriate, participate in the IEP team meeting and accept the recommendations of the team. (5)

THERAPEUTIC INTERVENTIONS

1. Refer the student to an audiologist and an otolaryngologist or otologist for audiological evaluation and physical evaluation of the inner, middle, and outer ear.
2. Refer the student for a psychoeducational evaluation to include use of best-practice procedures for evaluation of students with hearing deficits.
3. Refer the student for a speech and language evaluation to include use of best-practice procedures for

6. Parents select the mode of communication best suited for their child to learn in communication with others. (6)

7. Student, parents, and/or staff identify when the amplification equipment needs or seems to need adjustment, and seek assistance from a qualified adult. (7, 8, 9)

8. Implement the selected communication mode. (10, 11)

9. Demonstrate progress with intelligible speech. (12)

10. Exhibit gains with auditory training skills. (13, 14)

11. Master some or all aspects of speechreading. (15, 16)

12. Use Signing Exact English or American Sign Language and/or fingerspelling successfully as a first language. (17)

13. Show substantial progress in a curriculum tailored to his/her own needs and strengths. (18)

14. Effectively use visual strategies to master comprehension of literature, content materials, and/or vocabulary. (19, 20)

15. Obtain extra practice with specific skills or concepts using peer tutoring. (21)

16. Increase academic achievement through taking personal responsibility to

evaluation of students with hearing deficits.

4. Meet with the parents to obtain their input into the evaluation of their child's hearing impairment and its effect on learning potential and to interpret test data to them.

5. Organize an IEP team meeting with the parents to determine the student's eligibility for special education and to identify programs, services, goals, and objectives appropriate for the student.

6. Assist parents with selecting the mode of communication that best meets the student's needs (e.g., auditory-oral, total communication, or manual), taking into consideration the student's level of hearing loss and providing the parents with literature to review, program visitation, and opportunities to speak with other parents of hearing impaired or deaf students (see *Communication and Communication Disorders* [Plante and Beeson]).

7. The school audiologist, hearing impaired teacher consultant, and/or teacher of the hearing impaired will monitor amplification and other assistive devices used by the student to ensure their proper function.

cooperate with effective instructional methods. (22)

17. Demonstrate progress in academic and social adjustment within the general education setting. (23, 24, 25)

18. Verbalize positive self-descriptive statements and statements indicating confidence in self and own abilities. (26, 27, 28)

19. Eliminate frustration-based disruptive behavior that interferes with the educational process. (28, 29, 30)

20. Parents understand and accept their child's hearing loss, seek out supports and resources to meet their child's needs, and work collaboratively with school personnel in developing a quality treatment plan/program for him/her. (4, 5, 6, 31)

21. Parents report satisfaction with their child's program and general school progress. (32, 33, 34)

__. _____
   _____

__. _____
   _____

__. _____
   _____

8. The school audiologist, hearing impaired teacher consultant, and/or teacher of the hearing impaired will educate the student, the parents, and appropriate school personnel in the function and operation of amplification and other assistive devices in an attempt to ensure proper functioning of the equipment and greater independence on the part of the student.

9. Offer at least an annual audiological evaluation to provide updated information on the student's hearing loss, monitor the student's hearing devices, and educate the student and parents about these issues.

10. Coordinate efforts by the speech and language clinician, and/or the teacher of the hearing impaired, or teacher consultant for the hearing impaired, in following the established plan for step-by-step instruction in the targeted communication mode(s) for the student (e.g., instruct the student in voicing words, phrases, complex sentences or in American Sign Language).

11. Establish a classroom environment that promotes conversation, uses facilitative activities and systematic experiences so that the student has many opportuni-

ties to develop competency with communication.

12. If a verbal communication mode is selected, maintain an expectation that speech is to be used when communication occurs, model appropriate speech, make functional opportunities for the use of speech available to the student, and give realistic, positive encouragement to the student for speech use (see *Effectively Educating Students with Hearing Impairments* [Luetke-Stahlman and Luchner]).

13. Assess whether the student is an appropriate candidate for auditory training (e.g., Is the student's residual hearing adequate with amplification to benefit from this training method?) (see *Effectively Educating Students with Hearing Impairments* [Luetke-Stahlman and Luchner]); refer for auditory training if appropriate.

14. In teaching auditory training, try a natural conversation approach (e.g., give directions while seated behind or next to the student in the classroom) and/or use a moderately structured approach (e.g., select specific words, phrases, or a set of sentences that allow the student to practice language, speech, and auditory training all at once with

guided practice) (see *Effectively Educating Students with Hearing Impairments* [Luetke-Stahlman and Luchner]).

15. Provide instruction in speechreading to include lip movement, visual communication (e.g., gestures, facial expressions), and differences made by situational clues such as the location of and the participants in the communication.

16. Offer speechreading training by role-playing real situations using videotape as a means of feedback for the student (see "Speechreading as Communication" by Palmer in *Volta Review* [1988, 90(50): 33–44]).

17. Provide the student with consistent instruction in manual techniques of communication (i.e., Signing Exact English or American Sign Language) after the family has selected this communication mode (often due to the severity of the student's hearing loss).

18. Consider the student's learning needs, current level of achievement, and parental expectations when determining options for curriculum, which could include: a curriculum designed for hearing impaired or deaf students; the general education curriculum with the student working to the stan-

dards of general education peers but with related services and IEP defined accommodations; the general education curriculum with altered expectations; a lower grade level curriculum; or a curriculum designed for students with other special needs (see *Curriculum Based Instruction for Special Education Students* [Bigge]).

19. Teach semantic mapping, which involves organizing information (in particular, vocabulary) into meaningful graphic formats (e.g., if the student is to learn about coffee, the word *coffee* is placed in the center of the diagram in a circle or oval with relevant words/subtopics being diagrammed out of it—i.e., grown in mountainous areas, made from coffee beans, effects of caffeine) (see *Teaching Reading Vocabulary* [Johnson and Pearson]).

20. Use graphic representations/visualizations to organize material into different frameworks to teach concepts (e.g., cause and effect, compare/contrast) or use a sequence of stages of an event (e.g., diagram the sequence of events leading to the eradication of smallpox—Initiating Event: World Health Organization adopts The Smallpox Eradication Program in 1958;

Event 1: Intensive global eradication program launched in 1967; Event 2: Surveillance-containment strategies used to end chain of transmission; Event 3 [Final Outcome]: In October of 1977, last person found in the world outside of a laboratory setting to have smallpox) (see "Teaching Students to Construct Graphic Representations" by Jones, Pierce, and Hunter in *Educational Leadership* [1989, 46(4): 20–26]).

21. Carefully select and train a peer tutor(s) from the student's grade (or consider cross-age tutoring with an older student) to engage in salient practice activities with the hearing impaired student.

22. Implement formal, systematic instructional methods in the classroom to include well-organized lesson plans offering guided practice with concepts and skills, learning centers in different subject areas that target the student's specific learning needs, all in a learning environment emphasizing a high level of student responsibility in a warm, democratic classroom climate (see *Effectively Educating Students with Hearing Impairments* [Luetke-Stahlman and Luchner]).

23. The teacher consultant provides support to the general

education teacher of the student, including information on the student's hearing loss and communication method; impact of the student's hearing loss on academics, social skills, and overall development; routine scheduled consultation time to meet with the general education teacher; in-service training to cover techniques to be used with the student by the general education teacher; information/training on services the student may use (e.g., note taker, interpreter) (see *Effectively Educating Students with Hearing Impairments* [Luetke-Stahlman and Luchner]).

24. Collaborate with the general education teacher in following through with accommodations for the student as identified in the IEP team process, which might include such items as an alternative manner in which the student gives a response in class or takes a test, shortened or modified assignments, or alternative expectations for the final product of a project.

25. Organize opportunities for the student to socially interact with and be fully included by same-age peers across various settings (e.g., after-school activities, working in the school store, paired with peers in a

buddy system for classroom, lunchroom, special activities) (see *Effectively Educating Students with Hearing Impairments* [Luetke-Stahlman and Luchner]).

26. Promote positive self-worth in the student by providing positive role models and facilitating activities and attitudes that assist the student in developing a sense of connection, uniqueness, power, and accomplishment (see *Effectively Educating Students with Hearing Impairments* [Luetke-Stahlman and Luchner]).

27. Work with the parents in their efforts to encourage their child in positive ways, including accepting their child's deficits and needs.

28. Refer the student to a school mental health professional for assistance with self-esteem issues and/or behavioral difficulties.

29. Develop a positive behavior intervention support plan targeting the reduction of those disruptive behaviors that are most overt and interfere with the student's education.

30. Carefully evaluate the antecedent behaviors leading to the disruptive or difficult behavior by the student, and reorganize the learning environment or task as a measure to prevent the negative actions.

31. Provide the parents with information regarding local support groups and national organizations (e.g., Alexander Graham Bell Association for the Deaf and the American Speech, Language and Hearing Association).

32. Provide the parents with frequent, routine communication updates on their child's progress, needs, problems, and successes.

33. Hold communication meetings with the school staff and parents every four to six weeks or as needed to discuss needs and successes of the student, and to problem solve concerns.

34. As a new school year approaches, hold a meeting to pass on to new teachers and staff the documentation regarding the student's strengths, weaknesses, supports, and other salient information to ensure future success.

__. _____
   _____

__. _____
   _____

__. _____
   _____

LISTENING COMPREHENSION

BEHAVIORAL DEFINITIONS

1. Significantly lower achievement in the area of listening comprehension in contrast to learning potential as documented on standardized measures.
2. Misses salient auditorily presented information in the classroom resulting in not following oral directions, not being able to take competent notes from a lecture, or a restricted opportunity to enjoy a story as read by the teacher or a peer.
3. Difficulty attending to the auditory message.
4. Receptive language deficits as manifested by difficulty understanding simple words or sentences and/or longer, more complex statements.
5. Deficits in listening and receptive language development significantly interferes with academic, social, and/or daily living skills.
6. A deficit in language processing as documented by a speech and language pathologist.

__. _____
   _____
   _____
__. _____
   _____
   _____
__. _____
   _____

LONG-TERM GOALS

1. Show significant improvement with overall listening comprehension closer to, or commensurate with, learning potential.
2. Improve receptive language to level of potential.

3. Increase proficiency with basic listening tasks including attending to a listening task, following oral directions, comprehending main ideas from literature or content material as read aloud in the classroom by the teacher or a peer, and obtaining basic information from a speaker's message.

4. Become knowledgeable regarding own learning style and acquainted with the types of strategies needed to be successful in listening.

5. Learn the nonverbal aspects of listening (e.g., maintaining eye contact and noticing nonverbal cues), as well as the metacognitive skills necessary for the active process of listening.

6. Parents accept their child's listening and receptive language deficits, adjust to realistic expectations, and seek out resources and supports that may assist their child.

__. _____
   _____

__. _____
   _____

__. _____
   _____

SHORT-TERM OBJECTIVES

1. Participate in an audiological evaluation. (1)

2. Cooperate with a psychoeducational evaluation. (2)

3. Participate in a speech and language evaluation. (3)

4. Parents meet with school clinicians to provide input into the multidisciplinary evaluation team process and to listen to an interpretation of the evaluation data. (4)

5. Parents attend the Individualized Education Planning (IEP) team meeting and verbalize an acceptance of the recommendations developed. (5)

THERAPEUTIC INTERVENTIONS

1. Refer the student for an audiological evaluation.

2. Refer the student for a psychoeducational evaluation.

3. Refer the student for a speech and language evaluation.

4. Meet with the parents to obtain their input into the multidisciplinary evaluation and to interpret to them the evaluation data.

5. Collaborate with the parents through the IEP team process to ascertain the student's eligibility for special education and to determine appropriate programs and/or services.

6. Accurately identify sounds and their source while eyes are closed. (6, 7)

7. Identify and implement attending to the cues that indicate listening is needed and important. (8)

8. Sit in a classroom seat that will have limited distractions. (9, 10)

9. Utilize listening technology to improve performance in the classroom. (11, 12)

10. Keep a listening diary and identify different purposes for listening. (13, 14)

11. Follow one-step, two-step, and three-step verbal directions correctly 90 percent of the time. (15, 16, 17, 18)

12. Show competencies with story comprehension, being able to accurately respond to 80 percent of questions asked about the selection. (19, 20, 21)

13. Effectively use mental pictures as a memory strategy while listening. (22)

14. Effectively place information into categories as a comprehension/memory aid. (23)

15. Ask questions of the speaker when listening to a presentation to aid listening comprehension. (24, 25)

16. Engage in self-questioning to increase comprehension of a verbal presentation. (26)

6. Organize a listening activity in which the student must close his/her eyes and identify sounds in the environment purely by concentrating for 30 seconds (e.g., clock ticking, footsteps in the hall, etc.).

7. Create sounds for the student to identify as he/she concentrates with eyes closed (e.g., crumpling paper, drinking water, opening a window, etc.) (see *Listening* [White]).

8. Teach the student to give eye contact to the speaker, attend to the verbal prompts of the speaker (e.g., "Before we begin," "These are the main points," "Listen carefully"), and attend to the silent pauses of the speaker.

9. Choose for the student at the onset a prime seat in the classroom, explaining the reason why the seat is a good selection (e.g., away from the doorway and windows, where visual aids are in good view, etc.).

10. Strongly reinforce the student for positive selection of a seat on his/her own where there are limited distractions.

11. Give a simple listening pretest to the student in which he/she must answer a few questions about a story read or follow several oral directions.

12. Introduce the student to the use of an FM system or an

17. Identify critical elements and messages in a speech of persuasion. (27, 28, 29)

18. Acknowledge listening comprehension weaknesses and list ways to improve skills in this area. (30, 31)

19. Increase receptive vocabulary to within one standard deviation of age-appropriate norms. (32, 33, 34, 35)

20. Parents become actively involved with improving their child's receptive language abilities. (36)

21. Give appropriate responses to *who, what,* and *where* questions. (37, 38, 39)

22. Give appropriate responses to *how* and *when* questions. (40, 41)

23. Give socially appropriate responses to personal/conversational questions. (42)

24. Parents accept their child's deficit areas and work to support improvement with these skills. (43)

25. Parents report satisfaction with their child's progress in listening comprehension, receptive language skills, and with his/her general school programming. (44, 45)

—. _____
   _____

—. _____
   _____

—. _____
   _____

auditory trainer device into the classroom; after a month of frequent use, repeat the same pretest (described in intervention 11) as a posttest to ascertain the effectiveness of the technology in aiding his/her listening skills.

13. Have the student keep a listening diary for five days (young students will need teacher or parent assistance) where each day he/she listens to something and answers these questions: What was the source of the information? (e.g., news on the radio, a song, a talk show, a story); How many people were speaking?; Why were you listening?; Were you successful at listening?; If you were not successful, what were the problems? (see *Listening* [White]).

14. Involve the student in a small group or class discussion where the listening diary data is shared by different students, and purposes for listening are given (e.g., for enjoyment and appreciation such as music, for information and for critical evaluation such as a news program, for details such as an airline schedule, for personal fulfillment/therapeutic listening such as a phone conversation with a friend or family member).

15. Give directions to the student and then have him/her

repeat the direction(s) before beginning the task(s).

16. Give the student visual cues for more lengthy or complex directions (e.g., offer pictures, a model, a diagram, a flowchart, etc.) as meaningful prompts until the student obtains greater success with more difficult auditory directions.

17. For directions in a sequence, verbalize them to the student in the order to be done with numbers attached to each direction.

18. When giving oral directions, use only vocabulary with which the student is completely familiar.

19. Read aloud to the student an age-appropriate literature selection daily at the elementary level, at least once per week at the secondary level, and encourage the parents to read to their young child every day.

20. Involve the student in active listening when literature is read aloud by asking the student to answer questions in relation to: Predicting—setting a purpose for listening (e.g., What do you think a story with a title like this might be about?); Reasoning and predicting from the first part of the story—confirm or reject his/her predictions (e.g., What do you think will happen next? What would happen if . . . ?); Proving—

give reasons to support predictions (e.g., What in the
story makes you think that?
Where in the story do you
get information to support
that idea?) (see *Directing
the Reading-Thinking Pro-
cess* [Stauffer]).

21. After a story or a chapter of
literature is read, have the
student keep a response
reading log in which he/she
writes likes, dislikes,
events, and feelings regarding the story or chapter (the
younger student can por-
tray responses in picture
form) (see *Language Arts—
Content and Teaching
Strategies* [Tompkins and
Hoskisson]).

22. When listening to literature
or content material being
read aloud, instruct the student in using visual images,
details, or descriptive words
to create a visual picture in
his/her mind by asking the
student questions (e.g.,
What do you think the
house in the story looks
like? Describe what you
think the mountain road is
like to ride on, etc.).

23. While listening to content-
area material being read,
or while listening to a
speaker's message, categorize the pieces of information into like groups,
clusters, comparisons, con-
trasts, or patterns (e.g.,
create a graphic organizer
that depicts a cause and all
potential effects identified

in the information) (see *Language Arts—Content and Teaching Strategies* [Tompkins and Hoskisson]).

24. Instruct the student in asking salient questions to understand a speaker's message (e.g., questions about an opinion, a detail or fact given, the meaning of a word or phrase, asking for a point to be restated, etc.).

25. Model for the student ways in which to ask questions of a speaker and organize a role play with the student that portrays a situation in which a speaker is typically asked questions (e.g., a teacher teaching a content area, a government official giving a speech, etc.).

26. Teach the student metacognitive strategies whereby he/she engages in self-questioning to monitor his/her listening comprehension (e.g., a list of self-questions *prior to* the presentation could include What is my purpose for listening? What am I going to do with what I listen to? Will I need to take notes? A list of self-questions *during* the presentation could include Am I putting information into groups? Is the speaker giving me nonverbal cues such as gestures and facial expressions? A list of questions *after* listening could include Do I have questions for the speaker?

Is any part of the message unclear?) (see *Language Arts—Content and Teaching Strategies* [Tompkins and Hoskisson]).

27. Provide experiences for the student at his/her developmental level to listen to and examine commercials, political speeches, and other speeches of persuasion, looking for the speaker's purpose, bias, unsupported inferences, opinions, loaded words, claims; include organizing opportunities for the student to write and videotape his/her own campaign speech, advertisement, or other form of persuasive message (see *Language Arts—Content and Teaching Strategies* [Tompkins and Hoskisson]).

28. Have the student listen to different radio advertisements, listening for specific elements (e.g., descriptive words, messages of persuasion) and determine which advertisement is best and why (see *Listening* [White]).

29. Have the secondary student listen to an interview of a politician or a discussion between two politicians, requesting that the student analyze the main message of each speaker, identifying special political jargon and words of persuasion used to make critical points, and finally rating each speaker as to effectiveness and sincerity (see *Listening* [White]).

30. Discuss with the student his/her learning style and learning needs, summarizing various strategies to help him/her improve and giving ongoing words of encouragement.

31. Show the student evidence that he/she is making gains in the listening comprehension area by keeping daily work as evidence or illustrating progress on a formalized chart of completed activities.

32. Use precise language when speaking to the student, being specific about what you want him/her to understand.

33. Systematically introduce new vocabulary words each week to the student, using visual prompts (e.g., objects and pictures) to show meaning, and using the words in different settings and situations throughout the week (e.g., games, daily oral language, art projects, music, etc.).

34. Role-play targeted action words, pairing each verb with a familiar noun the student already knows (e.g., The dog growled.).

35. Have the student engage in various activities to learn and reinforce the new vocabulary, including drawing pictures, creating stories, and making photo albums (see *The Source for Down Syndrome* [Chamberlain and Strode]).

36. Train parents to explain, discuss, answer questions, clarify, and basically talk, talk, talk to their child as well as read to him/her daily and discuss together what they have read.

37. Model asking questions and giving responses in the midst of daily activities; give prompts to the student as needed as he/she is asked to respond, making certain you are mildly challenging the student as he/she advances.

38. Allow waiting time for the student to give a response; only prompt when it appears the student is stuck, then offer choices (e.g., Where did you find the dog? In the kitchen or in the backyard?).

39. Create picture or photo books that target the types of responses desired from question types and show appropriate responses (e.g., a *who* book with pictures of salient people; a *where* book that has pictures of favorite or common places) (see *The Source for Down Syndrome* [Chamberlain and Strode]).

40. Train the student to give appropriate responses by asking questions that he/she can, without a doubt, answer; train parents to do the same at home.

41. Using the game Twenty Questions, generate questions of *how* and *when* to the student as part of the format.

42. Role-play social questioning/response scenarios, modeling quality answers and allowing considerable practice for the student in answering questions.

43. Train the parents to work with their child at home on listening and receptive language tasks, giving appropriate materials to the parents and instructing them in various interventions that could be effective in the home environment (e.g., have the parent tape-record directions on how to do a specific task and then have the student play and replay it until the task is accurately completed).

44. Share the student's progress and concerns with the parents in an ongoing, frequent manner.

45. Gather salient interventions and strategies that are most effective with the student, passing this information on through the IEP team process and/or through a staff meeting with the teacher(s) in the new school year.

—. _____

_____

—. _____

_____

—. _____

_____

MATHEMATICS CALCULATION

BEHAVIORAL DEFINITIONS

1. Achievement in the area of mathematics substantially below learning potential.
2. Poor skills in math computation.
3. Little or no automaticity of math facts.
4. Limited understanding of basic math vocabulary.
5. Low confidence in math abilities caused by, or resulting in, math anxiety.
6. Mathematic deficits interfere with the student's general academic functioning and/or daily living skills.

—. _____
   _____

—. _____
   _____

—. _____
   _____

LONG-TERM GOALS

1. Increase overall mathematics achievement to a level commensurate with learning potential.
2. Master the basic operations of addition, subtraction, multiplication, and division.
3. Demonstrate abilities with functional math and show the skill to apply the correct math concepts and processes in daily living situations.
4. Significantly reduce any math anxiety and increase confidence in his/her math abilities.

5. Show mastery of mathematical vocabulary to the level of math achievement.

—. _____

_____

—. _____

_____

—. _____

_____

SHORT-TERM OBJECTIVES

1. Cooperate with hearing, vision, and/or medical examination. (1, 2)

2. Participate in a comprehensive math or psychoeducational evaluation. (3)

3. Parents participate in an interpretive meeting to hear test results. (4)

4. Parents take part in an Individualized Education Planning (IEP) team meeting or general meeting and agree to implementation of math improvement plan. (5)

5. Demonstrate accurate use of mathematical estimation strategies. (6)

6. Verbalize accurate number facts. (7)

7. Increase the accuracy of basic mathematical calculations involving addition and subtraction. (8, 9, 10)

8. Demonstrate competence in utilizing an electronic calculator to check for accuracy

THERAPEUTIC INTERVENTIONS

1. Refer the student for hearing, vision, and/or medical examinations to rule out any physical cause of his/her achievement problems in the math area.

2. Explore with the family any sensory modality reasons for their child's math difficulties (i.e., vision, hearing).

3. Refer the student for evaluation of his/her intellectual abilities and academic achievement.

4. School evaluation clinician(s) meets with the parents to discuss their child's assessment results.

5. Conduct an IEP team meeting or general planning meeting with the parents present to determine the student's eligibility for special education and/or ascertain general education math services.

6. Teach estimation strategies to ensure the student is

of his/her own computing process. (11)

9. Engage in repeated practice sessions to improve accuracy of memorization of number facts. (12, 13, 14)

10. Utilize a record-keeping system to chart progress with learning number facts. (15)

11. Increase accuracy of mathematical fact memorization by employing a Language Master to record and repeatedly listen to basic number facts. (16)

12. Participate in a math lab at least 10 minutes daily. (17)

13. Exhibit skills in using consumer math. (18, 19)

14. Exhibit skills in using independent living math. (20, 21)

15. Exhibit skills in using transportation math. (22, 23)

16. Exhibit skills in using vocational math. (24, 25)

17. Consistently engage in proofing strategies. (11, 26, 27)

18. Demonstrate accuracy in mathematical calculation, using accommodations in the general education math curriculum. (28, 29, 30)

19. Effectively use computer-assisted instruction to reinforce math skills. (31)

20. Verbalize long- and short-term goals for learning

continually asking, Does this answer make sense?

7. Teach number facts with manipulatives, having the student also use hands-on materials, moving from the concrete to the graphic (e.g., pictures, diagrams) to the symbolic (e.g., numbers) in calculating a response.

8. Allow the student to use visual materials (e.g., number lines for addition and subtraction) to improve accuracy and increase his/her comprehension of the process.

9. Utilize the Touch Math approach (Bullock, Pierce, and McClellan) to teach basic math operations.

10. Teach rules that assist the student to more competently calculate (i.e., with addition, using the one-up rule or using doubles: $6 + 6 = 12$ so $6 + 7 = 13$; or with multiplication, using the nine's rule) (see *Strategies For Success* [Meltzer, Roditi, Haynes, Biddle, Paster, and Taber]).

11. Instruct the student in calculator use to check for accuracy after computing number facts.

12. Provide visual data, giving many examples, to demonstrate the relationships among the number facts to the student (e.g., the communicative relationship of multiplication facts $3 \times 5 =$

mathematical calculation. (32)

21. Participate in peer-mediated instruction. (33)

22. Increase accuracy of mathematical calculation through participation in game formats for learning mathematical facts. (34)

23. Verbalize acceptance of the need for specialized instruction in mathematical concepts. (35)

24. Parents play math games and emphasize number usage within the daily home routine. (36)

25. Parents provide positive homework involvement and encouragement for their child. (37)

26. Parents report satisfaction with their child's overall school experience and progress. (38, 39)

—. _____
   _____

—. _____
   _____

—. _____
   _____

15 so $5 \times 3 = 15$) to reduce the need for memorization.

13. Consistently engage the student in intensive and frequent practice of newly introduced facts while systematically reviewing previously introduced facts (e.g., use a paired drill with another student in a flash-card or game format).

14. Use mathematic table grids (e.g., a multiplication chart), giving the student a quick visual format upon which to practice and check for accuracy of number facts.

15. Establish a record-keeping system coupled with a motivational reinforcement system whereby the student can monitor his/her gradual progress as number facts are mastered, with growth reinforced by instructional staff.

16. Have the student use a Language Master whereby he/she states the number facts with the correct answer into the Language Master and listens repeatedly to the recording as a practice and memorization task (see Language Master).

17. Set up a math lab in the classroom where 10 to 15 minutes of the school day are spent working on individualized number fact goals by the student alone or in a small group in math

strategy notebooks, game format, or computerized number fact activities (see *Mega Math Blaster* [Davidson and associates]).

18. Emphasize functional skills in relation to consumer math (e.g., comparison shopping, use of credit, computing sales tax, budgeting for basic needs, and paying bills).

19. Provide opportunities in the community for the student to apply and practice consumer math (e.g., grocery shopping for a special meal on a budget).

20. Emphasize functional skills in relation to math and independent living (e.g., contrasting renting or buying, computing monthly expenses, purchasing home-owner's or renter's insurance, buying appliances, purchasing materials for home care and upkeep, and calculating lawn-care costs).

21. Through field trips and practicing actual home-care scenarios, provide opportunities for the student to experience some of the math needs involved in independent living.

22. Emphasize the mathematical side of calculating the costs involved in personal transportation (e.g., buying or leasing an auto, monthly gasoline costs, auto insur-

ance expenses, purchasing bus and/or subway passes, and computing taxi fares).

23. Assist the student in visiting auto dealerships, riding the city bus and/or subway, as well as inviting an insurance salesperson and an auto mechanic to visit the classroom to replicate real-life transportation math scenarios.

24. Prepare the student for math needed in employment (e.g., calculating wages, understanding gross versus net pay, filing tax returns, computing overtime pay, and understanding benefits).

25. Provide opportunities for the student to compare/contrast wages for different jobs and careers and to explore the role math plays in different occupations.

26. Assist the student in developing a personalized checklist of questions to use when proofing his/her mathematical work (e.g., Did I write down the numbers correctly? or Is my answer close to my estimate?) (see *Strategies For Success* [Meltzer, Roditi, Haynes, Biddle, Paster, and Taber]).

27. Develop an error pattern system, examining the most frequently incurred errors by the math-challenged student, having the student keep a log of these error pat-

terns to refer back to, which could include regrouping errors, substitutions, omissions, directionality, attention to sign, and placement errors (see *Enright Diagnostic Inventory of Basic Arithmetic Skills* [Enright]).

28. Shorten or alter assignments for the student (e.g., assigning every fourth or fifth problem, providing worksheets to eliminate copying, organizing individualized learning packets so that the student can receive smaller increments of instruction and more intensive review).

29. Provide numerous opportunities for review and reteaching essential concepts to the student.

30. Provide consistent reinforcement of the student's accurate use of math vocabulary (e.g., provide material for the student to refer back to, and give frequent prompts to the student regarding meaning and use of essential terms).

31. Carefully select computer software to use with the student in deficit areas in which self-paced practice, prompts, and feedback of accuracy are given (i.e., Conquering Math Series).

32. Have the student use self-determination by participating in both long- and

short-term math goal setting (e.g., long-term goal: master the process of reducing fractions; short-term goal: completing 10 problems of long division for homework).

33. In the general education math classroom, create opportunities for the math-deficient student to participate in peer-mediated instruction.

34. Use game formats in the classroom for reinforcement of concepts and skills (e.g., devoting part of a class period per week to multiplication bingo where a number is stated as an answer, and the student must cover all multiplication problems that have that number as its answer).

35. For students whose math deficits are severe, offer an alternative curriculum at the elementary level and alternative courses (e.g., applied math) at the secondary level.

36. Organize family activities that can emphasize use of math (e.g., developing shopping lists and shopping, playing games [e.g., Racko, Monopoly, Risk]).

37. Encourage the parents to assist the student with homework and seek out tutorial support if necessary.

38. A school math specialist or resource teacher maintains

ongoing communication regarding the student's math needs, including techniques for parental assistance with homework.

39. A case manager (e.g., math specialist or resource teacher) gathers information on the strategies and supports that are most effective for the student to share with the teacher(s) prior to the new school year.

__. _____
   _____
__. _____
   _____
__. _____
   _____

MATHEMATICS REASONING

BEHAVIORAL DEFINITIONS

1. Achievement in the area of mathematics substantially below learning potential.
2. Difficulty with mathematical reasoning skills impacting word problems and understanding of concepts such as measurement, geometry, and algebra.
3. An inability to apply the correct computational processes to mathematic problem solving.
4. Limited understanding of basic math vocabulary.
5. Low confidence in his/her math abilities caused by, or resulting in, math anxiety.
6. Mathematic deficits interfere with the student's general academic functioning and/or daily living skills.

—. _____

_____

—. _____

_____

—. _____

_____

LONG-TERM GOALS

1. Increase overall mathematics achievement to a level commensurate with learning potential.
2. Substantially improve problem-solving skills in completion of word problems.

3. Demonstrate abilities with functional math and show the skill to apply the correct math concepts and processes in daily living situations.
4. Reduce significantly any math anxiety and increase confidence in his/her math abilities.
5. Show mastery of mathematical vocabulary to the level of math achievement.
6. Exhibit competency with estimation abilities.

—. _____

_____

—. _____

_____

—. _____

_____

SHORT-TERM OBJECTIVES

1. Cooperate with hearing, vision, and/or medical examination. (1, 2)

2. Participate in a comprehensive math or psychoeducational evaluation. (3)

3. Parents participate in an interpretive meeting to hear test results. (4)

4. Parents take part in an Individualized Education Planning (IEP) team meeting or general meeting and agree to implementation of a math improvement plan. (5)

5. Display skill with estimating answers in math reasoning problems. (6, 7, 8)

6. Verbalize and implement a systematic problem-solving

THERAPEUTIC INTERVENTIONS

1. Refer the student for hearing, vision, and/or medical examinations to rule out any physical cause of his/her achievement problems in the math area.

2. Explore with the family any sensory modality reasons for their child's math difficulties (e.g., vision, hearing).

3. Refer the student for evaluation of his/her intellectual abilities and academic achievement.

4. School evaluation clinician(s) meets with parents to discuss assessment results.

5. Conduct an IEP team meeting or general planning meeting with the parents present to determine the

approach to completing word problems. (9, 10, 11)

7. Create graphic organizers depicting a visual picture of the word problem to assist in successfully working toward an accurate solution. (12, 13)

8. Exhibit skills in using consumer math. (14, 15)

9. Exhibit skills in using independent living math. (16, 17)

10. Exhibit skills in using transportation math. (18, 19)

11. Exhibit skills in using vocational math. (20, 21)

12. Consistently engage in proofing strategies. (22, 23)

13. Demonstrate accuracy in mathematical reasoning using accommodations in the general education math curriculum. (24, 25, 26, 27, 28)

14. Effectively use computer-assisted instruction to reinforce math skills. (29)

15. Verbalize long- and short-term goals for learning mathematical concepts. (30)

16. Participate in peer-mediated instruction. (31)

17. Apply mathematical reasoning accurately to routine occurrences within personal life. (32)

18. Verbalize acceptance of the need for specialized instruction in mathematical concepts. (33)

student's eligibility for special education and/or ascertain general education math services.

6. Model for the student self-questioning strategies to ascertain which operation to use in a word problem: Will it make sense to add the numbers? Why not? Will it make sense to subtract the numbers? Why not? and so on (see *Dyslexia: Research and Resource Guide* [Spafford and Grosser]).

7. Teach the student to round up or round down and guess at an answer, making an attempt at a reasonable, rather than an exact, answer.

8. Instruct the student in the clustering method where numbers in a word problem are clustered together within a range and then computation takes place, leading to an estimated response (i.e., attendance at a series of sporting events are 80,000, 88,000, 89,000, and 81,000—What is the average? All numbers are in the same range, so the estimation is 80,000 for an average attendance) (see "Teaching Computational Estimation: Concepts and Strategies" by Reyes in *National Estimation and Mental Computation: 1986 Yearbook* [Schoen and Zweng, eds.]).

19. Parents emphasize the use of math in daily living within the family routine. (34)

20. Parents provide positive homework involvement and encouragement for their child. (35)

21. Parents report satisfaction with their child's overall school experience and progress. (36, 37)

__. _____

_____

__. _____

_____

__. _____

_____

9. Provide instruction in a four-step process to problem solving: (1) understand the problem—clarify the language, talk it out, ask for help; (2) devise a plan—determine the correct operations, identify steps to follow, estimate; (3) carry out the plan—confirm hypotheses; (4) look back—is the answer reasonable and in a useable form? (see *How To Solve It* [Polya]).

10. Offer the problem-solving strategy of SQRQCQ (Survey, Question, Read, Question, Compute, and Question) to the student (see *Teaching Content Area Reading Skills* [Forgan and Mangrum]).

11. Teach the secondary student an eight-step process to solving word problems: (1) read the problem aloud; (2) paraphrase the problem aloud; (3) visualize—create a graphic depiction; (4) state the problem; (5) hypothesize; (6) estimate; (7) calculate; (8) self-check (see "The Eight Steps in the Verbal Math Problem Solving Strategy" by Montague and Bos in *Journal of Learning Disabilities* [1986, 19: 27–28]).

12. Use a multisensory technique (e.g., the CSA method—Concrete, Semiconcrete, Abstract), which includes verbal, visual, and hands-on methods to in-

struct the student in solving problems (e.g., the student represents the word problem using manipulatives, then uses pictures of objects, and finally moves to using symbols alone).

13. Model for the student different examples of how to visually display a word problem to enhance comprehension of the problem and to work toward a viable solution.

14. Emphasize functional skills in relation to consumer math (e.g., comparison shopping, use of credit, computing sales tax, budgeting for basic needs, and paying bills).

15. Provide opportunities in the classroom and in the community for the student to apply and practice consumer math (e.g., simulating the use of a credit card and realizing the finance charge per month if not paid in full).

16. Emphasize functional skills in relation to math and independent living (e.g., contrasting renting or buying, computing monthly expenses, purchasing home-owner's or renter's insurance, buying appliances, purchasing materials for home care and upkeep, and calculating lawn-care costs).

17. Through field trips and practicing actual home-care scenarios, provide opportu-

nities for the student to experience some of the math needs involved with independent living.

18. Emphasize the mathematical aspects of calculating the costs involved in personal transportation, covering math areas (e.g., buying or leasing an auto, monthly gasoline costs, auto insurance expenses, purchasing bus and/or subway passes, and computing taxi fares).

19. Assist the student in visiting auto dealerships, riding the city bus and/or subway, as well as inviting an insurance salesperson and an auto mechanic to visit the classroom to replicate real-life transportation math scenarios.

20. Prepare the student for math needed in employment (e.g., calculating wages, understanding gross versus net pay, filing tax returns, computing overtime pay, and understanding benefits).

21. Provide opportunities for the student to compare/contrast wages for different jobs and careers and to explore the role math plays in different occupations.

22. Assist the student in developing a personalized checklist of questions to use when proofing his/her mathematical work (e.g., Did I write down the numbers cor-

rectly? or Is my answer close to my estimate?) (see *Strategies For Success* [Meltzer, Roditi, Haynes, Biddle, Paster, and Taber]).

23. Teach calculator skills to the student for rechecking computation in calculation and in word problem processes.

24. Provide visual interventions that include using graph paper upon which to write problems, color coding sequences of steps to problem solution, and creating charts to keep up in the classroom for different skills/concepts for use by the student as reference points.

25. Have the student read a problem with the correct answer into a tape recorder and listen to it as auditory reinforcement.

26. Shorten or alter assignments for the student (e.g., assigning every fourth or fifth problem, providing problems on worksheets to eliminate copying, and organizing individualized learning packets so that the student can receive smaller increments of instruction and more intensive review).

27. Provide numerous opportunities for review and reteaching essential concepts to the student.

28. Provide consistent reinforcement of the student's

accurate use of math vocabulary (e.g., provide material for the student to refer back to and give frequent prompts to the student regarding meaning and use of essential terms).

29. Carefully select computer software to use with the student in deficit areas in which self-paced practice, prompts, and feedback of accuracy are given (e.g., for elementary level: Exploring Measurement, Time and Money; for secondary level: Survival Math).

30. Have the student use self-determination by participating in both long- and short-term math goal setting (e.g., long-term goal: apply the metric system to everyday measurement; short-term goal: complete two geometric theorems for homework).

31. In the general education math classroom, create opportunities for the math-deficient student to participate in peer-mediated instruction.

32. Provide a math problem of the day using personalized information in its content (e.g., including names of the student's family, pets, local addresses, favorite television personalities, etc.) (see *Dyslexia: Research and Resource Guide* [Spafford and Grosser]).

33. For students whose math deficits are severe, offer an alternative curriculum at the elementary level and alternative courses (e.g., applied math) at the secondary level.

34. Organize family activities that can emphasize use of math (e.g., budgeting and purchasing school clothes, playing games [e.g., Life, Monopoly]).

35. Encourage the parents to assist the student with homework and seek out tutorial support if necessary.

36. A school math specialist or resource teacher maintains ongoing communication regarding the student's math needs, including techniques for parental assistance with homework.

37. A case manager (math specialist or resource teacher) gathers information on the strategies and supports that are most effective for the student to share with the teacher(s) prior to the new school year.

___. _____

_____

___. _____

_____

___. _____

_____

MILD MENTALLY
IMPAIRED—ADOLESCENT

BEHAVIORAL DEFINITIONS

1. Diminished intellectual abilities resulting in diminished learning capacity.
2. An intelligence quotient as measured on an individually administered intelligence test falling within a range from approximately 55 to 70 (with 100 as average).
3. Short- and long-term memory deficits.
4. Difficulty with thinking, reasoning, and communication skills apparent in both academic and social arenas.
5. Achievement at the sixth percentile or lower in basic skill areas (e.g., reading, math) as measured on an individually administered standardized test.
6. Mild to moderate impairments in self-care and functional, adaptive, and leisure skills.
7. Difficulty with generalizing/transferring acquired skills to practical settings.

__. _____

_____

__. _____

_____

__. _____

_____

LONG-TERM GOALS

1. Demonstrate achievement in basic academic skills to the level of potential.
2. Exhibit communication and social skill functioning to an acceptable level in the school and community.
3. Maintain evidence of a positive self-concept.
4. Demonstrate improved self-care and adaptive behaviors to the level of potential.
5. Develop prevocational and vocational skills to the level of potential and participate successfully in vocational training.
6. Function at the highest level of independence in relation to potential within the home, school, and community.

__. _____
_____
__. _____
_____
__. _____
_____

SHORT-TERM OBJECTIVES

1. Cooperate with a psychoeducational evaluation. (1)
2. Participate in a speech and language evaluation. (2)
3. Complete an evaluation by occupational and/or physical therapists. (3)
4. Parents meet for an interpretive meeting with the school clinicians. (4)
5. Parents attend the Individualized Education Planning (IEP) team meeting and accept the outcome recommendations of the meeting. (5)

THERAPEUTIC INTERVENTIONS

1. Refer the student for a psychoeducational evaluation to include intellectual, achievement, and adaptive behavior assessment.
2. Refer the student for a speech and language evaluation.
3. Refer the student for an occupational and/or physical therapy evaluation.
4. Arrange for a multidisciplinary evaluation team meeting in which test results are interpreted to parents, and they have an opportunity to provide

6. Increase the number of words read on sight. (6, 7)

7. Expand reading vocabulary. (8, 9)

8. Master essential survival words visible in the school and in the community, readily pronouncing and comprehending them on sight. (10)

9. Demonstrate reading comprehension at a level commensurate with learning potential. (11, 12, 13)

10. Use computerized instruction to improve overall reading skills. (14, 15)

11. Increase accurate spelling of carefully selected weekly spelling words to a 90 percent level. (16, 17, 18, 19)

12. Cooperate with an occupational therapist's suggestions in handwriting skills. (20)

13. Demonstrate greater competency with handwriting skills. (21, 22, 23)

14. Demonstrate an accurate implementation of sentence structure. (24, 25)

15. Write a story from a picture stimulus that is at least one paragraph and uses only complete sentences. (26, 27)

16. Show skill in neatly and accurately completing an employment application. (28, 29, 30)

17. Exhibit competencies with consumer math skills. (31, 32, 33)

input into the multidisciplinary evaluation process.

5. Arrange for an IEP team meeting, determining the student's eligibility for special education and appropriate programs and/or services.

6. Teach the student the most frequently used words from a familiar-sight word list (e.g., Dolch Word List), using visual strategies such as the configuration method where each word is outlined and memorized per its shape.

7. Provide sight word vocabulary instruction using a visual, auditory, kinesthetic, and tactile approach where the student sees the word, hears the word said aloud, traces the word, and feels the word as it is traced (see *Remedial Techniques in Basic School Subjects* [Fernald]).

8. Ensure the student increases the number of word meanings mastered by teaching a select vocabulary list each week whereby the student needs to read and define each word, making certain the selected words have relevance to the student; provide the word list to the parents so they can emphasize their use and post them prominently at home.

9. At his/her level, teach the student the easier aspects of using the dictionary (e.g.,

18. Exhibit competencies with math skills needed in an independent living situation. (34, 35, 36)

19. Exhibit math skill competencies needed with health care issues. (37)

20. Exhibit math skills needed in the area of employment and vocation. (38, 39, 40)

21. Show competencies with math related to daily living skills. (41, 42)

22. Care for personal needs in an effective manner. (43, 44)

23. Demonstrate autonomy with organizing and preparing food. (45, 46)

24. Show an interest in and awareness of a variety of recreational and leisure activities. (47, 48)

25. Demonstrate two positive social interactions per day with peers and adults. (49, 50, 51, 52)

26. Make positive statements regarding self and progress in learning. (53, 54)

27. Cooperate with assessment of prerequisite employability skills. (55, 56)

28. Show success with job sampling experiences in the community. (57)

29. Participate in the development of an individualized transition plan. (58)

30. Participate in visiting vocational training sites. (59)

31. Exhibit success with postsecondary employment. (60)

defining a word and pronouncing a word).

10. Through labeling, pictures matched with words, and practice, instruct the student in basic words that give direction in daily living (maneuvering through the school and the community) (e.g., exit, fire exit, bus stop, stop/walk/wait, men, women, restrooms).

11. Assist the student with a structure to organize the meaning of what he/she has read (e.g., RAP method includes three steps: R—Read the paragraph, A—Ask yourself what the paragraph is about, P—Put the main idea and two details in your own words) (see *Learning Strategies Curriculum: The Paraphrasing Strategy* [Schumaker, Denton, and Deschler]).

12. Instruct the student at his/her level in the reciprocal teaching method whereby comprehension of a passage is assimilated by the student through teacher-directed discussion, using the strategies of summarizing, questioning, clarifying, and predicting (see "Reciprocal Teaching of Comprehension-Fostering and Comprehension-Monitoring Activities" by Palinscar and Brown in *Cognition and Instruction* [1984, 1: 117–175]).

13. Use a direct instruction approach, structuring the

32. Parents verbalize an acceptance of their son/daughter and his/her cognitive disability, and verbalize realistic goals and expectations. (61, 62)

33. Parents report satisfaction with their son's/daughter's overall school experience and progress. (63)

—. _____
   _____

—. _____
   _____

—. _____
   _____

learning to use a repeated sequential pattern of tasks for improving both the student's word identification and reading comprehension skills (see *Corrective Reading Program* [Englemann, Becker, Hanner, and Johnson]).

14. Provide carefully selected software for the student that will enhance sight word identification skills (e.g., Word Man by Developmental Learning Materials has the student watch tracks of letters and he/she must decide when a word is formed; Word Radar by Developmental Learning Materials allows the student to match basic sight words).

15. Select software (e.g., Comprehension Power by Milliken) that provides the student with reading and comprehension practice, engaging the student in reading a selection of high interest and then responding to comprehension questions with prompt feedback as to accuracy.

16. Teach a four-sense modality process whereby the student sees the word, hears the word, traces the word, and spells the word throughout the study process (see *Remedial Techniques in Basic School Subjects* [Fernald]).

17. Provide the student with instructional exercises to increase his/her visual

recognition and recall of each word to be learned (e.g., show four choices of a word and have the student select the correct spelling).

18. Move the student from partial to total recall in a visual memory spelling task where he/she is first shown an entire word, studies its configuration and sequence of letters, and then is shown the word again, but must fill in omitted letters; at the end of the exercise, the student must spell/write the entire word from recall.

19. Engage the student in various games to master the weekly spelling word list (e.g., spelling bingo).

20. Reinforce the instructional directions of the occupational therapist as they are carried out by the student in the classroom (e.g., correct grasp of the writing tool, position of the paper, posture, etc.) as part of the writing skills to be mastered.

21. Give cursive handwriting instruction, concentrating on the student's signature and overall legibility.

22. Provide models of correct letter formations for the student with revisualization difficulties so a reference is *always* available.

23. Teach the motor-impaired student only manuscript or cursive to avoid frustration.

24. Teach the student the basics

of sentence structure (e.g., subject/predicate, noun/verb) by giving the student a format to follow (e.g., answering questions: Which? [my], Who or what? [dog], Does or did? [licked], What or whom? [the mail carrier], Where? [on the arm]) (see *Teaching Special Needs Students in the Regular Classroom* [Morsink]).

25. Assist the student with sentence-building activities where words or phrases are pieced together by the student to construct competent sentences, or the teacher gives a sentence starter and the student finishes it with correct structure.

26. Present a picture stimulus to the student and then assign him/her to write a story about it; brainstorm ideas with the student for his/her story, tapping into prior knowledge.

27. Assist the student with organizing and writing a story from a picture stimulus, using a specific organizational format: (1) look at the picture; (2) let your mind be free; (3) write down the story parts, identifying *who* the main character is, *when* the story takes place, *where* the story takes place, *what* the main character does, *what* happens when he or she tries to do it, *how* the main character feels; (4) write down story ideas for each

part; (5) write your story (see "Improving Composition Skills of Inefficient Learners with Self-Instructional Strategy Training" by Graham and Harris in *Topics in Language Disorders* [1987, 7: 66–77]).

28. Provide the student with models of completed job applications from local businesses.

29. Teach the student how to complete an application section by section, assisting him/her with creating a list of information needed to bring to the potential work site if the application must be filled out at the place of potential employment (e.g., social security number, driver's license or pictured identification, electronic speller).

30. Instruct the student in reviewing and editing his/her employment application using the COPS strategy: C—Have I Capitalized proper names?, O—How is the Overall appearance? (e.g., handwriting, margins, spacing), P—Have I used Punctuation correctly?, S—Do the words look correctly Spelled? (see "Learning Strategies: An Instructional Alternative for Low Achieving Adolescents" by Deschler and Schumaker in *Exceptional Children* [1986, 52(6): 583–590]).

31. Accompany the student into stores where comparison shopping can take place (e.g., the student compares the costs of a similar item at different types of stores [e.g., department, hardware, drugstore] or the student compares the costs of different kinds of orange juice, socks, and toothbrushes at a grocery store).

32. Create simulation scenarios in which the student must deal with establishing a budget and paying bills, receiving differing amounts of income from various types of imaginary work.

33. Encourage the parents to establish a financial account (i.e., savings, checking) for the student at a banking institution and to provide an allowance for tasks done at home to give the student practice with real money situations.

34. Using the newspaper, assist the student with understanding costs involved with renting an apartment versus renting or purchasing a house.

35. Teach the student to budget for household costs (e.g., electricity, telephone, water, insurance, and saving for maintenance and repair issues) by obtaining real data from an unidentified family or individual(s) to use for examining the needs and costs.

36. Make certain the student is able to tell time to five-minute intervals, read a nondigital clock or watch, and organize himself/herself to use time efficiently (e.g., being ready for work or appointments on time).

37. Spend time with the student at a physician's office or with the school nurse, working on teaching him/her about dosages of medication, blood pressure, pulse, and use of a thermometer.

38. Instruct the student in calculating his/her salary (e.g., computing a week's wages based on a part-time schedule and an hourly wage).

39. Provide examples of paychecks that clearly demonstrate the difference between gross and net pay, teaching the student about payroll deductions.

40. Initiate exposure for the student to the general processes of filing federal and state income taxes.

41. Give the student practice in establishing a weekly and monthly budget, including items (e.g., food, clothing, transportation, and recreational activities).

42. Consider use of a commercial math program that is designed to familiarize the student with real-life situations across the daily living spectrum (e.g., *Practical Mathematics: Consumer*

Applications [Frederick, Postman, Leinwand, and Wantuck]).

43. Provide health information to the student that models proper hygiene, grooming, fitness, nutrition, and illness prevention.

44. Give improvement prompts to the student when he/she shows deficits in personal care (e.g., dress, grooming, health).

45. Have the student participate in a daily living skills course where meal planning and food preparation is emphasized.

46. Accompany the student to community outings to provide instruction in the purchasing of food and planning of meals.

47. Organize a supervised evening recreational group for mildly mentally impaired secondary students centering around different monthly social activities (e.g., concerts, movies, plays, card parties, swimming).

48. Work with the student and the parents in developing recreational activity for the student: (1) developing one or two hobbies that can be shared with the family or done independently and (2) selecting social/recreational activities wisely, maintaining an awareness of choices outside of isolating selections such as video games or television.

49. Through development of a positive behavior support plan, identify several positive target behaviors of the student, which the teacher will reinforce in order to decrease the student's negative actions and replace them with prosocial behaviors.

50. Have the student work with a school mental health professional to role-play strategies to learn prosocial behaviors and positive cognitive self-talk to decrease overt behavioral difficulties.

51. Teach the student at his/her level of comprehension strategies demonstrating personal-best behavior in interpersonal problem solving (e.g., using the FAST strategy [F—Freeze and think, A—Alternatives, S—Solution, T—Try it] and the SLAM strategy [S—Stop, L—Look, A—Ask, and M—Make]) (see "Fast Social Skills with a Slam and a Rap: Providing Social Skills Training for Students with Learning Disabilities" by McIntosh, Vaugh, and Bennerson in *Teaching Exceptional Children* [1995, 28: 37–41]).

52. Use modeling by both the teacher and positive peers to instruct the student in prosocial behaviors.

53. Establish a warm, accepting classroom environment in which individual differences are applauded.

54. Assist the student in setting workable, achievable goals and then organize school staff and the parents to show positive recognition for attainment of the goals.

55. Conduct an assessment of the student's employability skills, using a systematic approach (e.g., the Targeted Employment Assessment Model from *Competitive Employment* [Wehman]) that examines vocational skills, independent living skills, parent attitudes and behavior, and job requirements to ascertain deficit employability areas and what type of employment model may best meet the student's needs (competitive employment versus some type of supported employment) (see *Competitive Employment* [Wehman]).

56. Implement the Life-Centered Career Education (Brolin) curriculum model with the student, which emphasizes instruction in daily living skills, personal social skills, and occupational guidance and preparation to work on deficit areas in the vocational/quality-of-life arena.

57. Establish a schedule for the student to experience job shadowing and a sampling of work in the community with various types of employment for (1) exposing the student to a number of

job options available in the community; (2) training the student in work-related skills such as time management and workplace behavior; (3) identifying employment interests of the student; and (4) gathering another piece of information upon which to ascertain the level of support needed for success in work settings (see *Secondary Programs for Students with Developmental Disabilities* [McDonnell, Wilcox, and Hardman]).

58. Using a collaborative model, write an individualized transition plan with the student, parents, school vocational training representative, community agencies, and potential employers (as appropriate), establishing short- and long-term goals for the student to make the transition from school to work, developing specific desired outcomes and identifying the necessary level of support (e.g., no special services, time-limited services, ongoing services) for the student to obtain those outcomes (see *Office of Special Education and Rehabilitative Services Programming for the Transition of Youth with Disabilities: Bridges from School to Working Life* [Will]).

59. Arrange for the student and his/her parents to visit potential vocational training

sites, focusing on programs providing the identified level of support needed for the student to be successful as an employee (e.g., sheltered workshop, enclave, supported work in a competitive employment setting).

60. Provide support to the student in his/her high school vocational training, working toward the goal of adult vocational programming leading to gainful, permanent employment.

61. Communicate with parents on a routine, frequent basis, reporting on the student's progress, successes, and concerns.

62. Refer the parents to a local parent support group for families with individuals maintaining cognitive challenges and/or to a national organization such as the American Association on Mental Retardation in Washington, DC.

63. Gather information on the strategies and supports that have been most effective for the student and arrange for this information to be shared with the teaching staff in the new school year.

__. _____

_____

__. _____

_____

__. _____

_____

MILD MENTALLY IMPAIRED—CHILD

BEHAVIORAL DEFINITIONS

1. Diminished intellectual abilities resulting in diminished learning capacity.
2. An intelligence quotient as measured on an individually administered intelligence test falling within a range from approximately 55 to 70 (with 100 as average).
3. Short- and long-term memory deficits.
4. Difficulty with thinking, reasoning, and communication skills apparent in both academic and social arenas.
5. Achievement at the sixth percentile or lower in basic skill areas (e.g., reading, math) as measured on an individually administered standardized test.
6. Mild to moderate impairments in self-care and functional, adaptive, and leisure skills.
7. Difficulty with generalizing/transferring acquired skills to practical settings.

__. _____
   _____
__. _____
   _____
__. _____
   _____

LONG-TERM GOALS

1. Demonstrate achievement in basic academic skills to the level of potential.

2. Exhibit communication and social skill functioning to an acceptable level in the school setting.
3. Maintain evidence of a positive self-concept.
4. Demonstrate progress with self-care and adaptive behaviors to the level of potential.
5. Parents develop an awareness and acceptance of their child's intellectual and cognitive capabilities so that they place appropriate expectations on his/her functioning.

—. _____
   _____
   _____

—. _____
   _____
   _____

—. _____
   _____

SHORT-TERM OBJECTIVES

1. Cooperate with a psychoeducational evaluation. (1)
2. Participate in a speech and language evaluation. (2)
3. Complete an evaluation by occupational and/or physical therapists. (3)
4. Parents meet for an interpretive meeting with the school clinicians. (4)
5. Parents attend the Individualized Education Planning (IEP) team meeting and accept the outcome recommendations of the meeting. (5)
6. Adjust positively to a new school schedule, which could include a full-time special education classroom, full inclusion in general education, or placement on

THERAPEUTIC INTERVENTIONS

1. Refer for a psychoeducational evaluation to include intellectual, achievement, and adaptive behavior assessment.
2. Refer the student for a speech and language evaluation.
3. Refer the student for an occupational and/or physical therapy evaluation.
4. Arrange for a multidisciplinary evaluation team meeting in which test results are interpreted to parents, and they have an opportunity to provide input into the mulitdisciplinary evaluation process.
5. Arrange for an IEP team meeting, determining the student's eligibility for spe-

the continuum between these two options. (6)

7. Build a sight word vocabulary to the level of expected achievement. (7, 8, 9)

8. Master introduced survival words visible in the school, readily identifying them on sight. (10)

9. Use context and picture cues to identify unknown words. (11)

10. Increase comprehension skills to the level of expected achievement. (12, 13, 14, 15)

11. Demonstrate greater fluency in oral reading. (16)

12. Apply the interactive model to all arithmetic tasks. (17)

13. Demonstrate comprehension of the processes required in computing number facts. (18, 19)

14. Engage in repeated practice sessions to improve accuracy of memorization of number facts. (20, 21, 22)

15. Utilize beginning applied math skills. (23)

16. Match the value of smaller coin denominations with small purchases. (24, 25)

17. Effectively use computer-assisted instruction to reinforce math skills. (26)

18. Show success in the general education curriculum. (27)

19. Participate in an alternative curriculum in specific subject areas. (28)

cial education and appropriate programs and/or services.

6. Per the IEP team, organize or reorganize the student's schedule, which could include placement in a special education classroom for part of the school day or in a general education setting for all or part of the school day.

7. Provide whole word instruction of basic sight words (e.g., the, is, was, this, etc.), such as using the configuration method where each word is outlined and memorized per its shape.

8. Instruct the student in a word-chunking system using visual and auditory skills to break a word into familiar, workable parts (see *Glass Analysis for Decoding Only* [Glass and Glass]).

9. Provide reading instruction using a visual, auditory, kinesthetic, and tactile approach where the student sees the word, hears the word said aloud, traces the word, and feels the word as it is traced (see *Remedial Techniques in Basic School Subjects* [Fernald]).

10. Through repetition, drill, and labeling of objects and locations in the school, instruct the student in basic words that give direction in daily living (e.g., exit, men, women, boys, girls, gym, and library).

20. Demonstrate motor skills to the level of potential. (29)

21. Demonstrate self-care skills to the level of potential. (30, 31)

22. Demonstrate two positive social interactions per day with peers and adults. (32, 33, 34, 35)

23. Make positive statements regarding self and progress in learning. (36, 37, 38)

24. Parents verbalize an acceptance of their child and his/her cognitive disability, and verbalize realistic goals and expectations for the child. (39, 40)

25. Identify personal preferences for types of work tasks. (41, 42, 43)

26. Recognize and master some of the behaviors required for success in the work world. (44, 45)

27. Parents report their satisfaction with their child's overall school experience and progress. (39, 46)

—. _____
   _____

—. _____
   _____

—. _____
   _____

11. Teach the student to follow these steps when faced with an unknown word: (1) read to the end of the sentence; (2) use picture cues (when available); (3) sound out the word; (4) ask for help (see *Mental Retardation— Foundations of Educational Programming* [Hickson, Blackman, and Reis]).

12. Use the language experience method with the student where a topic is drawn from the student's interests and background, the student verbalizes a sentence or sentences to an adult about the topic, the adult writes the sentence as dictated by the student, the student depicts what is written in picture form, and then reads aloud repeatedly what he/she has dictated (see *Teaching Reading in the Elementary School* [Barr and Johnson]).

13. Use a reading program that emphasizes high-interest stories with repetitive, limited vocabulary and a visual emphasis (e.g., *Reading Milestones* [Quigley, King, McAnally, and Rose]).

14. Read to the student several times during the school day in a small group for discussion and question of text.

15. Have the student listen and follow along with stories of interest on a CD-ROM at the computer.

16. Engage the student in the Neurological Impress

method where the teacher and the student read in unison, with the teacher initially reading more loudly and faster than the student as a model (see "A Neurological-Impress Method of Remedial-Reading Instruction" by Heckelman in *Academic Therapy* [1969, 4: 277–282]).

17. Instruct the student in the Interactive Unit of Arithmetic model, which involves the student showing four possible modes of output: manipulate, identify, say, and write (see *Best Practices in Mild Mental Disabilities* [Cawley, Miller, and Carr]).

18. Teach number facts with manipulatives, having the student use hands-on materials, moving from the concrete to the graphic (e.g., pictures, diagrams) to the symbolic (e.g., numbers) in calculating a response.

19. Utilize the Touch Math approach (see *Touch Math* [Bullock, Pierce, and McClelland]) in which the student learns basic math operations.

20. Provide visual data, giving many examples, to demonstrate the relationships among the number facts (e.g., the commutative relationship of multiplication facts: $2 \times 5 = 10$ so $5 \times 2 = 10$) to reduce the need for memorization.

21. Consistently engage the student in intensive and

frequent practice of newly introduced facts while systematically reviewing previously introduced facts (e.g., pair the student with a peer tutor to work on drills such as with flash cards or in a game format).

22. Instruct the student in self-instructional training to internalize the computational processes following these steps: modeling of self-instruction by the teacher; use of self-instruction by the student with teacher assistance; use of self-instruction by the student with just monitoring by the teacher; whispered self-instruction by the student with monitoring by the teacher; and finally, independent self-instruction by the student (see "Self-Instruction Training: Cognitive Behavior Modification for Remediating Arithmetic Deficits" by Leon and Pepe in *Exceptional Children* [1983, 50(1): 54–60]).

23. Have the student exercise practical use of math (e.g., matching digits from a phone number with digits on a telephone, matching different routine activities of the day with a time on the clock, and measuring ingredients for a cooking project).

24. Engage the student in counting and game playing with pennies, nickels, dimes,

and quarters to comprehend the worth of each coin.

25. Have the student participate in a classroom or school store activity every week to identify coins needed to purchase desired items (e.g., recognition of a dime to purchase a 10¢ pencil).

26. Seek out and utilize computer software that will help provide the student with individualized practice of math facts and other basic math concepts (e.g., *Academic Skill Builders in Math* [Chaffin and Maxwell]).

27. Identify adaptations in each subject area as needed to create success for the student in general education that could include increasing the level of support in general education with an assigned peer tutor, a cross-age student tutor, or a teacher assistant; adapting the manner in which the instruction is delivered to the student (e.g., using more visual aids, more concrete examples, and hands-on activities); altering the level of difficulty or skill level; and changing how the learner may respond (e.g., instead of an oral report, have the student exhibit learning by completion of a hands-on project).

28. Identify, establish, and monitor in what subject areas the student may

function in a general education curriculum at the integrated grade level with adaptations and in what subject area an alternative curriculum needs to be offered to the student (e.g., the student may do well in general education social studies in a general education fourth grade classroom with adaptations, but may exhibit reading skills at a first grade level and need specialized, individualized instruction to progress in the reading area).

29. Instruct the student in areas of fine and gross motor development by organizing meaningful activities and following these principles: (1) prioritize the skills to be taught as they relate to the student's daily functioning; (2) teach skills in natural environments; (3) organize goals of all services (e.g., physical therapy and occupational therapy) into an integrated instructional routine for the student; (4) organize the student's therapy to be carried out in a group when appropriate; (5) integrate participation by general education peers in the motor activities with the student when possible; (6) keep a detailed database of the student's performance and alter instruction as needed (see *Educating Children with Multiple Disabilities* [Orelove and Sobsey]).

30. Identify and prioritize self-care issues of the student with the family (e.g., dressing, undressing, brushing teeth, hair care) and develop routines for accomplishing established goals at school and at home.

31. Organize a visual chart that will allow the student to identify the targeted individual self-care goals he/she is working on and that can be used as a reminder by the student to complete these tasks (e.g., a visual prompt to brush teeth after lunch), and which will exhibit the progress the student is making with completing each goal in an independent manner.

32. Through development of a positive behavior support plan, identify several target behaviors that the teacher will work on with the student to decrease negative actions and replace them with prosocial behaviors.

33. Have the student work with a school mental health professional to role-play strategies to learn prosocial behaviors and positive cognitive self-talk to decrease overt behavioral difficulties.

34. Teach the student, at his/her level of comprehension, strategies demonstrating personal-best behavior in interpersonal problem solving such as using the FAST strategy (F—Freeze

and think, A—Alternatives, S—Solution, T—Try it) and the SLAM strategy (S—Stop, L—Look, A—Ask, and M—Make) (see "Fast Social Skills with a Slam and a Rap: Providing Social Skills Training for Students with Learning Disabilities" by McIntosh, Vaugh, and Bennerson in *Teaching Exceptional Children* [1995, 28: 37–41]).

35. Use modeling by both the teacher and positive peers to instruct the student in prosocial behaviors.

36. Establish a warm, accepting classroom environment in which individual differences are applauded.

37. Assist the student in setting workable, achievable goals and then organize school staff and parents to show positive recognition for attainment of the goals.

38. Praise the student for effort regardless if success is attained.

39. Communicate with parents on a routine, frequent basis, reporting progress, successes, and concerns.

40. Refer the parents to a local parent support group for families with individuals maintaining cognitive challenges and/or to a national organization such as the American Association on Mental Retardation in Washington, DC.

41. Organize various tasks in the classroom and in the school for the student to experience and perform.

42. Offer career awareness opportunities for the elementary student through literature, classroom guests, and community outings to observe people performing different jobs.

43. Encourage the parents to have the student participate in community activities and organizations that can promote responsibility and enjoyment (e.g., Scouts, 4-H, church groups).

44. When providing instruction in self-care, promote the importance of appropriate dress and grooming in the workplace.

45. Make the student accountable (to his/her potential) for beginning and ending work on time, working with accuracy, and turning in work.

46. Gather information on the strategies and supports that have been most effective for the student and arrange for this information to be shared with the teaching staff in the new school year.

—. _____
_____

—. _____
_____

—. _____
_____

ORAL EXPRESSION / LANGUAGE

BEHAVIORAL DEFINITIONS

1. Overall expressive language abilities as measured by standardized tests are substantially below learning potential.
2. Deficits in oral expression significantly interfere with academic performance.
3. Recurring evidence of word retrieval problems.
4. Inaccurate use of grammar and sentence structure, including an inability to follow the rules of grammar and sentence organization (syntax).
5. Difficulty with initiating a social conversational topic, topic maintenance, using appropriate nonverbal behaviors, and accurately interpreting the nonlinguistic cues of others.
6. An inability to produce expressive meaningful discourse due to inadequate grasp of the meaning of language (semantics).
7. Pattern of negative, overt behavior directly related to frustration due to limited or inaccurate oral expression.

—. _____

_____

—. _____

_____

—. _____

_____

LONG-TERM GOALS

1. Improve overall expressive language abilities to the level of potential.
2. Show progress in the skill of word retrieval.

3. Demonstrate gains in the areas of syntax and semantics.
4. Parents develop an understanding and acceptance of their child's oral expression deficits and establish realistic expectations for his/her functioning and progress.
5. Decrease and eventually extinguish negative behaviors related to frustration over expressive language difficulties.

—. _____
   _____
   _____

—. _____
   _____
   _____

—. _____
   _____

SHORT-TERM OBJECTIVES

1. Cooperate with an audiological assessment. (1)
2. Cooperate with a psychoeducational evaluation. (2)
3. Participate in a speech and language assessment. (3)
4. Parents participate in an interpretive meeting with school clinicians. (4)
5. Parents participate in the Individualized Education Planning (IEP) team meeting, and verbalize acceptance of the recommendations of the staff for their child's education. (5)
6. Demonstrate awareness of syllables in individual words. (6)
7. Identify root words, suffixes, and prefixes to 80 percent accuracy. (7)

THERAPEUTIC INTERVENTIONS

1. Refer the student for an audiological evaluation to rule out hearing loss as a reason for an oral expression deficit.
2. Refer the student for a psychoeducational evaluation.
3. Refer the student for a speech and language evaluation.
4. Staff meets with the parents to gather parental input and interpret test data.
5. School personnel collaborate with the parents at the IEP team meeting to determine the student's eligibility for special education programs and/or services.
6. Teach the student to recognize individual syllables in words by asking him/her to listen to the syllables emphasized by a teacher model and then to repeat the syl-

8. Use verb tenses in daily oral language to 80 percent accuracy. (8)

9. Identify and use pronouns in daily oral language to 80 percent accuracy. (9)

10. Use plurals in daily oral language with 80 percent accuracy. (10, 11)

11. Use sentences of six words or more that contain descriptive phrases. (12, 13)

12. Accurately define and currently use five new words per week. (14, 15, 16, 17)

13. Effectively use semantic mapping strategies (diagrams) to increase knowledge of word meanings. (18)

14. Demonstrate accurate and appropriate use of quantitative, qualitative, spatial, and temporal relational words. (19, 20, 21)

15. Increase proficiency with word retrieval skills. (22, 23, 24, 25)

16. Demonstrate progress with word retrieval skills through general education adaptations. (26)

17. Utilize oral expression skills accurately within a functional context in the classroom. (27, 28)

18. Show mastery of age-appropriate telephone conversation skills. (29, 30)

19. Demonstrate competency with requesting and giving information. (31)

lables orally, clapped out in a rhythm.

7. Instruct the student as to how to break words apart verbally, recognizing the base or root of the word and identifying prefix and suffix components.

8. Using daily activities (e.g., a storytelling activity or art project), prompt the student to describe and discuss what he/she is doing at present, did previously, or what the next sequence or event will be (see *Language Disorders* [Owens]).

9. Model the correct use of specific pronouns to be learned by the student, beginning with first person (I) before teaching the second person (you) (see *Language Disorders* [Owens]).

10. Teach the concept of one, more than one, then easier plural words such as those ending with just an *s*, waiting to introduce irregular plurials (e.g., hippopotami, mice) until the student appears developmentally able to comprehend them (see *Language Disorders* [Owens]).

11. Use sentence completion and fill-in-the-blank statements as practice for selecting the correct plural (see *The Source for Down Syndrome* [Chamberlain and Strode]).

12. Use pictures or photos to have the student practice target phrases, adding

20. Show an awareness of the other person's (listener's) needs in a conversational setting. (32, 33, 34)

21. Initiate and maintain on-topic behaviors in a conversational setting. (35, 36)

22. Demonstrate an increased accuracy in reading the non-linguistic cues of others. (37)

23. Accurately use nonlinguistic cues effectively in conversation. (38)

24. Demonstrate competencies with taking turns in conversation. (39)

25. Decrease disruptive or angry behaviors due to frustration with expressive language deficits (40, 41, 42)

26. Parents verbalize an acceptance of the language deficits of their child, adjust their expectations realistically, and seek resources of support. (43, 44)

27. Parents express satisfaction with their child's progress in oral expression skills and with his/her school program and/or services. (45)

—. _____
   _____
—. _____
   _____
—. _____
   _____

words and phrases as he/she describes the visuals.

13. Teach specific phrases, modeling them for the student and having him/her practice them in contrived scenarios with prompts for him/her to add specificity and descriptiveness to sentences.

14. Assist the student in building and extending his/her knowledge of word meanings, focusing on these strategies: (1) build on prior experiences and knowledge of the student to link new words; (2) provide instruction in meaningful contexts; and (3) provide repeated and varied exposures to the vocabulary to be learned (see "Learning Word Meanings From Context During Normal Reading" by Nagy, Anderson, and Herman in *American Educational Research Journal* [1987, 24: 237–270]).

15. Teach the student to describe the features of his/her world, using specific descriptive words, thus expanding vocabulary (e.g., instead of calling it hot chocolate, it could be identified as a warm, steaming, delicious cup of chocolate drink) (see *Language Disorders* [Owens]).

16. Provide instruction in the meaning of types of words (e.g., homonyms, antonyms, synonyms) to assist the stu-

dent with categorizing/organizing meanings of words.

17. Engage the student in vocabulary-building games (e.g., Pictionary, Boggle, Scrabble Jr., and Scrabble).

18. Instruct the student in using diagrams to master the meaning of an individual word (e.g., creating a spider-gram [e.g., using *frog*], where the word is in the center and associations of the word surround it [e.g., green, amphibian, eats insects], or creating a compare/contrast matrix where the meanings of two words [e.g., dog and cat] are contrasted in terms of similarities and differences) (see *Practical Procedures for Children with Language Disorders* [Nelson] and *Teacher's Handbook for Elementary Social Studies* [Taba]).

19. Introduce the concepts of qualitative (e.g., heavy, light) and quantitative (e.g., some, few) terms with positive comparisons being taught prior to negative comparisons (e.g., "bigger than" is introduced prior to "smaller than") (see *Language Disorders* [Owens]).

20. Teach the student spatial terminology (e.g., in front of/behind), initially using objects that have a front and back, moving to familiar objects less defined, and then to teaching vertical terms (e.g., above/below)

prior to horizontal terms (e.g., left/right) (see *Language Disorders* [Owens]).

21. Introduce temporal terminology to the student (e.g., time, order) through concrete events (e.g., time—making the student aware that art time is later in the afternoon at 3:00) or using pictures of scheduled events to show time and order (see *Language Disorders* [Owens]).

22. Provide cues for the student that give practice in word finding (e.g., use naming/descriptive tasks: It's a frog. It is green. It hops and eats insects; use association/beginning/middle/end: e.g., red, white, and _____; or use fill-in-the-blank format: The frog is sitting on the _____.) (see *Language Disorders* [Owens]).

23. Give opportunities for the student to practice categorizing terms (e.g., book, newspaper, magazine are all things to be read).

24. Have the student play games (leaving out any racing against a timer aspect) that encourage word retrieval (e.g., Taboo and Upwords by Milton Bradley and Word From Words by Game Concepts).

25. For secondary students, organize instruction using the keyword strategy whereby a familiar concept is associated to a new term

by a memorable link (e.g., melancholy is linked to a sad melody the student knows) (see "How Does the Keyword Method Affect Vocabulary Comprehension and Usage?" by Pressley, Levin, and Miller in *Reading Research Quarterly* [1981, 16: 213–225]).

26. Implement adaptations in the general education classroom to promote success for the student in the area of word finding: (1) Use a multiple-choice format for questioning and testing; (2) provide frequent prompts that cue the student to the target word, such as giving a beginning sound or syllable; (3) at times, question the student in a way that requires only a yes/no or true/false response; (4) have the student prepare for a class discussion/questioning format by giving him/her an opportunity to study the material in advance with assistance in focusing on new and salient vocabulary; and (5) allow additional response time for oral questioning (see "Word-Finding Interventions for Children and Adolescents" by German in *Topics in Language Disorders* [1992, 13(1): 33–50]).

27. Provide remediation of the student's functional language skills within a functional context (e.g., a request by the student for

information or materials for a real-life situation).

28. Role-play and/or videotape situations for the student to identify errors in how he/she requested information, action, or material inadequately, inaccurately, or inappropriately (see "Children's Awareness of Communication" by Lloyd, Baker, and Dunn in *The Origins and Growth of Communication* [Garvey, Feagans, and Golinhoff, eds.].

29. Teach opening, topic maintenance, and closing skills in answering, initiating, and ending a phone conversation.

30. Role-play with the student different voices on the other end of the phone as well as different situations to which the student needs to respond (e.g., the other voice is lost and needs directions, the other voice is that of a person without sight needing assistance).

31. Engage the student in activities that provide opportunities for exchanging information with others (e.g., have the student describe objects seen through a view master; have the student describe objects felt in a bag; have the student play I Spy and Twenty Questions) (see *Language Disorders* [Owens]).

32. Teach the student what information is salient to relay

to the listener by various descriptive or directive tasks with the student as speaker (e.g., the student gives directions to the listener on how to complete a simple task such as drawing an object; the student gives directions for a task from behind a screen to the listener; the student verbally directs the listener through an obstacle course).

33. Assign the student the role of the listener, giving him/her incomplete, vague, or confusing messages/directions and have the student identify the needed missing information.

34. Train the student to give sufficient, but not too much information to the listener by learning to monitor his/her own conversation (e.g., role-play and videotape situations that allow the student prompt feedback).

35. Instruct the student in initiating a topic by a sequential process (e.g., maintain eye contact with the student for 10 seconds without speaking; if the student does not speak, explain the purpose of the conversation; return to the waiting strategy; if the student still does not initiate a topic, give a prompt such as having the student look for something of interest in a magazine; if the student still does not initiate, model the desired behavior)

(see "Conversational Skills Training: Teaching Adolescents with Mental Retardation to be Verbally Assertive" by Downing in *Mental Retardation* [1987, 25:147–155]).

36. Assist the student with continuing on a topic by commenting on the topic brought up by the student and giving the student cues to continue speaking (e.g., "Tell me more about your dog," or "Then what happened next?").

37. Model nonverbal cues for the student that are frequently used as part of conversational skills (e.g., eye contact, head nodding, specific facial expressions, body posture) and organize opportunities for the student to practice interpreting those behaviors of others in conversation.

38. Organize opportunities for the student to practice using nonverbal cues in conversation, providing prompt feedback to the student regarding miscues either verbally or by using videotape.

39. Structure activities for the student that teach the importance of turn taking in conversation (e.g., play the game Twenty Questions, speak into walkie-talkies or into an intercom system).

40. Establish a charting/reinforcement system for docu-

menting language progress and discuss this progress with the student on a frequent basis.

41. Collaborate with the parents in writing a positive behavior support plan for student, selecting several target behaviors to be decreased or extinguished using a hierarchy of reinforcements and consequences as appropriate.

42. Use adaptations in the general education setting with the student, offering prompts and cues of support, thus lowering his/her frustration level.

43. Provide the parents with oral expression materials/ strategies and train them to positively work with their child at home on such skills.

44. Offer the parents information regarding support to parents from organizations such as the American Speech-Language-Hearing Association.

45. Keep in close communication with the parents, reporting progress on a frequent basis, and actively responding to questions and concerns they may have.

__. _____
_____

__. _____
_____

__. _____
_____

PHYSICALLY HEALTH IMPAIRED

BEHAVIORAL DEFINITIONS

1. Presence of a physical disorder that can limit mobility and movement, and distort posture (e.g., cerebral palsy, muscular dystrophy, spina bifida, osteogenesis imperfecta [brittle bone disease], amputation [limb deficiency], spinal cord injuries).
2. No known cure has been identified for the medical condition, which is considered permanent.
3. The medical condition is life threatening.
4. Strength and stamina are compromised.
5. Continuing issues with incontinence and bowel control are present.
6. Depression due to a lack of independence and an ongoing need for assistance from others.

LONG-TERM GOALS

1. Maintain the maximum mobility and access within the school environment.
2. Maintain the greatest independence possible given restrictions caused by the condition.
3. Routinely engage in the greatest self-care management possible.
4. Demonstrate positive self-esteem.

5. Demonstrate ongoing progress with attaining academic, vocational, and communication skills.
6. Exhibit self-advocacy in making requests to have basic or mobility needs met in the school setting.
7. Parents work closely with school staff to establish a quality educational program for their child.

—. _____

_____

—. _____

_____

—. _____

_____

SHORT-TERM OBJECTIVES

1. Parents provide initial information to school personnel regarding student's condition and give permission for access to the child's medical records and treating personnel. (1)
2. Parents meet with school personnel to assist with the development of specific health-related plans for the student at school. (2, 3)
3. Cooperate with a psychoeducational evaluation. (4)
4. Participate in a speech and language assessment. (5)
5. Cooperate with a physical therapy assessment. (6)
6. Cooperate with an occupational therapy assessment. (7)
7. Parents meet with school personnel to discuss evaluation outcomes. (8)

THERAPEUTIC INTERVENTIONS

1. Arrange for a consultation with the family and obtain a release of information from parents for medical personnel to give pertinent information on the student.
2. Organize a school-based team of pertinent members, including a school nurse to review health issues of the student as they relate to the educational setting.
3. The school nurse meets with the family and medical personnel to create any protocols necessary for the daily health care issues of the student (e.g., catheterization) and/or medical crisis response plans.
4. Conduct a psychoeducational evaluation of the student's academic, cognitive, emotional, and personality strengths and weaknesses.

8. Parents agree to recommendations of the Individualized Education Planning (IEP) team and/or Section 504 team meeting. (9, 10)

9. Perform routine self-care needs as independently as possible. (11, 12, 13, 14)

10. Cooperate with activities that can maximize mobility and physical participation in school activities. (15, 16, 17)

11. Engage in fine motor activities or alternative activities with adaptations. (18, 19, 20, 21)

12. Demonstrate progress in maximizing communication skills. (22)

13. Utilize an augmentative communication system. (23, 24)

14. Master selected age-appropriate functional activities of daily living (ADLs) skills. (25, 26)

15. Show progress within the general education curriculum through the use of adaptive teaching techniques. (27, 28, 29, 30)

16. Teachers and the parents consult with mental health professionals regarding the student's special emotional and behavioral needs. (31)

17. Verbalize positive comments about self and accomplishments. (32, 33, 34)

18. Use self-advocacy to get medical, emotional, and

5. Refer the student for a speech/language evaluation.

6. Refer the student for a physical therapy assessment.

7. Refer the student for an occupational therapy assessment.

8. The multidisciplinary evaluation team meets with the parents to review evaluation findings.

9. Conduct an IEP team meeting and/or Section 504 planning meeting to determine the student's eligibility for programs and/or services and needed classroom and school accommodations.

10. Through meetings with the family and in-service, assist all need-to-know school personnel in acquiring insight and knowledge about the pertinent health issues of the student; also encourage strict adherence to matters of confidentiality.

11. Collaborate efforts among the teacher, occupational therapist, health care/management aide, and family that concentrate on identifying and teaching targeted self-care routines that the student can fully or partially engage in (e.g., feeding, toileting, dressing).

12. Break down each self-care task into simple behaviors that are rewarded, workable pieces to assist the student in achieving a successful outcome (e.g., removal of

academic needs met.
(35, 36, 37, 38)

19. Show successful preparation (prerequisites) for vocational training. (39, 40, 41)

20. Participate in a variety of leisure interests and activities. (42, 43, 44)

21. Parents take an active role in clearly communicating needs of the student to school staff. (45, 46)

22. Parents express satisfaction with their son's/daughter's overall progress and care in the school environment. (47)

—. _____
   _____

—. _____
   _____

—. _____
   _____

socks: push sock down on leg below ankle, pull sock off over heel, pull sock completely off).

13. Therapists identify assistive devices and/or technical aids that may help the student achieve greater independence with carrying out daily self-care skills.

14. Create a written procedure for the student's essential and repeated routines at school (e.g., the lunch procedure that identifies the goals, seating, and equipment, setup, feeding assistance needed, communication plan, and cleanup) (see *Teaching Individuals with Physical and Multiple Disabilities* [Bigge]).

15. Therapists (occupational therapist, physical therapist) collaborate with the family and equipment specialists in evaluating and/or adapting positioning equipment so that the student has appropriate alignment, body support, and seating for school needs (e.g., appropriate height of a wheelchair for access to desks, computer workstations, library tables).

16. School staff organizes safe access for the student to move in and outside of the building (e.g., to a bathroom, the lunchroom, the playground, various classrooms).

17. In collaboration with the family, therapists (physical)

instruct school staff in safe procedures for transferring the student (e.g., out of a wheelchair onto the toilet, into and out of a desk).

18. Organize the student's work surface to meet his/her needs (e.g., an occupational therapist arranges for the student to have a slant board to make paper/pencil activities workable).

19. Provide adaptations for students with limited motor control to complete fine motor activities (e.g., use wrist weights, use paper holders to steady the paper).

20. For the student unable to facilitate any grasp, organize equipment so that the student is able to use other body parts to draw, color, write, and so on (see *Teaching Individuals with Physical and Multiple Disabilities* [Bigge]).

21. Provide switch systems to allow the student to operate equipment ordinarily requiring fine motor abilities (e.g., connecting a large switch to a fan or radio to turn it on and off, which can be accessed with a hand, head, or foot).

22. The speech and language therapist reinforces strengths of the student while working on deficit areas that could involve receptive and/or expressive language, and areas of articulation.

23. For the student with unintelligible, partially intelligible, or total lacking in speech, an augmentative communication evaluation completed by an augmentative specialist or at a specialized center should be considered by the family and school.

24. Develop an augmentative communication system for the student, considering selection of salient vocabulary and symbols that allow for motivating interaction with others as well as meeting the basic communication needs of the student.

25. Identify the student- and parents-selected functional ADL skills that meet a specific need for the student (e.g., using the telephone, using bus transportation) and need to be learned.

26. Break each identified functional ADLs skill into small sequential steps and practice each step as a classroom activity, as a role play, and then, as appropriate, in the community (see *Teaching Individuals with Physical and Multiple Disabilities* [Bigge]).

27. Use the questioning strategy *who, what, why, when, where, with whom, to what degree,* and *how* when systematically attempting to identify the modifications needed for the student to maintain physical partici-

pation in general education lessons and activities (see *Teaching Individuals with Physical and Multiple Disabilities* [Bigge]).

28. Train teaching staff and a management/health care aide (as needed) to organize adaptations of instruction for the student (e.g., the student responds verbally instead of writing out answers to comprehension questions; the student is quizzed over science information using questions only requiring yes/no answers to make the response expectations more attainable).

29. Integrate technology into lessons for the student (i.e., a process of studying spelling words with a student without adequate speech and writing skills could include having the teacher or management aide acting as the voice of the student and pronouncing each word; the student uses eye gaze on a specially designed computer to identify the correct spelling of each word from several choices (see "A Spelling Study Strategy for Physically Disabled Augmentative Communication Users" by Koppenhaver and Yoder in *Communication Outlook* [1989, 10(3): 10–12]).

30. Offer alternative instructional periods, such as adaptive physical educa-

tion, when integration into the general education curriculum shows no benefit to the student's needs.

31. Provide consultation by a school mental health professional to the teacher and parents in helping the student by implementation of these guidelines: (1) Assist the student with accepting the disability; (2) set and maintain expectations for performance and accomplishment; (3) support and encourage the student's attempts at independence; (4) provide experiences in the student's areas of strength; (5) provide appropriate discipline (see *The Exceptional Child in the Family* [Ross]).

32. Encourage and facilitate the student's participation in individual counseling sessions with a school mental health professional, emphasizing improved self-concept.

33. Refer the student and his/her family to a mental health professional outside of the school setting (preferably someone who specializes in working with children/adolescents with disabilities) should negativity and depression become paramount.

34. In the classroom, concentrate on curriculum tasks that are motivating and rewarding to the student, allowing frequent success,

promoting a positive self-image, and following guidelines to include targeting appropriate teaching strategies for the student, setting high but realistic expectations, building on strengths and competencies, providing feedback with support and encouragement, and keeping a record to show student progress (see *Teaching Children with Learning and Behavior Problems* [Wallace and Kauffman]).

35. Encourage the student to communicate his/her needs in an assertive manner; reinforce all efforts toward being assertive.

36. Establish a subtle type of communication with the student should he/she indicate a need for assistance with a private concern (e.g., a need for help with toileting).

37. As a classroom teacher or service provider, offer a periodic opportunity for the student to privately share current frustrations, health issues, and fears.

38. Role-play activities where the student can practice scenarios such as explaining his/her condition to a stranger, requesting assistance from an adult or peer, letting others know he/she is in an emergency situation and requires immediate response, and showing he/she can perform certain

self-care and mobility functions without assistance.

39. Create a strand of instruction from early childhood into adolescence that focuses on these areas: (1) physical self-reliance, self-evaluation, and adaptability; (2) opportunities for career awareness, career exploration, and career preparation; and (3) social skills needed for employment (see *Teaching Individuals with Physical and Multiple Disabilities* [Bigge]).

40. Implement the Life-Centered Career Education model that emphasizes instruction in ADL skills, personal-social skills, and occupational guidance and preparation (see *Life-Centered Career Education: A Competency-Based Approach* [Brolin]).

41. Write a vocational plan with the student and his/her family that targets experiences in natural settings, matches the strengths of the student with task analysis of specific jobs, transitions the student into actual work settings, identifies and implements needed job and task adaptations, and eventually moves the student into adult vocational programming leading to employment (see *Vocational Preparation and Employment of Students with Physical and Multiple Dis-*

abilities [Sowers and Powers]).

42. Provide opportunities for the student during and after the school day to explore different enjoyable leisure activities (e.g., adaptive horseback riding, board games, downhill skiing, arts and crafts, aquatics).

43. Organize an evening recreation group for secondary students and young adults with varying disabilities, centering around different monthly social activities (e.g., concerts, movies, plays, card parties, restaurant-hopping, swimming).

44. Assist the student in a task analysis of one or two activities or hobbies with which he/she may achieve some independence, matching the student's strengths and interests with viable options.

45. Encourage and facilitate the parents in communicating the student's needs (e.g., placing in writing requests for medical procedures that need to be implemented during the school day, reporting changes in the student's condition, reporting new information from surgeries/medical interventions); always contact the parents when emergencies involving their child's medical condition arise.

46. The school nurse and the physical and/or occupa-

tional therapist remain as medical and treatment liaisons to the family and medical personnel treating the student.

47. Convey the supports and care plan in place for the student, the successes and what works best with the student, to the new teaching and therapy staff prior to the onset of the new school year.

___. _____

_____

___. _____

_____

___. _____

_____

PRESCHOOL CHILDREN WITH DEVELOPMENTAL DELAYS

BEHAVIORAL DEFINITIONS

1. A significant delay apparent in one or more areas of development that cannot be readily resolved by medical or nutritional means of intervention.
2. A severe sensory, physical, or neurological system impairment that impacts one or more areas of development (e.g., visual impairment or blindness, hearing impairment or deafness, seizure disorder, cerebral palsy, autism, attention-deficit disorder, Down syndrome, muscular dystrophy, traumatic brain injury).
3. An impairment in attachment relationships with caregivers and others including peers.
4. A chronic and significant medical/health concern that compromises development and participation in age-appropriate activities (e.g., asthma, cancer, diabetes, congenital heart disease, cystic fibrosis, sickle-cell anemia).
5. Delayed or disordered language in one or more areas of the subskills of language (e.g., pragmatics, semantics, syntax, morphology, phonology) impacting verbal and/or nonverbal communication.
6. Delayed cognitive development that slows the rate of acquisition of various mental processes and impacts progress in areas of learning, self-care, and communication.

__. _____
   _____
__. _____
   _____
__. _____
   _____

LONG-TERM GOALS

1. Resolve the area of delayed development and demonstrate functioning commensurate with age level.
2. Begin the process of compensating for the physical, medical, or sensory deficits and learning developmentally critical skills and information.
3. Show steady progress in the curriculum in the areas of physical, social, communication, self-care, and cognitive development.
4. Meet or exceed all goals and objectives as identified on the Individualized Education Plan (IEP).
5. Adjust readily to a preschool integrated with nondisabled, same-aged peers for part or all of the school experience with special education support services provided as needed.
6. Exhibit self-confidence and enthusiasm for learning, showing an ongoing willingness to try new experiences and challenges.
7. Parents accept support from school staff in understanding their child's disability, develop positive coping strategies for the stress and demands they encounter, seek out resources and supports for their child and themselves, and work collaboratively with school personnel in developing and implementing a proactive treatment plan for their child.

—. _____

_____

—. _____

_____

—. _____

_____

SHORT-TERM OBJECTIVES

1. Parents participate in pre-assessment consultations. (1, 2)

2. Parents share developmental, social, and medical histories of their child with a member of the school multidisciplinary evaluation team. (3)

THERAPEUTIC INTERVENTIONS

1. School professionals make contact with the parents, share information about how the assessment will be conducted, and identify the referral question(s) from the parents' perspective.

2. School professionals collaborate with the parents on the types of assessments to

3. Participate cooperatively with all aspects of the evaluation, with a parent nearby as needed. (4)

4. Parents collaborate with school clinicians at the multidisciplinary evaluation team meeting. (5)

5. Parents participate in the IEP team meeting and agree to the recommendations given. (6)

6. Successfully make the transition from home to school-based learning. (7, 8, 9)

7. Parents separate from their child and accept the child's placement in a school program. (9, 10, 11)

8. Adjust to and work cooperatively with related service providers. (12, 13)

9. Demonstrate steady progress with individualized or selected curriculum. (14, 15)

10. Show abilities as an active and engaged learner. (16, 17)

11. Advance in deficit areas and show overall progress in the least-restrictive environment. (18)

12. Increase independence through mastery of adaptive behavior skills. (19, 20)

13. Demonstrate self-confidence by showing a willingness to attempt new challenges. (21, 22, 23)

14. Show progress in meeting communication objectives. (24)

be completed (e.g., speech and language, occupational therapy, physical therapy, psychological).

3. A representative from the multidisciplinary evaluation team meets with the parents to obtain information regarding the child's developmental, social, and medical history and to discuss current issues.

4. Refer the child for evaluations (e.g., speech and language, occupational therapy, physical therapy, psychological) as identified through the collaborative preassessment process.

5. Conduct a multidisciplinary evaluation team meeting with the parents to obtain their input and to interpret the evaluation findings to them.

6. Conduct an IEP team meeting with the parents to determine the child's eligibility for special education, develop goals and short-term objectives in the areas of need, determine programs and/or related services and any modifications and accommodations needed by the child to progress.

7. Make a visit to the student's home to meet him/her in the most secure environment, talking with the parents and engaging the child in play and communication.

8. Have the parents bring their child to visit the

15. Parents maintain involvement with learning about their child's disability and effective interventions for progress. (25, 26, 27, 28)

16. Parents work as full partners with school staff in maintaining a quality program for their child and express satisfaction with his/her progress. (29, 30, 31)

—. _____
   _____

—. _____
   _____

—. _____
   _____

school and the classroom prior to the first day, giving them a tour of a few salient places in the school (e.g., therapy room, speech and language office), emphasizing the classroom where the child will attend, and identifying potential favorite toys with the child.

9. Assist the student and parents with a specific plan when separation problems are an issue (e.g., the teacher greets the parent and student at the door of the school and escorts the student to the classroom without the parent, talking intensely to the child about a favorite activity or toy waiting for him/her in the room).

10. Answer all questions raised by the parents prior to the student beginning the school program, responding to concerns such as special health procedures, bathrooming procedures, the daily, weekly, and monthly schedules, procedures for arrival and departure, and the process of communicating about the child's progress.

11. Establish an open-door policy for the parents to visit the classroom as a means of reassuring them regarding any fears and providing opportunities for them to see their child engaged in activities and skills at school.

12. Plan for the related service providers to the student

(e.g., occupational therapist, speech and language clinician) to frequent the classroom routinely, initially delivering instruction in the classroom with the student (unless and until the IEP identified a model that stipulates that the child is to be given one-to-one therapy in a separate setting).

13. Integrate related service delivery content with classroom curriculum and instruction as a best practice (i.e., use materials on the same topic as the thematic unit being followed in the classroom).

14. Consider the student's curriculum needs by responding to these questions: What can the child do independently? What skills are in the process of being acquired? What critical developmental skills must the child attain? What seems to work best with the child? (see *Special Educational Needs in the Early Years* [Wilson]).

15. Match the curricular needs of the student in the context of physical, instructional, and social aspects with the individual characteristics of the student to create meaningful content (see *Early Intervention/Early Childhood Special Education: Recommended Practices* [Odom and McLean]).

16. Organize the student's environment so that he/she has

ample opportunity to explore and experience the classroom, facilitating the interactions the student has with toys, materials, activities, peers, and adults (see *Special Educational Needs in the Early Years* [Wilson]).

17. Use a variety of instructional approaches with the student that vary by the amount of teacher direction, ranging from strategically altering the physical structure of the classroom as a means of intervention to direct instruction with the teacher-led lessons and frequent prompts to the student.

18. Early childhood special education staff work collaboratively with early childhood education staff to provide the related services, supports, and resources needed for the targeted student to be successful in an integrated environment with nondisabled/same-aged peers.

19. Select adaptive behavior skills that are appropriate for the student based on his/her developmental level, which address any or all of the subdomains of self-care (e.g., dressing, eating, toileting, grooming), community self-sufficiency (e.g., functioning with adult supervision in restaurants, churches, the neighborhood), and personal-social and social adjustment (e.g., inde-

pendent play/self-occupation, cooperation and interaction in play, responsibility) (see *Early Intervention / Early Childhood Special Education: Recommended Practices* [Odom and McLean]).

20. Organize adaptive behavior activities using materials and training to accommodate the student's developmental level and physical, health, or sensory needs; teach the parents to use similar procedures for tasks at home to provide consistency for the student.

21. Give opportunities for participation in a task or activity to be a privilege rather than something that absolutely has to be accomplished, allowing some choice using high-interest materials and strategies as motivation (see *Special Educational Needs in the Early Years* [Wilson]).

22. Provide the student with various roles in activities and tasks that match his/her skill level and allow for success that builds self-confidence and self-esteem (e.g., leader, assistant, collector of information) (see *Special Educational Needs in the Early Years* [Wilson]).

23. Reinforce the student with verbal and/or extrinsic rewards when he/she shows success, attempts, or self-initiation in trying new or difficult tasks.

24. Speech and language therapist provides individualized services to the child and provides direction to the classroom teacher as to current objectives and interventions recommended.

25. Establish a parent participation component to the student's program that provides in-services for parents on salient topics for their needs (e.g., working with the child on language strategies, teaching the child social skills in a community setting).

26. Encourage the parents to self-define their needs, priorities, and concerns, and to identify what supports/strategies/activities would be best for their family; provide assistance in helping the parents locate these identified resources (see *Special Educational Needs in the Early Years* [Wilson]).

27. Refer the parents to a specialist with background in working with families and disabilities should the challenges of coping, adapting, and/or accepting the realities of having a child with a disability become paramount.

28. Refer the parents to a local parent support group and/or a national organization to facilitate their information gathering (e.g., Division for Early Childhood of the Council for Exceptional

Children or the Federation for Children with Special Needs).

29. Establish and maintain frequent, open communication with the parents regarding issues, concerns, and successes of their child; select a method of communication most acceptable to the parents (e.g., home/school communication notebook, weekly phone call, e-mail, etc.).

30. Choose a school team member as a primary contact to any community agencies involved with the student to coordinate all efforts in best meeting the child's needs and those of his/her family (e.g., public health department, social services, physician's office, private language clinician).

31. Coordinate interdisciplinary team meetings involving the parents, school staff, and representatives of community agencies to exchange information in more complex situations to better serve the student.

—. _____

_____

—. _____

_____

—. _____

_____

READING COMPREHENSION

BEHAVIORAL DEFINITIONS

1. General reading achievement is significantly below learning potential.
2. Reading comprehension is substantially reduced and impairs the ability to succeed across subject areas.
3. Reading rate is slow and/or halting; general dysfluency is present.
4. Difficulty with attending to the focus of the text being read; lacks self-monitoring skills.
5. Demonstrates limited application of basic study skills to break apart the text and obtain meaning.

—. _____

_____

—. _____

_____

—. _____

_____

LONG-TERM GOALS

1. Increase reading achievement to a level commensurate with learning potential.
2. Improve reading comprehension abilities to obtain skills necessary to assimilate grade level material, or to be commensurate with learning potential.
3. Use reading to effectively carry out daily living needs including acquisition of vocational training.
4. Show progress with reading rate.

5. Parents accept the student's achievement deficits and provide supports to improve remedial areas.

—. _____

—. _____

—. _____

SHORT-TERM OBJECTIVES

1. Cooperate with hearing, vision, and/or medical examination. (1, 2)
2. Participate in a comprehensive reading or psychoeducational evaluation. (3)
3. Parents participate in an interpretive meeting to hear test results. (4)
4. Parents take part in an Individualized Education Planning (IEP) team meeting or general planning meeting and agree to implementation of a reading improvement plan. (5)
5. Demonstrate increased accuracy in reading comprehension. (6, 7, 8, 9, 10)
6. Identify the main characters and their actions in a literary piece or text. (11, 12)
7. Identify the main idea and subtopics of the literary piece or text. (13, 14)
8. Use self-monitoring skills to improve comprehension. (15, 16)

THERAPEUTIC INTERVENTIONS

1. Refer the student for hearing, vision, and/or medical examinations to rule out any physical impairment that could be the cause of his/her deficit achievement in the reading area.
2. Explore with the family any sensory modality reasons for their child's reading difficulties (i.e., vision, hearing).
3. Refer the student for a psychoeducational evaluation.
4. School evaluation clinician(s) meets with the parents to discuss assessment results.
5. Conduct an IEP team meeting or general planning meeting with the parents present to determine the student's eligibility for special education and/or ascertain general education reading services.
6. Establish a purpose for reading a given selection by having the student activate

9. Successfully engage in practice with reading comprehension tasks using computer software programs. (17)

10. Exhibit improved oral reading fluency and increased reading rate. (18, 19, 20, 21)

11. Demonstrate competent study skill techniques. (22, 23, 24)

12. The student and parents advocate for needed and appropriate accommodations. (25)

13. Use effective time-management and organizational skills. (26)

14. Increase the amount of time spent weekly on leisure reading. (27, 28, 29, 30, 31)

15. Parents demonstrate a more accepting attitude and understanding of their child's reading deficit. (30, 32, 33)

16. Parents report satisfaction with their child's overall school experience and progress. (34)

—. _____
   _____

—. _____
   _____

—. _____
   _____

his/her prior knowledge on the topic.

7. Provide instruction for the elementary student in identifying and developing the story's main strategy where the main idea of a story is placed in the center, and extensions are drawn that contain other main ideas, concepts, events, and characters to break down the selection into meaningful visual information (see "Story Maps Improve Comprehension" by Reutzel in *The Reading Teacher* [1985, 38: 400–405]).

8. Assist the student in organizing the meaning of a selection by using story grammar, which is a system to consistently describe text features such as setting, responses by characters, goals and consequences (see *Stories, Scripts and Scenes: Aspects of a Schema Theory* [Mandler]).

9. Instruct the secondary student in the use of graphic organizer diagrams created to visually depict the order and organization of text content examining cause and effect, descriptive or enumerative, sequential, compare and contrast, or problem and solution (see "Improving Comprehension: Causal Relations Instruction for Learning Handicapped Learners" by

Varnhagen and Goldman in *The Reading Teacher* [1985, 38:400–405]).

10. Teach paraphrasing skills whereby the student orally restates in his/her own words what was read prior to organizing the information into a written language task.

11. Have the student compare a main character in the readings to someone in his/her family or to a well-known actor to help create visualization of the character (e.g., personality, physical attributes) (i.e., Who would Anne Frank have looked like that you know?).

12. Have the student describe personality and physical traits, create significant quotes from the character, and identify with whom the character associates in the readings.

13. Assign the student to create a new cover for the book or article, or make a poster of what the text would be as a movie or video.

14. Have the student categorize the setting, characters, conflict(s), and outcome with assistance from marginal glosses, which are notes written by the teacher in the margin of the readings to the student, giving prompts such as vocabulary highlights, clarification of points, and interpretation of events.

15. Model for the student desired on-task behaviors, which involve periodic self-checking and self-recording to ensure he/she is concentrating during silent reading.

16. Teach the student a self-questioning procedure as an inner dialogue while he/she is reading silently such as: Why am I reading this? How is it organized? Does this make sense as I read? (see *Educational Assessment of Learning Problems: Testing for Teaching* [Wallace, Larsen, and Elksnin]).

17. Provide computer software programs (e.g., The Twistaplot Reading Adventures from Scholastic) to allow the student to independently practice comprehension skills.

18. Lead a large group with the targeted student included in a choral reading activity, modeling proper phrasing, tempo, and voice intonation and expression.

19. Give the student a media script as if he/she is an announcer with the opportunity to read and rehearse the material before the broadcast.

20. Engage the student in the Neurological Impress method where the teacher and student read together in unison, with the teacher initially reading more loudly and faster than the

student as a model (see "A Neurological-Impress Method of Remedial-Reading Instruction" by Heckelman in *Academic Therapy* [1969, 4: 277–282]).

21. Arrange for the student to work with a proficient reader for oral reading activities where, as each reader finishes a part, they retell what happened in the selection to their partner.

22. Allow the secondary student to use the guided notes method where the teacher creates a sparse outline of the material to be covered with the student, then fills in the outline as the teacher lectures or as reading text is covered (see "Guided Notes, Review and Achievement of Learning Disabled Adolescents in Secondary Mainstream Settings" by Lazarus in *Education and Treatment of Children* [1991, 14:112–128]).

23. Teach the secondary student the PORPE method, which involves Predicting, Organizing, Rehearsing, Practicing, and Evaluating study material (see "An Initial Validation of a Study Strategy System" by Simpson, Hayes, Stahl, Connor, and Weaver in *Journal of Reading Behavior* [1988, 20: 149–180]).

24. Integrate reading strategies and study skills into all

subject areas to allow the student to practice needed skills across the curriculum.

25. Consider accommodations that will allow the student to work to his/her potential without penalty with regard to the reading disability, such as untimed tests, slower pace of coverage of material, taped lecture notes, credit/no credit grading, individual tutoring, shortened reading tasks, and homework adaptations.

26. School personnel and parents provide instruction and support to the student in organizing a study schedule, maintaining an assignment agenda, and using calendars for short- and long-term planning of projects.

27. Organize daily reading activities in a positive classroom climate with praise and encouragement for reading accomplishments and progress.

28. Create a visual chart to display the increased reading time for the student and/or offer extrinsic rewards for reading goals attained.

29. Seek out recreational reading materials that are at the student's independent reading level and that match his/her interests.

30. Encourage the parents to create a family reading time and activities that promote practice for the student's

reading skills and reading for enjoyment.

31. Encourage the student to participate in after-school activities that value reading such as poetry club, drama club, school newspaper, and/or a book club.

32. Communicate with the parents frequently to keep them well-informed of their child's learning needs and progress.

33. Assist the parents with seeking out information and support on reading disabilities from such organizations as the International Reading Association and the Council for Exceptional Children—Division for Learning Disabilities.

34. A case manager (reading specialist, resource teacher) gathers information on the strategies and supports that are most effective for the student to share with the teacher(s) prior to the new school year.

___. _____

_____

___. _____

_____

___. _____

_____

SEVERELY MULTIPLY IMPAIRED

BEHAVIORAL DEFINITIONS

1. Learning is seriously impacted by severe multiple impairments in areas of intelligence, health, and/or physical capabilities.
2. The modalities of vision and/or hearing are severely impaired limiting communication and/or independent mobility.
3. A severe physical impairment is present and limits activities of daily living (ADLs).
4. A severe health impairment places the student seriously at risk.
5. Cognitive functioning is in the mildly mentally impaired range.
6. Cognitive functioning is in the moderately mentally impaired range.
7. Cognitive functioning is in the severely mentally impaired range.

__. _____
    _____

__. _____
    _____

__. _____
    _____

LONG-TERM GOALS

1. Develop communication skills to the level of potential.
2. Exhibit daily living and adaptive behavior skills to the greatest level of independence possible in the home, school, and community.
3. Show progress with fine and gross motor skills and/or with adaptations needed to maximize these skill areas.
4. Maintain the maximum mobility and access possible across various settings.
5. Parents accept the student's cognitive and physical challenges, es-

tablish realistic expectations for the student, and seek out resources and means to assist their child.

6. Parents work closely with school staff to establish and maintain a quality educational program for their child.

___. _____
  _____
  _____

___. _____
  _____
  _____

___. _____
  _____
  _____

SHORT-TERM GOALS

1. Parents provide initial information to school personnel regarding the student's condition and give permission for access to the child's medical records and treating personnel. (1)

2. Parents meet with school personnel to assist with the development of specific health-related plans for the student at school. (2, 3)

3. Cooperate with psychoeducational and adaptive behavior evaluations. (4)

4. Participate in a speech and language assessment. (5)

5. Cooperate with a physical therapy assessment. (6)

6. Cooperate with an occupational therapy assessment. (7)

7. Parents meet with school personnel to discuss evaluation outcomes. (8)

THERAPEUTIC INTERVENTIONS

1. Arrange for a consultation with the family and obtain a release of information from the parents for medical personnel to give pertinent information about the student to the school staff.

2. Organize a school-based team of pertinent members including a school nurse to review health issues of the student as they relate to the educational setting.

3. Arrange for the school nurse to meet with the family and medical personnel to create any protocols necessary for the daily health care issues of the student (e.g., catheterization) and/or medical crisis response plans, and to exchange information regarding medication regimens.

4. Conduct a psychoeducational and adaptive/functional behavior evaluation

8. Parents agree to the recommendations of the Individualized Education Planning (IEP) team. (9, 10)

9. Perform routine personal hygiene tasks as independently as possible. (11, 12, 13, 14)

10. Master selected age-appropriate skills in the domain of self-care. (14, 15)

11. Demonstrate mastery of ADLs to the level of potential. (16, 17)

12. Express wants and needs in a verbal or nonverbal manner. (18, 19, 20)

13. Respond to requests or directions of others. (19, 20, 21)

14. Cooperate with activities that can maximize mobility and build physical strength. (22, 23)

15. Access all appropriate areas of the school facility as independently as possible. (24, 25, 26)

16. Engage in fine motor activities or alternative activities with adaptations. (27, 28, 29)

17. Demonstrate progress with functional reading skills through identifying survival words accurately 90 percent of the time. (30, 31)

18. Identify coins correctly 90 percent of the time. (32)

19. Match time on the clock to a scheduled activity to 90 percent accuracy. (33)

to include observation, inventories, and interviews with the parents, staff, and the student as appropriate.

5. Refer the student for a speech/language evaluation and to an augmentative communication specialist as appropriate.

6. Refer the student for a physical therapy assessment.

7. Refer the student for an occupational therapy assessment.

8. Arrange for the multidisciplinary evaluation team to meet with the parents to review evaluation findings regarding their child.

9. Conduct an IEP team meeting to determine the student's eligibility for programs and/or services and needed classroom and school accommodations.

10. Through meetings with the family, assist all need-to-know school personnel in acquiring insight and knowledge about the pertinent health issues of the student; also encourage strict adherence to matters of confidentiality.

11. Based on the adaptive/functional behavior evaluation and concerns of the student and parents, prioritize personal hygiene tasks as those that can be mastered (e.g., washing and/or drying hands and/or face, blow-

20. Reduce the frequency of inappropriate self-stimulating behavior by 80 percent. (34)

21. Initiate greetings to and respond to greetings from peers and adults. (35)

22. Demonstrate effective use of the telephone. (36)

23. Terminate angry outbursts of temper and make requests calmly. (37)

24. Interact appropriately with same-age peers. (38)

25. Participate in leisure/recreational activities. (39, 40)

26. Increase on-task behavior and reduce distractibility. (41, 42)

27. Comply with classroom rules. (43)

28. Parents and the student visit potential training sites and examine employment training opportunities. (44, 45, 46)

29. Parents show acceptance of available resources to support them in the care of their child. (47, 48)

30. Parents state their satisfaction with their child's school progress and program. (49, 50)

__. _____
   _____

__. _____
   _____

__. _____
   _____

ing/wiping nose when requested, taking care of all or some aspects of toileting and bathing, brushing teeth, combing hair).

12. Break down each personal hygiene task to be mastered into simple behaviors to assist the student in achieving a successful outcome (e.g., take comb from drawer, move to the mirror, raise hand to top of head with comb, make combing strokes through hair, return comb to drawer).

13. Physical and occupational therapists identify assistive devices and/or technical aids that may help the student achieve greater independence with carrying out personal hygiene skills.

14. Create a written procedure for each essential personal hygiene and self-care routine used at school (e.g., the eating procedure for lunch, snacks, etc., identifying the small steps for the student to accomplish: washing hands, moving to the table, using utensils, cleaning face and hands after) (see *Teaching Individuals with Physical and Multiple Disabilities* [Bigge]).

15. Work with the family, based on the adaptive/functional assessment, to prioritize the self-care skills the student can master (e.g., dressing, self-feeding).

16. Prioritize teaching of independent living skills that the student is capable of mastering (e.g., setting the table in a partial or complete manner, making a sandwich, using a switch to start the mixer to create a cake), establishing frequent opportunities for the student to practice.

17. Break each identified functional activity of daily living skills into small sequential steps and practice each step as a classroom activity, as a role play, and then, in the community as appropriate (see *Teaching Individuals with Physical and Multiple Disabilities* [Bigge]).

18. Collaborate with the speech and language therapist to develop a communication plan for the student that meets his/her individual needs.

19. Work with the augmentative communication specialist in identifying adaptive communication equipment that will allow the student a language output (e.g., switch, electronic computer-based speech device).

20. Develop the augmentative communication system, selecting salient vocabulary and symbols that motivate the student to interact with others.

21. Routinely establish/structure situations in which the

student has an opportunity to communicate with adults and peers in the school setting (e.g., student presses device every morning with same-age peers for the joke of the day).

22. The physical therapist, school staff, and family agree upon and carry out activities and procedures that are relevant to the education of the student in expanding and/or maintaining range of motion, ambulation, and general gross motor movements.

23. The occupational and physical therapists collaborate with the family and equipment specialists in evaluating and/or adapting positioning equipment so that the student has appropriate alignment and/or support for school needs (e.g., walking with a correct-fitting brace, accurate seating in a wheelchair to a height allowing access to work space, sinks).

24. School staff organizes safe access for the student to move in and outside of the building (e.g., onto the playground, into the lunchroom, into the gymnasium, having workable elevators, making certain that facilities are *at least* American Disabilities Act–approved).

25. For the blind student, provide braille markers

throughout the building, working closely with a plan collaboratively organized with the orientation and mobility specialist.

26. For the student with physical challenges, collaborate with the family and physical/occupational therapists in developing safe procedures for transferring/moving the student (e.g., out of a wheelchair onto the toilet, into and out of a desk, having safe activities in physical education class).

27. Organize the student's work surface to meet his/her needs (e.g., an occupational therapist arranges for the student to have a slant board to make paper/pencil activities workable).

28. Provide adaptations for limited motor control to allow the student to complete fine motor activities (e.g., use wrist weights, use paper holders to steady the paper).

29. Provide switch systems to allow the student to operate equipment ordinarily requiring fine motor abilities (e.g., connecting a large switch to a fan or radio to turn it on and off, which can be accessed with a hand, head, or foot).

30. Clearly label locations in the school with a survival word and a survival sign to designate basic areas of importance in the school for

the student to recognize (e.g., danger, restroom [men/women]).

31. Assist the student with identifying survival words and signs in the community.

32. Teach the student to identify specific coins that will allow him/her access to certain desired products (e.g., four quarters in a soda machine equate to a can of soda pop).

33. Instruct the student in matching salient times of the school day with hourly times on the clock (e.g., the student recognizes 12:00 as time for lunch and 3:00 as time to depart for home).

34. Establish a positive behavior support plan to reinforce socially acceptable self-stimulating behaviors and to extinguish inappropriate self-stimulating behaviors, using a hierarchy of positive reinforcements and consequences as agreed upon between family and staff.

35. Utilize repetition and modeling to teach the student initiation of socially appropriate greetings and farewells with peers and staff, and engagement in reciprocation of greetings initiated by others.

36. Use modeling and behavior rehearsal to teach the verbal student appropriate phone etiquette and use of the phone for safety issues.

37. Create a positive behavior support plan targeting anger management and tantrum behaviors, extinguishing unreasonable outbursts, and replacing those with calm communication to make wants and needs known.

38. Integrate the student with same-age peers who provide socially appropriate modeling and encourage positive social reciprocity.

39. Expose the student to various potential hobbies or sport recreational activities in the school and community that match the strengths of the individual student.

40. Instruct the secondary student in various activities of interest to him/her using a task-analysis approach in which each activity is segmented into small, workable steps to success (see "Assessment and Selection of Leisure Skills for Severely and Profoundly Handicapped Persons" by Wehman and Schleien in *Education and Training of the Mentally Retarded* [1980, 14: 50–58] and "Leisure Skills Programming for Severely Handicapped Children" by Wehman and Schleien in *Teaching Social Skills to Exceptional Children* [Cartlege and Cartwright, eds.]).

41. Assist the student with increasing the time of on-task

behavior and lengthening work at a particular activity.

42. Provide opportunities for the student to work next to others, reinforcing for the student the amount of production of the task, avoiding distraction, and not leaving the activity to be completed.

43. Reinforce the student for compliance with classroom rules and point out the parallel to employment rules.

44. Consult with the occupational therapist regarding the potential types of work that may be appropriate for the student's given strengths and any fine motor deficits.

45. Seek out potential sheltered workshops, work activity programs, and other training opportunities appropriate for the student's needs, setting up visits for the family to view such sites.

46. Conduct an assessment of the secondary student's employability skills, using a systematic approach (e.g., the Targeted Employment Assessment Model from *Competitive Employment* [Wehman]) that examines vocational skills, independent living skills, parent attitudes and behavior, and job requirements to ascertain deficit employability areas and if the student

maintains skill acquisition potential to be employed.

47. School mental health professionals seek out, on behalf of the parents or in conjunction with the parents, individuals, agencies, and resources that can provide respite to the family in caring for the severely multiply impaired child/adolescent.

48. Encourage the parents of secondary students to seek information regarding independent living situations and foster and group home facilities in the community as considerations for future living for the student at a later age.

49. Establish an ongoing partnership with the student's parents in communicating frequently about successes and concerns, and provide a listening ear of support to the parents as issues arise.

50. Compile a list of supports and interventions that provide success for the student and share with staff and family at conferences, with new or changing staff, and at the IEP team meetings.

__. _____
  _____

__. _____
  _____

__. _____
  _____

SPEECH DISORDERS

BEHAVIORAL DEFINITIONS

1. Consistent and significant difficulty with producing and using developmentally expected speech sounds.
2. Deficits in sound production interfere substantially with communication in the home, school, and community.
3. Inaccurate speech patterns involving leaving off the beginnings or endings of words, distorting vowels, leaving out syllables within longer words, and/or being generally unintelligible to people outside of the family.
4. Oral-motor weaknesses (apraxia) with limited control over movement of the mouth, sometimes involving a tongue thrust, all impacting the quality of speech sounds produced.
5. Repeated dysfluency (stuttering) as demonstrated by impairment in the normal fluency and time patterning of speech.
6. Deficits in fluency that are at a frequency to interfere with competency in communication, impacting academic and social functioning.
7. Voice disorders (pitch, loudness, vocal quality, and/or resonance) originating from vocal misuse, disease, congenital defects, laryngeal trauma, or neurological disorders.

__. _____
_____
__. _____
_____
__. _____
_____

LONG-TERM GOALS

1. Achieve the speech goals identified in the Individualized Education Plan (IEP).
2. Achieve mastery of the expected speech sounds that are appropriate for age, learning potential, and dialect.
3. Show substantial progress with intelligibility, improving communication with others in settings outside of the home.
4. Demonstrate improvement in oral-motor control, leading to progress with speech clarity.
5. Reduce or eliminate dysfluency; speak with greater fluency at a normal rate on an increasingly frequent basis.
6. Reduce voice problems including improvement of pitch, loudness, vocal quality, and/or resonance.
7. Develop an awareness and acceptance of speech and language deficits, and work to overcome and/or compensate for these deficits in the school, home, and community settings.
8. Parents establish realistic expectations for their child's speech and language abilities, and work collaboratively with school personnel for a quality treatment plan for their child.

—. _____
   _____

—. _____
   _____

—. _____
   _____

SHORT-TERM OBJECTIVES

1. Cooperate with a medical evaluation. (1, 2)
2. Participate willingly in a speech evaluation. (3)
3. Parents participate in the multidisciplinary evaluation team process and the interpretation of evaluation information. (4)
4. Parents participate in an

THERAPEUTIC INTERVENTIONS

1. Parents seek a medical evaluation for their child from a family physician or from a otolaryngologist (ear/nose/throat physician) to identify any organic basis for a speech or voice disorder.
2. Parents share educationally relevant medical informa-

IEP team meeting and accept the recommendations given. (5)

5. Comply with the therapy interventions offered by the speech and language pathologist to correct the identified articulation errors. (6, 7)

6. Parents take an active role in positively working with their child on articulation issues. (8)

7. Cooperate with strategies to improve pronunciation miscues. (9)

8. Show progress with phonemic awareness skills as part of a metalinguistic approach to improving pronunciation miscues. (10)

9. Participate willingly in oral-motor exercises leading to improved articulation or phonological skills. (11)

10. Participate openly and willingly in speech sessions to increase fluency. (12, 13)

11. Become desensitized to fluency disruption in natural settings. (14, 15, 16)

12. Parents readily engage in collaboration with the speech therapist to assist their child with fluency issues. (17)

13. Cooperate with the speech therapist in activities geared to improve voice quality. (18)

14. Parents accept their child's deficit areas within the speech and language do-

tion related to potential speech needs of their child.

3. Refer to a speech pathologist for an evaluation in the area(s) of need.

4. Have the parents provide input into the multidisciplinary evaluation and establish an interpretive meeting in which speech evaluation information is discussed with the parents.

5. Conduct an IEP team meeting to determine the student's eligibility for special education and the service delivery needs of the student.

6. Select individualized, therapeutic speech targets to be remediated and select strategies that will assist the student in correcting the articulation errors.

7. Provide practice in articulation training methods, allowing the student ample opportunities for correction of misarticulated sounds to take place.

8. Introduce the parents to ways in which they can work with their child in daily routines and activities at home, correcting articulation miscues without undue pressure or stress on the student.

9. Implement metalinguistic approaches into interventions for remediating pronunciation errors (e.g., deleting final consonants),

main, develop realistic expectations for progress, and seek out positive resources of support. (19, 20)

15. Parents report satisfaction with their child's school speech and language treatment plan and overall progress. (21)

—. _____

    _____

—. _____

    _____

—. _____

    _____

working on correction of deletion of final consonants by pairing a keyword with other words so that the student realizes that, when given a different ending, the word has a different meaning (*see* paired with seed, seat, and seal) (see *Language Disorders* [Owens] and "A Language Approach to Treatment of Phonological Process Problems" by Young in *Language, Speech, and Hearing Services in Schools* [1983, 14: 47–53]).

10. Provide instruction in phonemic awareness to include strategies of rhyming, clapping out syllables, identifying words with like initial or final sounds (see *Phonemic Awareness in Young Children—A Classroom Curriculum* [Adams, Foorman, Lundberg, and Beeler] and *Sound Practice: Phonological Awareness in the Classroom* [Layton, Deeny, and Upton]).

11. Select nonspeech interventions (e.g., lip exercises) as appropriate to provide the student with greater oral-motor control, thus contributing to improved speech.

12. Use play therapy as an intervention to develop a relationship with the young student or use a candid, warm, friendly approach with the older student.

13. Model a simple, fluent style for the student to emulate, with many pauses and silent periods injected into the speech used with the student (see *Stuttering: An Integrated Approach to Its Nature and Treatment* [Peters and Guitar] and *The Treatment of Stuttering* [Van Riper]).

14. After obtaining a basal level of fluency of the student, begin a process where the student is interrupted more and more frequently in a systematic manner of desensitization to increase the student's tolerance for fluency disruption at home and school (see *Stuttering: An Integrated Approach to Its Nature and Treatment* [Peters and Guitar] and *The Treatment of Stuttering* [Van Riper]).

15. Use a counterconditioning process by matching a pleasant experience for the student with answering questions and having his/her fluency disrupted (see *Stuttering: An Integrated Approach to Its Nature and Treatment* [Peters and Guitar] and *The Treatment of Stuttering* [Van Riper]).

16. After the student stutters and completes his/her utterance, the word or phrase that was dysfluent is restated by the therapist/teacher/parent in a

calm, normal manner, thus instilling a positive memory of the student's utterance rather than the painful recollection of the stuttering (see *Stuttering: An Integrated Approach to Its Nature and Treatment* [Peters and Guitar] and *The Treatment of Stuttering* [Van Riper]).

17. Spend time counseling the parents, discussing the identification of fluency disrupters for the student in the home environment; explore with the parents ways to eliminate or decrease the disrupters and ways for the parents to assist their child in lessening his/her awareness of the dysfluency (see *Stuttering: An Integrated Approach to Its Nature and Treatment* [Peters and Guitar] and *The Treatment of Stuttering* [Van Riper]).

18. The speech therapist develops a treatment plan for the student to improve voice quality (e.g., elimination of harmful daily vocal habits, learning new techniques to use his/her voice without strain) and engages in collaboration with the parents and teachers, involving their participation with the student's voice problems (see *Communication and Communication Disorders: A Clinical Introduction* [Plante and Beeson]).

19. Maintain ongoing, frequent contact with the parents, reporting progress and concerns regarding the student's speech and language needs.

20. Refer the parents to another parent for support, to a local organization of support, or to a national organization such as the American Speech-Language-Hearing Association.

21. Gather the interventions and supports most effective with the student and communicate this information to the staff working with the student in the new school year.

___. _____

_____

___. _____

_____

___. _____

_____

TOURETTE'S DISORDER

BEHAVIORAL DEFINITIONS

1. Presence of simple motor tics (e.g., sudden and brief movements such as eye blinking, shoulder shrugging, or facial grimacing).
2. Presence of one or more vocal tics (e.g., throat clearing, grunting, sniffing, or snorting).
3. Tics occur many times in a day.
4. Tics occur intermittently with many days between incidents.
5. Tics cause a disruption in home and school environments, especially in areas of social functioning.
6. Coprolalia (involuntary uttering of obscenities) is present.
7. Poor social skills and low self-esteem.
8. Symptoms of obsessive-compulsive disorder, anxiety, and/or depression.
9. Comorbidity with attention-deficit hyperactivity disorder and/or learning disabilities.
10. Anxiety, fatigue, excitement, and psychosocial stressors increase symptomatology.
11. Academic functioning is lower than peers, with specific difficulties noted in visual-motor, mathematics, and handwriting skills.

__. _____

_____

__. _____

_____

__. _____

_____

LONG-TERM GOALS

1. Reduce feelings of stress related to family, school, and/or peers to improve daily functioning.
2. Take prescribed medication and recognize its benefits.
3. Student, family, and school staff accept the diagnosis, recognizing that the behaviors are not voluntary or spiteful.
4. Utilize self-monitoring techniques to improve daily functioning.
5. Improve social skill functioning, self-esteem, and peer relationships as evidenced by positive participation in school activities.
6. Achieve academics at the level of intellectual potential.

—. _____

_____

—. _____

_____

—. _____

_____

SHORT-TERM OBJECTIVES

1. Describe and demonstrate in vivo how the tic occurrence is impacting daily academic functioning. (1, 2, 3, 4)

2. Cooperate with psychoeducational evaluation of the tic disorder. (2, 5)

3. Complete a speech and language evaluation. (2, 6)

4. Participate in an occupational therapy assessment of the tic disorder. (2, 7)

5. Parents and student receive evaluation feedback and agree to comply with the Individualized Education Planning (IEP) team or Section 504 recommendations. (3, 8)

THERAPEUTIC INTERVENTIONS

1. Compile baseline data to include classroom observation, teacher information, and parent and student information to ascertain if the symptoms of Tourette's Disorder are interfering with the student's education experience.

2. If a formal evaluation is needed, conduct an evaluation review plan with the parents to determine what different components should be involved in the assessment.

3. Organize a school-based multidisciplinary evaluation team to conduct an assessment of the student's visual-motor integration, achievement—particularly

6. Follow directions and accurately complete assignments. (9, 10, 11)

7. Increase the amount of time spent on tasks and reduce the frequency of distraction from tasks in the classroom. (12, 13, 14, 15)

8. Increase the percentage of accurately completed assignments. (16, 17, 18)

9. Utilize areas of strength to learn new material. (19)

10. Take tests in a calm and confident manner. (20)

11. Rely on a study partner to provide confirmation of homework assignments and directions. (21, 22)

12. Proofread written assignments before submitting them. (23, 24)

13. Utilize a calculator for math work. (25)

14. Implement whisper reading to help focus attention. (26)

15. Utilize self-talk and relaxation techniques to reduce tic frequency. (27, 28, 29)

16. Implement competing responses to reduce tic frequency. (28, 30)

17. Practice assertiveness to explain to others the involuntary nature of the tic. (31)

18. Release tic behaviors from all attempts at control, only in a private designated environment. (32)

19. Cooperate with a behavior modification program de-

in math and written language, attention, language-based problems, and social/emotional/behavioral adjustment; gather data from the student and his/her parents, teachers, and counselor.

4. Consult with medical personnel involved with the student as part of gathering evaluative information, obtaining a signed release of information form from the parents.

5. Conduct or refer the student for psychoeducational testing to include a functional behavioral analysis of the tic stimuli and consequences.

6. Refer the student for a speech and language evaluation to assess the impact of the tic on language development.

7. Refer the student for an occupational therapy evaluation to assess motor functioning in academic and nonacademic settings.

8. Conduct an IEP team meeting and/or a Section 504 planning meeting to determine the student's eligibility for special education programs and/or services and the accommodations that are required.

9. Implement strategies in the classroom to enhance student functioning (e.g., teacher/support staff model-

signed to decrease tic behaviors. (5, 28, 33, 34)

20. Demonstrate increased positive peer interaction and
prosocial behavior. (35, 36)

21. Verbalize improved feelings
of self-esteem and self-
worth. (37, 38, 39)

22. Parents and family report
efforts to reduce pressure to
perform on the student.
(40, 41)

23. Take prescribed medication
and verbalize an under-
standing of its benefits.
(42, 43, 44, 45)

24. Parents report satisfaction
with progress of the stu-
dent. (40, 46, 47)

__. _____
   _____

__. _____
   _____

__. _____
   _____

ing acceptance and positive
regard for the student, allowing the student short breaks
to provide for reduction of
stress, sharing information
on Tourette's Disorder) with
other students.

10. Utilizing both visual and auditory instructional formats,
keep directions limited to
one or two steps, and provide
additional support prompts
to aid the student as needed.

11. Have the student repeat instructions aloud to check for
understanding.

12. Provide preferential seating
where the focus of instruction takes place.

13. Maintain a quiet place in
the classroom or elsewhere
when, at times, reduced
distractions are imperative
to assist the student with
focusing.

14. Plan for routine short
breaks to allow the student
physical movement when
symptoms require it.

15. Develop a signal that can
be implemented in a subtle
manner with the student
that indicates a need for the
student to refocus.

16. Create a contract with the
student to specify the
amount of work required
and expected time of com-
pletion.

17. Modify written tasks, focusing on what knowledge/skill
the student has mastered

rather than the quantity of work.

18. Train the student in self-talk in which the student verbally reminds himself/herself of a task that must be completed or verbally rehearses a task.

19. Configure instructional formats to match the learning style of the student, emphasizing the student's stronger modalities.

20. Arrange for an extended time, alternative format, and/or a private area for the student to take tests.

21. Allow the student access to competently produced lecture notes.

22. Arrange for a homework partner for the student in a discreet manner who can be a source of information of assignments and directions on how to complete them.

23. Grade the student's handwriting on effort.

24. Encourage the student to proofread written expression tasks and to use a word processor with spell check.

25. Provide hands-on manipulatives (e.g., unifix cubes, objects of interest to the student [little toys, checkers, poker chips]) and allow use of a calculator with math tasks.

26. Establish a quiet area for more lengthy reading tasks where the student can whis-

per read if necessary to remain on task and increase
comprehension.

27. Provide instruction to the
    student in using silent self-
    talk strategies to reduce or
    better manage tic behavior
    (e.g., teach the student with
    the onset of a tic episode to
    think several positive
    thoughts and, if needed, to
    seek out a previously deter-
    mined reinforcer in the class-
    room [beanbag corner with
    favorite books], continuing to
    think positive thoughts).

28. Teach the student to
    keep a written log of tic
    behavior to track success
    at tic reduction and to note
    environmental triggers and
    consequences that main-
    tain the tic.

29. Instruct the student in
    relaxation techniques and
    general stress-management
    strategies to reduce tic
    behavior.

30. Train the student in com-
    peting response practices
    (i.e., clearing one's throat in
    place of emitting vocal tic).

31. Provide the student with
    instruction and support in
    self-advocacy (assertive-
    ness) skills so that he/she is
    able to explain his/her med-
    ical condition to others.

32. Provide an alternative envi-
    ronment in which the stu-
    dent has an opportunity to
    release anxiety and tic be-
    haviors in private.

33. Develop with the parents, teachers, and student a behavior intervention plan based on the evaluation and functional behavioral assessment, which includes an incentive plan (positive reinforcement) to increase positive target behaviors and extinguish inappropriate behaviors.

34. Review and revise the student's behavior intervention plan with the parents as needed.

35. Include the student in small group, age-appropriate social skills training with a school mental health professional that includes an emphasis on problem solving, behavioral rehearsal, and role playing.

36. Organize opportunities for the student to practice positive social interaction with peers and adults in an accepting environment.

37. Arrange for the student to participate in individual counseling sessions with a school mental health professional to focus on low self-esteem.

38. Encourage the student to participate in school activities and promote with the parents his/her involvement in age-appropriate activities in the community.

39. Refer the student and his/her family to an outside

therapist if emotional issues become paramount.

40. Encourage the school staff to maintain ongoing dialogue with parents about Tourette's Disorder and the specific strengths and deficits of their son/daughter.

41. Discuss with the parents the symptom-exacerbating role of anxiety on Tourette's Disorder and concerns with undue or excess pressure on their son/daughter to perform.

42. Refer the student to a physician for an evaluation regarding the need for a presription for psychotropic medication to reduce tic occurrence.

43. Involve the school nurse in educating pertinent staff regarding any issues related to the student's medication regimen.

44. Gather observational data in the school setting, as requested by medical personnel and the family, related to medication and the student's functioning and performance.

45. Reinforce the student for consistent use of prescribed medication; ask the school nurse to explain the benefits of the medication to the student.

46. Maintain periodic school/home communication meetings to maintain

an open exchange of information on the student's
progress and needs.

47. Identify a school team
leader as the case coordinator to keep channels of communication open among all
involved parties.

__. _____
    _____
__. _____
    _____
__. _____
    _____

TRAINABLE MENTALLY IMPAIRED—ADOLESCENT

BEHAVIORAL DEFINITIONS

1. Lack of development, primarily in the cognitive domain, impairing learning capacity.
2. An intelligence quotient, as measured on an individually administered intelligence test, falling within a range from 30 to 55.
3. Moderate to significant impairment in functional and adaptive skills.
4. Limited interaction with peers and adults.
5. Deficits in expressive and/or receptive language processing and communication skills.
6. Deficits in fine motor, gross motor, and eye-hand coordination.

___. _____

_____

___. _____

_____

___. _____

_____

LONG-TERM GOALS

1. Exhibit daily living and adaptive behavior skills demonstrating the greatest level of independence possible in the home, school, and community.
2. Master basic academic skills to the extent possible.
3. Develop communication skills to the level of potential.

4. Increase prosocial interactions with peers and adults, diminishing noncompliant and aggressive behaviors.
5. Develop basic employability skills and participate successfully in vocational training opportunities.
6. Parents accept the student's level of intellectual and learning capabilities, establish realistic expectations, and seek out resources and means to assist their child.

—. _____

_____

—. _____

_____

—. _____

_____

SHORT-TERM OBJECTIVES

1. Cooperate with a psychoeducational evaluation. (1)
2. Participate in a communication evaluation. (2)
3. Cooperate with an evaluation by occupational and/or physical therapists. (3)
4. Parents meet with a multidisciplinary evaluation team to receive testing results. (4)
5. Parents attend the Individualized Education Planning (IEP) team meeting and accept outcome recommendations of the meeting. (5)
6. Recognize survival words and/or signs in the school and community to an 80 percent accuracy level. (6, 7)
7. Read items of choice on a simple menu. (8, 9)

THERAPEUTIC INTERVENTIONS

1. Refer for a psychoeducational evaluation to include intellectual and adaptive behavior.
2. Refer the student to the speech and language therapist and to an augmentative communication specialist as appropriate.
3. Refer the student for an occupational and/or physical therapy evaluation.
4. Arrange for a multidisciplinary evaluation team meeting in which test results are interpreted to the parents, and they have an opportunity to provide input into the multidisciplinary evaluation process.
5. Arrange for an IEP meeting, determining the student's eligibility for special

8. Identify, sort by size, and name various coins with 90 percent accuracy. (10, 11)

9. Use a computer with minimal assistance. (12, 13, 14)

10. Demonstrate self-determination of curriculum interests and cooperate with the required instruction. (15, 16)

11. Show progress with writing own signature. (17)

12. Exhibit an increase in effective verbal communication abilities. (18, 19)

13. Give essential personal information to 100 percent accuracy. (20, 21)

14. Show independence in performing personal hygiene tasks. (22, 23, 24)

15. Demonstrate the skills necessary for a quality personal appearance. (25, 26, 27, 28)

16. Assist in food preparation. (29, 30, 31, 32)

17. Cooperate with an assessment of personal safety skills. (33)

18. Implement personal safety skills and reduce high-risk and dangerous behaviors, protecting self from harm. (34, 35, 36, 37)

19. Demonstrate proper use of the telephone for personal safety. (38, 39, 40)

20. Engage in purposeful, enjoyable leisure/recreational activities. (41, 42, 43)

21. Engage in positive social in-

education and appropriate programs and/or services.

6. Clearly label locations in the school with a word and a sign to designate critical areas that the student must learn to identify (e.g. restrooms, school office, unsafe walking areas due to traffic outside of the school).

7. Take the student on repeated community-based instructional outings to work on recognizing and identifying the meanings of various survival words and signs (e.g., danger, wait/walk/stop, men, women).

8. Use the student's food and drink preferences to teach him/her to identify the words indicating those preferences by creating a menu in the classroom that shows a word with a picture (e.g., a picture of french fries by the word *fries* and a picture of milk next to the word *milk*).

9. Help the student transfer the word knowledge from the classroom and school menu to experiences in the community (e.g., identifying words on menus at various restaurants), and ordering preferences from these menus.

10. Create different activities for the student to sort, initially, a pile of coins that are very different in size and color (e.g., quarter and penny) and move to sorting coins that are more alike

teraction with same-age peers. (44, 45, 46, 47, 48)

22. Participate in job sampling experiences. (49, 50)

23. Cooperate with assessment of prerequisite employability skills. (51)

24. Participate in the development of an individualized transition plan. (52)

25. Visit vocational training sites. (53)

26. Exhibit success with post-secondary employment. (54)

27. Parents verbalize an acceptance of their child and his/her cognitive disability. (4, 55, 56)

28. Parents report satisfaction with their child's overall school experience and progress with transition to work. (57)

__. _____
   _____
__. _____
   _____
__. _____
   _____

(e.g., dimes and nickels), always having the student name the coins he/she is working with.

11. Develop scenarios in which the student must identify coins for certain tasks (e.g., telling the student to find two quarters and a dime to place in a snack machine for a desired product).

12. Ask the occupational therapist to assess the student for general abilities needed for operating a computer and write an instructional plan whereby the student becomes familiar and competent with its use.

13. Model for the student (if needed, the adult places his/her hand on the student's hand) all steps required to start the computer and to initialize familiar or preferred software.

14. Create a step-by-step picture sequence of the process required to use the computer for desired activities and place this sequence next to the computer.

15. Select a packaged curriculum from which the teacher can choose what aspects are most important for the student to work on (e.g., the IMPACT model, which is a functional curriculum placing an emphasis on ascertaining what the student wants to accomplish) (see *IMPACT: A Functional Curriculum Handbook for*

Students with Moderate to Severe Disabilities [Neel and Billingsley]).

16. Use a research-based packaged curriculum (e.g., the Teaching Research Curriculum) that provides a step-by-step curriculum, outlining development in the areas of gross motor, fine motor, self-help, and cognitive (see *The Teaching Research Curriculum for Moderately and Severely Handicapped: Gross and Fine Motor* and *The Teaching Research Curriculum for Moderately and Severely Handicapped: Self-Help and Cognitive* [Fredericks and associates]).

17. Teach the student cursive by working on individual letter formations, concentrating on the student's signature and general legibility with a user-friendly approach modified for the student (e.g., *Cursive Success* [Olsen]).

18. Work closely with the speech and language therapist and/or augmentative communication specialist, following a specific plan designed to improve the student's communication skills.

19. Use incidental teaching techniques in which the student initiates a communication opportunity (e.g., making a request for something verbally or nonverbally), the teacher focuses his/her full attention on the student, creating joint at-

tention on the topic selected by the student, requesting the student to elaborate on the request, and providing prompts to the student to expand his/her communication responses (see *Curricular and Instructional Approaches for Persons with Severe Disabilities* [Cipani and Spooner]).

20. Work daily with the student in giving his/her name, address, and phone number, using visual and auditory means to teach this skill.

21. Teach the student through role plays, discussions, and stories, situations when personal information should and should *not* be told to others.

22. Talk with the family to ensure there is no medical basis for any toileting difficulties.

23. Develop an incentive plan to reinforce the student for competent completion of designated hygiene tasks.

24. Pair the student with an age-appropriate peer to model good hygiene skills for the student and to provide prompts to the student in the process of attempting to competently complete hygiene tasks.

25. Instruct the student in the process of laundering clothes and provide opportunities to practice laundering skills (e.g., use of detergent, fabric softener, water amount and

temperature, understanding dryer heat).

26. Organize community-based outings with the parents' support that emphasize selection of clothes, delineating the correct size and style for the student.

27. Provide a full length mirror in the classroom (or another designated place) where the student can check his/her appearance on a routine basis.

28. Pair the student with a same-age peer who can model quality personal appearance; provide reinforcement to the student for positive aspects of quality appearance and give cues for areas that need improvement.

29. Involve the student in meal planning, using a chart of the four basic food groups and a pictorial recipe script for each dish to be made; organize grocery shopping outings with the student to purchase needed items for each planned meal; prepare the food through a step-by-step process.

30. Invite a cook to come into the classroom and model for the student the preparation of different and favorite foods.

31. Create a picture board or picture book for the student that outlines the steps needed for him/her to make certain favorite foods inde-

pendently (e.g., steps to cook a hot dog: (1) a picture of a sauce pan on the stove with water heating and the hot dog already in the pan; (2) a picture showing a hot dog bun and all the desired toppings for the hot dog; (3) a picture illustrating the approach to taking the hot dog out of the water; (4) a picture showing the hot dog being put in the hot dog bun and placed on a plate; and (5) finally, the condiments being placed on the hot dog (see "Pictorial Instruction: Training Daily Living Skills" by Spellman, DeBriere, Jarboe, Campbell, and Harris in *Systematic Instruction of the Moderately and Severely Handciapped* [Snell, ed.]).

32. Break into small increments the task of setting the table, using a visual depiction of the steps necessary and the final product.

33. Through observation and family report, identify several target behaviors of the student that place him/her at greatest safety risk.

34. Create a positive behavior support plan that reinforces appropriate safety behaviors and extinguishes the targeted high-risk and dangerous behaviors.

35. Use structured repetition to visually and auditorily present safety information related to the student's target safety behaviors.

36. Play educational games to promote the student's learning of safety skills (e.g., *Safety Skills: Learning to Be Careful* [Haugen]).

37. Role-play with the student various unsafe scenarios and provide the correct response (e.g., using assertiveness skills when someone is doing something one does not like, not going with a stranger, obtaining permission before going someplace).

38. Instruct the student how to independently dial 911 (or the appropriate emergency number), role-playing various emergency situations in which this would be the appropriate response.

39. Invite a police officer to the classroom to demonstrate the importance of using the telephone for emergencies and the various scenarios in which this action is needed.

40. Use pictorial representations of different dangerous situations for which the telephone would be used to call for assistance, having the student match the correct response with each scenario.

41. Assist the student (with parent support) in developing one or two hobbies and/or recreational skills that can be shared with the family or done independently.

42. Instruct the student in various activities of interest to him/her, using a task-

analysis approach where each activity is segmented into small, workable steps to success (see "Assessment and Selection of Leisure Skills for Severely and Profoundly Handicapped Persons" by Wehman and Schleien in *Education and Training of the Mentally Retarded* [1980, 14: 50–58] and "Leisure Skills Programming for Severely Handicapped Children" by Wehman and Schleien in *Teaching Social Skills to Exceptional Children* [Cartlege and Cartwright, eds.]).

43. Organize adaptations for the student to make desired or favorite activities viable (e.g., make two-handed basketball dribbles acceptable as a rule for the student, place his/her finger on the camera button for picture-taking prior to raising the camera to eye level) (see *Curricular and Instructional Approaches for Persons with Severe Disabilities* [Cipani and Spooner]).

44. Integrate the student with repeated experiences into social situations in which he/she is with age-appropriate peers who can model positive social-personal interactions.

45. Set up social scenarios in which the student is coached to observe peers who are modeling prosocial behavior.

46. Engage the student in role-

playing activities of social scenarios with prompt feedback and reinforcement given to the student for prosocial behavior.

47. Have the student practice the social skills role played in a natural environment to generalize skills to different settings (see *Students with Severe Disabilities: Current Perspectives and Practices* [Brimer]).

48. Write a positive behavioral support plan designed to decrease and extinguish aggressive or maladaptive behaviors.

49. Create opportunities for the secondary student to shadow various workers in the community to identify interests of the student.

50. Place the student at several work sites where he/she can try some unpaid work experiences to begin to learn employability skills (e.g., being on time, showing motivation, maintaining a positive attitude, taking direction, and working through to complete designated tasks).

51. Conduct an assessment of the student's employability skills using a systematic approach (e.g., the Targeted Employment Assessment Model from *Competitive Employment* [Wehman]) that examines vocational skills, independent living skills, parent attitudes and behavior, and job require-

ments to ascertain deficit employability areas and what type of supported employment model may best meet the student's needs.

52. In a collaborative model, write an individualized transition plan with the student, parents, school vocational training representative, community agencies, and potential employers (as appropriate), establishing short- and long-term goals for the student to make the transition from school to work, developing specific desired outcomes and identifying level of support (e.g., no special services, time-limited services, ongoing services) necessary for the student to obtain those outcomes (see *Office of Special Education and Rehabilitation Services—Programming for the Transition of Youth with Disabilities: Bridges from School to Working Life* [Will]).

53. Arrange for visits to potential vocational training sites for the student and his/her parents, focusing on programs providing the identified level of support needed for the student to be successful as an employee (e.g., sheltered workshop, work activity programs, supported work in a competitive, integrated employment setting).

54. Provide support to the student in his/her high school

vocational training (e.g., per the IEP some possibilities might be teacher consultant services, consulting by the occupational or speech and language therapist), working toward the goal of adult vocational programming leading to gainful, permanent employment.

55. Communicate with the parents on a routine, frequent basis, reporting the student's progress, successes, and concerns; assess their realistic acceptance of their child's limitations as well as his/her potential.

56. Refer the parents to a local parent support group for families with individuals who have cognitive challenges and/or to a national organization (e.g., American Association on Mental Retardation in Washington, DC and Association for Retarded Citizens in Arlington, TX).

57. Gather information on the strategies and supports that have been most effective for the student and arrange for this information to be shared with the teaching staff in the new school year.

___. _____

_____

___. _____

_____

___. _____

_____

TRAINABLE MENTALLY IMPAIRED—CHILD

BEHAVIORAL DEFINITIONS

1. Lack of development, primarily in the cognitive domain, impairing learning capacity.
2. An intelligence quotient, as measured on an individually administered intelligence test, falling within a range from 30 to 55.
3. Moderate to significant impairment in functional and adaptive skills.
4. Limited interaction with peers and adults.
5. Deficits in expressive and/or receptive language processing and communication skills.
6. Deficits in fine motor, gross motor, and eye-hand coordination.

__. _____
    _____
    _____
__. _____
    _____
    _____
__. _____
    _____

LONG-TERM GOALS

1. Exhibit daily living and adaptive behavior skills demonstrating the greatest level of independence possible in the home, school, and community.
2. Master basic academic skills to full potential.
3. Develop communication skills to the level of potential.

4. Increase prosocial interactions with peers and adults, diminishing noncompliant and aggressive behaviors.
5. Parents accept the student's level of intellectual and learning capabilities, establish realistic expectations, and seek out resources and means to assist their child.

—. _____

_____

—. _____

_____

—. _____

_____

SHORT-TERM OBJECTIVES

1. Cooperate with a psychoeducational evaluation. (1)
2. Participate in a communication evaluation. (2)
3. Cooperate with an evaluation by occupational and/or physical therapists. (3)
4. Parents meet with a multidisciplinary evaluation team to receive an evaluation of results. (4)
5. Parents attend the Individualized Education Planning (IEP) team meeting and accept outcome recommendations of the meeting. (5)
6. Recognize survival words and/or signs in the school and community. (6, 7)
7. Identify letters and essential words with 80 percent accuracy as beginning reading skills. (8, 9)
8. Identify, sort by size, and name various coins with 90 percent accuracy. (10, 11)

THERAPEUTIC INTERVENTIONS

1. Refer for a psychoeducational evaluation to include intellectual and adaptive behavior.
2. Refer the student to the speech and language therapist and to an augmentative communication specialist as appropriate.
3. Refer the student for an occupational and/or physical therapy evaluation.
4. Arrange for a multidisciplinary evaluation team meeting in which test results are interpreted to the parents, and they have an opportunity to provide input into the multidisciplinary evaluation process.
5. Arrange for an IEP meeting, determining the student's eligibility for special education and appropriate programs and/or services.

9. Recognize numbers and demonstrate counting skills to 95 percent accuracy. (12, 13)

10. Follow a visual schedule of the school day matching several marked times of the day with the time on the clock. (14)

11. Demonstrate 90 percent accuracy with addition skills. (15, 16, 17)

12. Demonstrate 90 percent accuracy with subtraction skills. (18, 19, 20)

13. Show competency with beginning computer skills. (21, 22, 23)

14. Show improvement with basic handwriting skills. (24)

15. Exhibit an increase in effective verbal communication abilities. (25, 26)

16. Verbalize essential personal information to 100 percent accuracy when appropriate. (27, 28)

17. Achieve independence with toileting. (29, 30, 31, 32)

18. Master dressing and undressing skills. (33, 34, 35)

19. Show progress with personal hygiene tasks. (36, 37)

20. Demonstrate very basic food preparation skills. (38)

21. Use personal safety skills, reducing high-risk and dangerous behaviors and protecting self from harm. (39, 40, 41, 42)

6. Clearly label locations in the school with a word and a sign to designate critical areas that the student must learn to identify (e.g. restrooms, school office, unsafe walking areas due to traffic outside of the school).

7. Take the student on repeated community-based instructional outings to work on recognizing and identifying the meanings of various survival words and signs (e.g., danger, wait/walk/stop, men, women).

8. Using visual and tactile strategies, provide daily instruction with letter and word identification, introducing preprimer books with high-interest, repetitive vocabulary (e.g., the *Reading Milestones* [Quigley, King, McAnally, and Rose]).

9. Provide practice in using community-based instructional outings to assist the student with identifying letters and words on storefronts, restaurants, and so on.

10. Create different activities for the student to sort, initially, a pile of coins that are very different in size and color (e.g., quarter and penny) and move to sorting coins that are more alike (e.g., dimes and nickels), always having the student name the coins he/she is working with.

22. Demonstrate proper use of the telephone for personal safety. (42, 43, 44)

23. Participate in a hobby or sport skill activity. (45)

24. Engage in positive social interaction with same-aged peers. (46, 47, 48, 49)

25. Parents verbalize an acceptance of their son/daughter and his/her cognitive disability, establishing realistic goals and expectations. (4, 50, 51)

26. Parents report satisfaction with their child's overall school experience and program. (52)

___. _____

_____

___. _____

_____

___. _____

_____

11. Develop scenarios in which the student must identify coins for certain tasks (e.g., telling the student to find two quarters and a dime to place in a snack machine for a desired product).

12. Implement repeated visual and tactile activities to teach the student numbers 1 through 10 and above (as appropriate) (e.g., match the numerical symbols with objects equalizing the same number; have the student trace a numeral made out of sandpaper, trace the number on paper, then write the numeral).

13. Have the student engage in rote counting on a daily basis while following along with a visual portrayal of each number.

14. Assist the student with telling time by the hour by selecting several on-the-hour times in the school day (e.g., 8:00 opening, 12:00 lunch, 3:00 departure time), visually matching the activity at this time with a visual identification on a nondigital clock and verbally correlating each day for the student the time and the activity.

15. Repeatedly model for the student combining two sets of a few objects together to make one total set.

16. Have the student engage in placing sets together and

counting the number of objects in the total set.

17. Ask the student to count and write down the number of objects in the first set, identify and write the number of objects in the second set, and finally, identify and write the number of objects in the combined set.

18. Repeatedly model for the student, taking a few objects away from a larger set.

19. Have the student engage in taking a few objects away from a larger set and counting the remaining objects in the initial, larger set.

20. Ask the student to identify and write down the number of objects in the initial set, count and write the number of objects taken away, and finally, identify and write the numeral representing the objects left.

21. Ask the occupational therapist to assess the student for general abilities needed for operating a computer, and write an instructional plan whereby the student becomes familiar and competent with its use.

22. Model for the student (if needed, the adult places his /her hand on the student's hand) all steps required to start the computer and to initialize familiar or preferred software.

23. Create a step-by-step picture sequence of the process

required to use the computer for desired activities and place this sequence next to the computer.

24. Teach the student manuscript or cursive writing, working on individual letter formations with a user-friendly approach (e.g., *Handwriting Without Tears* or *Cursive Success* [Olsen]).

25. Work closely with the speech and language therapist and/or augmentative communication specialist, following a specific plan designed to improve the student's verbal communication skills.

26. Use incidental teaching techniques in which the student initiates a communication opportunity (e.g., making a request for something verbally or nonverbally), the teacher focuses his/her full attention on the student, creating joint attention on the topic selected by the student, requesting the student to elaborate on the request, and providing prompts to the student to expand his/her communication responses (see *Curricular and Instructional Approaches for Persons with Severe Disabilities* [Cipani and Spooner]).

27. Work daily with the student in giving his/her name, address, and phone number, using visual and auditory

techniques to teach this skill.

28. Teach the student through role plays, discussions, and stories, situations when personal information should and should *not* be told to others.

29. Establish with the parents a routine for offering the student bathroom opportunities at school; as needed, offer incentives/reinforcers to the student for demonstrating desired toileting behaviors.

30. Talk with the family to ensure there is no medical basis for any of the student's toileting difficulties.

31. Make certain the student has no difficulties with prerequisites to independence with toileting (e.g., dressing and undressing).

32. Enlist the expertise of a behavioral consultant to establish a plan that reinforces independence with toileting and decreases or extinguishes difficulties.

33. Use the IEP team process to identify with the family which of the student's functional skills are appropriate to work on in the school setting (e.g., manipulating pants for toileting, taking off and putting on a coat, boots, mittens, gloves).

34. Model and assist the student repeatedly with dressing tasks to be mastered.

35. Work closely with the occupational therapist on ways to teach the student dressing skills (e.g., the manipulation of buttons, zippers, shoelaces).

36. Teach the student hygiene by incorporating into the daily routine appropriate tasks for the school setting (e.g., brushing teeth, combing hair, washing hands and face after eating, and nail care).

37. Develop an incentive plan to reinforce the student for competent completion of designated hygiene tasks.

38. Create a picture board or picture book for the student that outlines the steps needed for him/her to make certain favorite foods independently (e.g., steps to make chocolate milk: (1) a picture of a spoon, instant chocolate, glass, milk; (2) a glass with a carton of milk pouring; (3) a teaspoon of chocolate pouring into the milk; (4) and finally a picture showing stirring of the instant chocolate into the milk) (see "Pictorial Instruction: Training Daily Living Skills" by Spellman, DeBriere, Jarboe, Campbell, and Harris in *Systematic Instruction of the Moderately and Severely Handicapped* [Snell, ed.]).

39. Create a positive behavior support plan that reinforces

appropriate safety behaviors and extinguishes the targeted high-risk and dangerous behaviors.

40. Use structured repetition to visually and auditorily present safety information related to the student's target safety behaviors.

41. Role-play with the student various unsafe scenarios and provide the correct response (e.g., using assertiveness skills when someone is doing something one does not like, not going with a stranger, obtaining permission before going someplace).

42. Instruct the student how to independently dial 911 (or the appropriate emergency number), role-playing various emergency situations in which this would be the appropriate response.

43. Invite a police officer to the classroom to demonstrate the importance of using the telephone for emergencies and the various scenarios in which this action is needed.

44. Use pictorial representations of different dangerous situations for which the telephone would be used to call for assistance, having the student match the correct response with each scenario.

45. Assist the student (with parent support) in developing one or two hobbies and/or recreational skills that can

be shared with the family or done independently.

46. Integrate the student with repeated social situations in which he/she is with age-appropriate peers who can model positive social-personal interactions.

47. Set up social scenarios in which the student is coached to observe peers who are modeling prosocial behavior.

48. Engage the student in role-playing activities of social scenarios with prompt feedback and reinforcement given to the student for prosocial behavior.

49. Write a positive behavioral support plan designed to decrease and extinguish aggressive or maladaptive behaviors.

50. Communicate with the parents on a routine, frequent basis, reporting the student's progress, successes, and concerns; assess their realistic acceptance of their child's limitations as well as his/her potential.

51. Refer the parents to a local parent support group for families with individuals who have cognitive challenges and/or to a national organization (e.g., American Association on Mental Retardation in Washington, DC and Association for Retarded Citizens in Arlington, TX).

52. Gather information on the strategies and supports that have been most effective for the student and arrange for this information to be shared with the teaching staff in the new school year.

___. _____
      _____

___. _____
      _____

___. _____
      _____

TRAUMATIC BRAIN INJURY

BEHAVIORAL DEFINITIONS

1. Injury sustained to the head that impairs brain functioning to a mild, moderate, or severe degree.
2. Disrupted learning pattern in contrast to the learning pattern prior to the incident.
3. Impaired functioning in cognitive areas that may include disturbances in memory, planning, reasoning, attention, concentration, perceptual motor abilities, and/or language.
4. Deficits with social functioning due to impaired reasoning involving impulsivity, poor anger control, skewed problem-solving skills in social situations, agitation, and/or aggression.
5. Feelings of low self-esteem, depression, alienation, and anxiety that develop from frustration due to cognitive and social deficits.
6. Physical problems such as blurred vision, headaches, and reduced stamina.
7. Physical and psychosocial stress of caregivers related to postinjury needs/problems of the brain-injured child.
8. Lowered achievement in one or more areas of learning.
9. Decreased ability to attend to and complete classroom tasks.

—. _____

_____

—. _____

_____

—. _____

_____

LONG-TERM GOALS

1. Demonstrate cognitive processing abilities to the expected performance level based on neurological prognosis.
2. Demonstrate achievement in deficit areas to the level of expected potential.
3. Resolve motor and language deficits to the level of expected potential.
4. Demonstrate problem-solving strategies when confronted with social situations with peers.
5. Exhibit self-monitoring techniques in remaining on-task and with completion of classroom work.
6. Develop an awareness and understanding of the injury and its potential resulting implications and an acceptance of potential limitations in future functioning.
7. Parents recognize realistic expectations for the student's recovery in relation to academic and psychosocial functioning.

—. _____

_____

—. _____

_____

—. _____

_____

SHORT-TERM OBJECTIVES

1. Cooperate with psychoeducational evaluation. (1, 2, 3, 4, 5)

2. Participate in speech/ language assessment. (1, 2, 3, 4, 6)

3. Cooperate with physical/occupational therapy assessment. (1, 2, 3, 4, 7)

4. Parents provide information regarding changes in the family and the student that

THERAPEUTIC INTERVENTIONS

1. Arrange for a consultation with relevant medical specialists to obtain postinjury status about the student prior to reentrance to school.

2. Organize a school-based multidisciplinary evaluation team to include a staff member with considerable knowledge of traumatic brain injury to review all critical and relevant information/evaluations completed during the student's hospitalization.

have occurred since the brain injury. (8)

5. Parents and the student receive assessment feedback and agree to Individualized Education Plan (IEP) recommendations. (9)

6. Utilize compensatory learning aids. (10)

7. Demonstrate improved attention and less reactivity to the learning environment. (11)

8. Follow a specific homework plan to include the use of a daily agenda taken between school and home, keeping track of both short- and long-term assignments. (12, 13)

9. Parents utilize proven instructional methods while working with the student on academic material at home. (12, 13, 14)

10. Parents maintain contact with the student's teachers on a daily or weekly basis. (14)

11. Receive all necessary medical accommodations available within the school setting. (15, 16)

12. Perform up to academic potential as determined by multidisciplinary analysis of tasks and abilities. (17)

13. Demonstrate increased time spent on-task and increased percentage of completed assignments. (16, 17, 18, 19)

14. Increase prosocial behaviors and reduce negative inter-

3. Staff complete reentry guidelines/checklists for traumatic brain injury to ensure that the reintegration of the student is done in a comprehensive manner (see "Children and Adolescents with Traumatic Brain Injury: Reintegration Challenges in Educational Settings" by Clark in *Journal of Learning Disabilities* [1996, 29(6): 633–642]).

4. Multidisciplinary evaluation team meets to ascertain other necessary assessments that are pertinent to the student's special education eligibility, Section 504 eligibility, and/or programming needs.

5. Conduct or refer the student for psychoeducational testing.

6. Refer the student for speech/language evaluation.

7. Refer the student for a physical/occupational therapy assessment.

8. Consult with the parents to gather information about the student's functioning prior to and since the injury as part of the reentry process for the student and to provide a psychosocial background for school evaluations as needed.

9. Conduct an IEP team meeting and/or Section 504 planning meeting to determine the student's eligibility for such programs and/or services and necessary classroom accommodations.

actions with peers and teachers. (20, 21)

15. Increase frequency of positive peer contacts and enhance peer friendships. (21, 22)

16. Verbalize improved feelings of self-esteem. (21, 23, 24, 25)

17. Attend individual counseling sessions for emotional and behavioral problems. (23, 25)

18. Verbally acknowledge limitations in relation to the injury and state realistic goals in future planning. (25, 26, 27, 28, 29)

19. Parents cease denial in relation to their child's deficits as a result of the injury. (25, 29, 30, 31)

20. Parents verbalize reasonable expectations regarding their child's abilities and terminate all undue pressure. (29, 30, 32)

21. Identify vocational interests and goals. (33, 34, 35)

22. Participate in visual and/or hearing acuity testing. (36, 37)

23. Demonstrate ongoing academic progress as measured objectively between set evaluation cycles. (38, 39)

24. Parents report satisfaction with progress and planning for the student. (37, 38, 39, 40)

10. Provide compensatory aids for the student's use (e.g., tape-recording notes, computer-based programs, memory notebooks, shortened assignments, extended time lines, and larger assignments segmented into briefer tasks).

11. Modify the learning environment by decreasing distractions with the use of special work areas, retaining routine and structure by maintaining a regular schedule, and giving advanced organization information to the student prior to any changes.

12. Provide the parents with specific materials (e.g., study guides, worksheets, textbooks) on how they may best assist their son/daughter at home.

13. Model instructional strategies (e.g., categorizing and labeling new concepts and vocabulary, rote review of the student's memory notebook [retrieval of lost vocabulary and lost concepts], and direct instruction with visual prompts) for the parents to use at home.

14. Encourage the parents to maintain regular (i.e., daily or weekly) communication with teachers to help the student remain organized and current with school assignments.

15. Involve the school nurse in educating pertinent staff re-

___. _____
    _____

___. _____
    _____

___. _____
    _____

garding any issues related to the student's medication regimen.

16. Gather observational data in the school setting, as requested by medical personnel and the family, related to medication and the student's functioning and performance.

17. Conduct a task analysis to ascertain the quantity and levels of academic tasks the student is capable of performing.

18. Train the student in self-talk in which the student verbally reminds himself/herself of the task at hand or verbally rehearses a task.

19. Create an incentive-based plan that reinforces the student's ability to self-monitor his/her time on-task, complete class assignments, and establish short-term goals.

20. Develop a behavior intervention plan based on a functional behavioral assessment to reinforce prosocial behavior and to extinguish inappropriate behaviors.

21. Involve the student in short- or long-term small group social skills training with a school mental health professional, including emphasis on problem solving, social skill rehearsal, and social interaction role playing.

22. Include the student in an orchestrated friendship group

where the school staff provides structure and mediation to create positive peer
contacts for the afflicted student (see "Building Social
Networks for Children and
Adolescents with Traumatic
Brain Injury: A School-
Based Intervention" by
Glang, Todis, Coolery, Wells,
and Voss in *Journal of Head
Trauma Rehabilitation*
[1997, 12(2): 32–47]).

23. Arrange for the student to
participate in individual
counseling sessions with a
school mental health professional.

24. Establish affective goals
(e.g., using positive "I" statements [identifying two per
week about his/her performance in school], engaging
in a positive social activity
with a peer once per week)
with the student to increase
self-esteem, which are then
addressed by all members
of the school team.

25. Refer the student and
his/her family to an outside
therapist if emotional, behavioral, or denial issues
become paramount.

26. School staff frequently reinforces student's strengths.

27. Instruct the student in attribution retraining to avoid
learned helplessness and decrease frustration tolerance
by leading the student
through a series of instructional steps over a three-
week period involving both

easy and difficult tasks, always modeling specific self-correction strategies for the student (see "An Attribution Training Program with Learning Disabled Children" by Shelton, Anastopoulous, and Linden in *Journal of Learning Disabilities* [1985, 18(5): 261–265]).

28. Provide project-based learning tasks to allow the student a greater sense of accomplishment with creating and completing a major activity successfully.

29. At the secondary task level, arrange for a meeting to discuss future, appropriate course selections with the student and his/her parents.

30. Educate the parents about traumatic brain injuries and the specific deficits of their child.

31. Invite the parents to visit their child's classroom and to observe his/her participation in instructional periods.

32. Discuss with the parents the negative consequences of them placing undue pressure(s) to perform on their child.

33. Organize visits for the student and his/her parents to vocational training sites that match the student's interests and abilities.

34. Contact agencies in the community that provide resources applicable to the student's present and/or fu-

ture educational/vocational needs.

35. Arrange a transition planning meeting to identify the student's goals and the resources necessary to obtain such goals.

36. School nurse makes contact with the family and, if appropriate, to medical specialists regarding the status of physical anomalies of the student.

37. Have the student participate in visual and/or hearing acuity screenings performed at the school.

38. Arrange monthly communication meetings of the student's school team to competently process crucial issues.

39. Reconvene the IEP team or Section 504 team on an informal or formal basis prior to the annual review to communicate progress and concerns with the family (and with the student when appropriate).

40. Identify a school team leader as the case coordinator to keep channels of communication open among all involved parties.

__. _____

_____

__. _____

_____

__. _____

_____

VIOLENT AND DANGEROUS

BEHAVIORAL DEFINITIONS

1. Exhibits direct aggression toward others by physical and/or verbal means (e.g., arguing, threatening, fighting, using a weapon, or showing cruelty to people and/or animals).
2. Poor impulse control and a low frustration tolerance.
3. Has poor social skills, feels repeatedly rejected by peers, and is socially isolated.
4. Has been a victim of bullying by peers and feels constantly disrespected.
5. History of conflict with and disrespect for authority figures.
6. Lack of academic achievement and motivation.
7. Access to or fascination with weapons, especially guns (may have had a gun in his/her possession).
8. Has a history of lying, stealing, truancy, fire setting, or other forms of property destruction.
9. Membership in a group engaged in delinquent-type conduct (gang affiliation).
10. Engages in drug or alcohol use frequently.
11. Has written or talked about plans for violent acts of revenge.
12. Antisocial conduct is evident across home, school, and community settings, and significantly interferes with educational functioning and interpersonal interactions.

—. _____
   _____

—. _____
   _____

—. _____
   _____

LONG-TERM GOALS

1. Terminate expressions of anger and increase positive social interactions with peers and adults.
2. Learn social skills and increase positive interactions with peers and adults.
3. Cooperate with persons of authority (e.g., teachers or principals) in a reasonable, nonoppositional manner.
4. Improve self-concept through positive involvement in a particular activity or sport for which he/she has a skill, talent, or interest.
5. Pass grade-level expectations for the current level of placement or pass courses to receive credit toward graduation, demonstrating improved academic attitude and performance.
6. Parents work with school staff and other officials/supports in the community to provide their child with greater structure, higher expectations, and improved functioning.

—. _____

_____

—. _____

_____

—. _____

_____

SHORT-TERM OBJECTIVES

1. Cooperate with a psychoeducational evaluation. (1, 2, 3)

2. Participate in a psychiatric evaluation/consultation. (4)

3. Parents participate in the multidisciplinary evaluation team process and collaborate on, and agree to, a positive behavior intervention support plan. (5)

4. Parents, and the student as appropriate, participate in the Individualized Education Planning (IEP) team meeting and accept identi-

THERAPEUTIC INTERVENTIONS

1. Refer the student for a psychoeducational evaluation to include an assessment of social/emotional, academic, intellectual, and adaptive functioning.

2. Complete a functional behavioral assessment of the student's maladaptive behaviors, examining the situational antecedents, the nature of the negative behaviors, and the consequences of the negative behaviors.

fied recommendations.
(6, 7, 8)

5. Parents consult with a physician who will evaluate the student for psychotropic medication and share school-related recommendations with selected school staff. (9)

6. Assimilate all components of the positive behavior intervention support plan and agree to its implementation. (10, 11)

7. Establish several goals for improved personal conduct. (12, 13)

8. Increase the frequency of targeted positive behaviors as a result of systematic monitoring, self-evaluation, and an extrinsic reward system. (13)

9. Extinguish aggressive acts by mastering self-control skills. (14, 15, 16, 17, 18)

10. Demonstrate improved problem solving through the practice of personal accountability. (19)

11. Implement effective techniques for problem solving. (20)

12. Attend a social skills training group and use prosocial skills to replace aggression. (21)

13. Become involved in a school-related activity or sport. (22, 23)

14. Reduce aggressive behavior in response to school-wide

3. Organize the data from the functional behavioral assessment, along with input from the student, parents, and school staff, resulting in a report that describes the maladaptive behavior(s), predicts when the behavior(s) may occur, hypothesizes reasons for the behavior(s), and proposes interventions that lead to the resolution of the problem(s) (see *Positive Behavior Support for ALL Michigan Students: Creating Environments That Assure Learning* [Michigan Department of Education—Office of Special Education and Early Intervention Services]).

4. Refer the student for a psychiatric consultation/evaluation.

5. Meet with the parents to obtain their input into the multidisciplinary evaluation team process, interpret evaluation results to them, and collaborate on the development of a positive behavior intervention support plan.

6. Collaborate with the family at the IEP team meeting to determine the student's eligibility for special education, establish goals and short-term objectives in deficit areas, identify appropriate programs and/or services, decide on needed accommodations and modifications, and finalize a positive behavior intervention support plan.

prevention measures.
(24, 25, 26)

15. Participate in service learning projects to increase self-esteem and to learn empathy. (27, 28)

16. Exhibit steady progress in and a more positive attitude toward academics.
(29, 30, 31)

17. Parents demonstrate willingness to learn a variety of child disciplinary methods and how to effectively use each method. (32)

18. Parents participate in a parent training program.
(33, 34, 35)

19. Parents indicate a level of trust with school staff and work cooperatively in the best interest of their son/daughter. (36, 37, 38)

—. _____
   _____
—. _____
   _____
—. _____
   _____

7. Should a more restrictive environment outside of the present school placement be decided by the IEP team, organize a visit for the student and parents to view the program and have their questions answered.

8. Should the student be determined by the IEP team to be ineligible under special education administrative rules for special education programs and/or services, develop a multimodal treatment plan to be implemented through general education with adaptations (i.e., shortened school day, ongoing monitoring/shadowing) or in an alternative small group setting where the student has access to needed components of behavior management, self-control/anger management strategies, social skills training, problem solving, and/or cognitive restructuring.

9. Refer the parents to a physician to evaluate the student as to the need for psychotropic medication; discuss with the parents any implications for the school setting from their medical consultation.

10. Select keystone target behaviors in which a target behavior is selected for reinforcement based on its incompatibility with a secondary negative behavior (e.g., John will follow directions as given by the teacher

on the first or second request: decreases noncompliance and reduces the opportunity for negative verbiage [e.g., swearing] by the student) (see "Relationships Between Assessment and Treatment Within a Behavioral Perspective" by Nelson in *Journal of Psychopathology and Behavioral Assessment* [1988, 10: 155–170]).

11. Review and discuss with the student and family all aspects of the positive behavior intervention support plan and have them sign an agreement that outlines specifically a hierarchy of reinforcers (e.g., earning more rights and privileges, time to play computer games, free time to socialize with peers, etc.) and of consequences (e.g., in-school suspension, home/school reporting, reporting incidents to interested parties [parole officer, community mental health counselor], moving to a lower level in the special education classroom as related to rights and privileges).

12. Work with the student to establish several goals (begin with one if necessary) for improved personal conduct in school, developing a plan to meet each goal by answering the questions: What is my goal? What is my plan to achieve my goal? What if the plan does not work? With whom will I check my plan? What reward will I give

myself when I have done all I can to achieve my goal? (examples of a goal could be: My goal is to walk away if someone bumps into me in the hall and not fight, or My goal is to not swear at people in authority at school) (see *As Tough As Necessary: Countering Violence, Aggression, and Hostility in Our Schools* [Curwin and Mendler]).

13. Have the student share his/her goal(s) with the parents and any other important individuals involved in his/her life at the time (e.g., parole officer, community mental health counselor, coach).

14. Teach the elementary student the turtle technique: When the cue word *turtle* is used, the student is to act like a turtle by physically closing his/her eyes and pulling arms and legs close to the body similar to a turtle going into its shell; the student then uses a muscle tensing, muscle relaxation process, releasing all tension from his/her body; the student identifies with the teacher or school mental health professional the conflict/problem and reviews these problem-solving questions: What's my goal? What am I doing? Is what I am doing helping me achieve this goal? What can I do differently? (see "The Turtle Technique: A Method for the

Self-Control of Impulsive Behavior" by Schneider and Robin in *Counseling Methods* [Krumboltz and Thoreson, eds.]) and *Treating Conduct and Oppositional Defiant Disorders in Children* [Horne and Sayger]).

15. Teach the secondary student alternative responses to conflict (e.g., leaving the conflict, using calming methods, identifying other solutions); videotape and role-play the student's use of alternative responses, and reassure the student that the alternative response may not feel right at first) (see *Treating Conduct and Oppositional Defiant Disorders in Children* [Horne and Sayger]).

16. Teach the student self-control skills that match his/her strengths and cognitive abilities (e.g., relaxation training, thought stopping, replacing negative thoughts with calm ones, self-selected time-outs, using words instead of actions) (see *Treating Conduct and Oppositional Defiant Disorders in Children* [Horne and Sayger]).

17. Refer the student to or conduct a group program for anger coping intervention with other aggressive students that integrates the components of perspective taking, awareness of physiological arousal, use of self-instruction to inhibit

impulsivity, and social problem solving in weekly sessions using discussion, activities, role playing, videotaping, and goal setting (see "Anger Coping Intervention with Aggressive Children: A Guide to Implementation in School Settings" by Lochman, Lampion, Gemmer, and Harris in *Innovations in Clinical Practice: A Source Book* [Keller and Heyman, eds.] and "An Intervention and Consultation Model from a Social Cognitive Perspective: A Description of the Anger Coping Program" by Lochman, Dunn, and Klimes-Dougan in *School Psychology Review* [1993, 22(3): 458–471]).

18. Assist the student with regaining self-control through using a crisis prevention/intervention model that could involve physical management of the student when harmful to self or others (see *Nonviolent Crisis Intervention* [Caraulia and Steiger]).

19. Implement the Responsible Thinking Process, which involves giving the student a choice of remaining in class and following rules or moving to a Responsible Thinking Classroom where he/she is taught effective problem solving; the premise is to place the responsibility for thinking/problem solving on the student, asking him/her salient questions to teach responsibility for actions

and behavior (see *Discipline for Home and School, Book One* [Ford] and *Discipline for Home and School, Book Two* [Ford]).

20. Provide instruction to the student in a six-step process for solving problems prior to hurting self or others: (1) *Stop and calm down*—attend to the signs of tension in one's body; (2) *Think*—consider options; (3) *Decide*—What do I want to happen? What will be the consequences?; (4) *Choose a second solution*—have a backup plan; (5) *Act*—carry out the choice; and (6) *Evaluate*—Did I reach my goal? What will I do next time? Who might help me figure out a solution? (see *As Tough As Necessary: Countering Violence, Aggression, and Hostility in Our Schools* [Curwin and Mendler]).

21. Refer the student to a social skills training group in which instruction, modeling, rehearsal (role-playing), feedback, and generalization will be used to assist him/her in replacing maladaptive social responses with more adaptive choices (see *Skillstreaming the Adolescent: New Strategies and Perspectives for Teaching Prosocial Skills* [Goldstein and McGinnis]; *Aggression Replacement Training* [Goldstein, Glick, and Gibbs]; *The Prepare Curriculum: Teaching Prosocial*

Competence [Goldstein]; or *Anger Management for Youth: Stemming Aggression and Violence* [Eggert]).

22. Seek out choices of activities that might be of interest to the student and present options to the student and parents (e.g., after-school intramural sports, card collecting [Magic cards/baseball cards], tech-ed, auto shop, wood shop); replace negative behaviors and low interest with positive outlets and high motivation.

23. Assist the student in solving logistical problems (e.g., cost, transportation) that might prevent the student's participation in school-related, extracurricular activity.

24. Work with administration and school staff in implementing schoolwide interventions that teach all students conflict resolution, respect for diversity, peer mediation, and anger control methods to deal with disputes in nonviolent ways (see *Discipline With Dignity* [Curwin and Mendler]).

25. Require training and implementation of positive modeling of alternative expressions of anger and frustration by all school staff to include lunchroom personnel, bus drivers, custodians; in this way, the student *always* sees nonviolent, reasonable responses to hos-

tile situations (see *As Tough As Necessary: Countering Violence, Aggression, and Hostility in Our Schools* [Curwin and Mendler]).

26. Establish a core set of schoolwide values that are the principles in developing the rules of the school (e.g., value—school is a place where people feel safe, so no one is to be ridiculed, shunned, or hurt inside or outside of the school; rule—no weapons allowed on school grounds) (see *As Tough As Necessary: Countering Violence, Aggression, and Hostility in Our Schools* [Curwin and Mendler]).

27. Implement a supervised cross-age tutoring experience in which an older, alienated student assists a younger student or a student with severe disabilities with learning tasks.

28. Create a project in which the behaviorally challenged student is part of the group volunteering or entertaining at a nursing home, a preschool, or a facility for developmentally challenged children or adults.

29. Match the student's academic needs carefully with his/her abilities, so the student is frequently engaged in academic tasks in which he/she can succeed.

30. Develop a specialized curriculum in a strength area or interest area of the stu-

dent at which he/she can be successful and can become very intensely engaged, thus replacing negative thoughts or actions (e.g., create an independent study with the student in woodworking where he/she has talent and construct a major project from design to completion of the structure).

31. Refer the student to a mentoring program in which he/she is matched with a volunteer adult to assist him/her with schoolwork, motivation, and positive behavior, and with whom the student can build a relationship of trust.

32. Have the parents meet on a weekly basis with a school mental health professional to learn different methods of child discipline, instructing them in each method and teaching them to match the method to fit the crime (include tried-and-true strategies: ignoring, grandma's law [the child is allowed a privilege *after* compliance], use of natural or logical consequences, time-out, extra chores, and loss of privileges); process with the parents each week as to what occurred and problem solve any need for change (see *Treating Conduct and Oppositional Defiant Disorders in Children* [Horne and Sayger]).

33. Provide a comprehensive parent training program for

the parents of children from ages three to eight that involves a number of varied components including child-directed play, use of differential attention, effective use of commands, time-out, logical and natural consequences, close monitoring of the child, and problem-solving and communication strategies with their child (see *Troubled Families—Problem Children: Working with Parents—A Collaborative Process* [Webster-Stratton] or *Helping the Noncompliant Child* [Forehand and McMahon]).

34. Provide a comprehensive parent training program for the parents of preadolescent or adolescent youth involving five basic management practices: (1) identify problem behaviors, (2) use social and tangible reinforcers, (3) learn effective discipline procedures, (4) provide close supervision of the child, and (5) teach problem-solving skills (see *A Social Learning Approach to Family Intervention* [Patterson, Reid, Jones, and Conger] and *A Comparative Evaluation of Parent Training for Families of Chronic Delinquents* [Marlowe, Reid, Patterson, Weinrott, and Bank]).

35. Refer the parents to a therapist who is equipped to work with aggressive youth and/or antisocial family structures should school in-

terventions prove insuffi-
cient or if parents prefer to
seek counseling assistance
from outside the school.

36. Maintain routine contact
with the parents, reporting
successes of their child and
the problem-solving difficulties encountered.

37. Obtain a confidential release of information agreement from the parents to
allow communication be-
tween designated school
staff with community agencies or supportive people involved with the student
outside of school (i.e., law
enforcement, social services,
public health, community
mental health).

38. Designate the student to
have a case manager in the
school setting (e.g., special
education teacher, school
mental health professional)
to maintain a positive focus
on the student and his/her
ongoing needs over the long
term, act as an advocate in
times of adversity or crisis,
maintain a relationship
with the family, and take a
leadership role in problem-
solving concerns.

—. _____
   _____

—. _____
   _____

—. _____
   _____

VISUALLY IMPAIRED AND BLIND

BEHAVIORAL DEFINITIONS

1. A loss or deficit that adversely impacts overall development and/or functioning in the educational environment.
2. Identified as legally visually impaired or blind as a result of a comprehensive evaluation by an ophthalmologist or optometrist.
3. One eye has vision equal to, or less than, 20/70 after refractive correction, with the other eye presenting with an even more severe loss.
4. Impairment results from trauma before, during, or after birth, infection, or retinopathy of prematurity.
5. Impairment results from a congenital eye condition (e.g., albinism, amblyopia, cataracts, or glaucoma).

—. _____

_____

—. _____

_____

—. _____

_____

LONG-TERM GOALS

1. Attain goals and objectives that are identified in the Individualized Education Planning (IEP) team process and that seek to build self-esteem, self-confidence, academic performance, and social skills.
2. Achieve academic functioning to the level of potential, considering visual impairment.
3. Develop listening and tactile skills commensurate with learning potential that can be used at home, in school, and in the community.

4. Develop movement and mobility skills sufficient to realize maximum independence with travel through environments in the home, at school, and in the community.
5. Learn to effectively use residual vision and visual aids to the maximum extent possible.
6. Demonstrate increased feelings of competence and self-esteem.
7. Parents understand and accept their child's visual deficits, establish realistic expectations, and seek out resources to meet his/her needs.

—. _____
_____
—. _____
_____
—. _____
_____

SHORT-TERM OBJECTIVES

1. Cooperate with a comprehensive visual examination. (1)

2. Participate in a multifaceted multidisciplinary evaluation of visual, academic, intellectual, physical, language, and psychosocial strengths and weaknesses. (2)

3. Parents participate in the multidisciplinary evaluation team process. (3)

4. Parents, and student as appropriate, participate in the IEP team meeting and accept the recommendations of the team. (4)

5. Parents work with specialists to determine the most appropriate mobility system for their child. (5)

THERAPEUTIC INTERVENTIONS

1. Refer the student to an ophthalmologist or optometrist for a comprehensive vision examination.

2. Organize a multidisciplinary evaluation team of qualified professionals who will assess the student in the areas of functional vision, vision efficiency, low vision aids, intellectual functioning, gross and fine motor development, achievement, language development, listening skills, social learning, orientation and mobility, and daily living skills.

3. Meet with the parents to collaborate on the vision and medical information they received from vision

6. Cooperate with instruction and recommendations provided by the orientation and mobility specialist. (6)

7. Parents collaborate with school staff regarding their child's mobility needs. (7, 8)

8. Engage successfully in community-based instruction by using effective orientation and mobility strategies. (9, 10)

9. Demonstrate increasing proficiency with the use of braille. (11, 12)

10. Listen to tape recordings to learn to accurately identify critical sounds and content. (13, 14)

11. Accurately understand and follow verbal directions given by the teacher within the classroom. (15, 16)

12. Utilize braille study notes to guide listening to verbally presented material. (17)

13. Cooperate with a technology assessment. (18)

14. Effectively use low-level technology visual assistance equipment for school tasks. (19)

15. Effectively use high-level technology visual assistance equipment for school tasks. (20)

16. Master optimization of listening and vision skills. (21, 22)

specialists, to obtain parent input into the evaluation of their child's visual deficits, and to interpret results of the test data and findings of the various school professionals.

4. Organize an IEP team meeting with the parents to determine the student's eligibility for special education and to identify programs, services, goals, and objectives appropriate for the student.

5. The orientation and mobility specialist, using information from parents, school staff, and the psychosocial evaluation, makes recommendations as to the best mobility system for the student (e.g., walker, cane, an alternative mobility device, electronic travel aid, sighted guide, or dog guide), taking into consideration the specific needs of the student, the complexity of environments the student travels in, the student's physical and cognitive abilities, and motivational/attitudinal issues.

6. The orientation and mobility specialist trains the student with regard to movement (e.g., travel through the school, playground, and neighborhood as well as topography [hilly, slope], textures [bumpy, concrete, pavement], and

17. Effectively work in the general education curriculum with adaptations to the teaching methods. (23, 24, 25, 26, 27, 28)

18. Demonstrate 80 percent mastery of academic material in a curriculum tailored to own needs and strengths. (29)

19. Exhibit successes with activities of daily living (ADLs) and independent activities for daily living (IADLs). (30)

20. Establish prevocational employability skills by age 16. (31, 32, 33)

21. Parents and the student participate in the development of an individualized transition plan (school to work). (34, 35)

22. Attend a peer-mediated social skills training group. (36)

23. Follow rules of games and social encounters. (37)

24. Terminate dysfunctional, maladaptive, or antisocial behavior. (36, 38)

25. Verbalize positive self-descriptive statements and statements indicating confidence in self and own abilities. (39, 40)

26. Parents understand and accept their child's vision loss, seek out supports and resources to help meet their child's needs, and work collaboratively with school

positional concepts [front, back], maneuvering through traffic, crossing busy streets, riding public transportation, moving in shopping malls, planning routes of travel) (see *Children with Visual Impairments: A Parents' Guide* [Holbrook]).

7. Encourage the parents to incorporate the orientation and mobility techniques used at school into daily home routines to provide consistency and advancement of progress in movement for the student.

8. Make a home visit to assist the parents with incorporating orientation and mobility strategies into the student's movement such as getting to and from the bus, and throughout the home and yard, attending to issues of safety, use of space, and accessibility to essential items.

9. Plan instructionally sound outings in the community (e.g., grocery store, mall, park) where the student can learn new concepts of orientation and mobility and can practice skills already acquired.

10. Teach the parents the strategies of mobility their child has been taught to use in the community so there can be consistency of instruction between home and school for the student.

personnel in developing a quality treatment plan for him/her. (3, 4, 41, 42)

27. Parents report satisfaction with their child's educational program and general school progress. (43, 44, 45)

___. _____
_____

___. _____
_____

___. _____
_____

11. Provide instruction in pre-braille literacy to the student, to include training in tactile discrimination, fine motor skills, tactile tracking, concept development, access to and activities with books in braille, and writing activities in braille (see *Blind and Visually Impaired Students: Educational Service Guidelines* [Pugh and Erin]).

12. Provide specific braille instruction to the student, to include orientation to braille books, mechanics of braille reading, writing with tools (e.g., the braille writer), implementing routine use of braille reading and writing skills, learning the literacy braille code involving punctuation, numbers, and special symbols, learning nemeth braille code (math), interpreting graphic materials (e.g., charts and graphs), and eventually mastering codes (e.g., music or a foreign language) (see *Blind and Visually Impaired Students: Educational Service Guidelines* [Pugh and Erin]).

13. Provide listening practice for the student by playing tapes identified for different listening purposes that include: (1) listening for factual details; (2) selective listening in which the student must discriminate and identify certain sounds or

phrases from distracting background noise; (3) informative listening in which the student must identify the main or topic sentence in a passage; and (4) evaluative listening in which the student identifies opinions and supporting evidence (see *Teaching the Visually Limited Child* [Bishop]).

14. Have the student listen to material from a tape recorder, slowly increasing the speed at which the information is presented at each practice session to a listening maximum speed (similar to a process used to learn speed reading) (see *Teaching Children with Visual Impairments* [Best]).

15. Organize verbal directions in the classroom by giving a clear and decisive prompt that directions are being given (e.g., "Everyone listen carefully now"); make the directions concise, specific, sequential, and repeatable.

16. Assist the student in selecting classroom seating that is away from noise sources such as sinks and hallways, with close proximity to the speaker in a more quiet, well-designed space with a discrete, identifiable sound environment (see *Children with Visual Impairments* [Webster and Roe]).

17. When the student is listening to books on tape or to a

classroom lecture, provide
study notes in braille that
indicate main headings,
summarize main ideas, and
list salient questions to be
answered, or provide a basic
outline of the material to be
covered to allow the student
a guide through the mate-
rial for more effective listening (see *Teaching Children
with Visual Impairments*
[Best]).

18. Conduct a technological
    evaluation to determine
    the student's needs in rela-
    tion to assistive technology
    devices and his/her visual
    impairment.

19. Provide the student with
    low-level technology visual
    assistance equipment (e.g.,
    braille writer, magnifiers,
    telescopic devices, talking
    calculators/dictionaries/
    watches, tape recorders),
    and instruct him/her in
    their use as they relate to
    different academic and
    functional tasks.

20. Provide the student with
    high-level technology visual
    assistance equipment (e.g.,
    screen enlargement systems,
    braille translation systems,
    speech-based screen access
    technology, electronic note
    taker for the blind, systems
    that produce tactile graph-
    ics, closed-circuit televison
    system and other magnifica-
    tion devices) and instruct
    the student in their use as

they relate to different academic and functional tasks.

21. Establish a classroom environment in which advantaged lighting and contrast and distractions can be controlled to meet the individual vision needs of the student.

22. Teach the student to use an appropriate viewing posture, use of touch in combination with vision, maximum lighting, and the appropriate distance from an object all as means to maximize low vision abilities.

23. Provide advanced organizer instruction to the student in essential skills and concepts prior to the instruction in the general education classroom and review key points after the lesson in a posttutoring session (see *Children with Visual Impairments* [Webster and Roe]).

24. Provide 95 percent of instruction using a hands-on experience (e.g., models, tools, music, community-based outings).

25. Individualize the expectations for assignment completion by reducing the number of items to be learned or answered and/or adapting the time allotted for learning or task completion.

26. Offer classroom dialogue and questioning to audito-

rily involve and engage the student.

27. Increase the amount of personal assistance the student receives (e.g., paraprofessional who knows braille works one-on-one, assign a peer tutor to provide auditory information, organize a cooperative/consensus learning group for a lesson or task).

28. Allow for flexibility in how the student may respond to questions or assignments (e.g., having the student give verbal instead of written responses to tests, allowing audio-recorded answers to assignments, etc.).

29. Consider the student's learning needs, current level of achievement, and parental expectations in determining the best curriculum option: a lower grade-level curriculum, a curriculum designed for students with other special needs, use of individualized adaptations/accommodations to meet the student's visual needs.

30. Collaboratively work with the family and the student to target goals for ADLs instruction (e.g., areas of personal hygiene, eating habits, grooming), and later, IADLs skills (e.g., cooking, laundry, home care, money management), coordinating efforts between home and school.

31. Organize community-based instructional outings for the student to learn about different types of employment, to have many opportunities to meet individuals at their work, to talk with them about their jobs, and to be able to ask questions.

32. Provide opportunities for the student to interview adults with visual disabilities about their occupations, training, and experiences.

33. Teach and reinforce work habits that replicate those needed in the workplace (e.g., positive attitude, motivation, initiative, time on task, concern for quality and accuracy, punctuality).

34. Arrange for an assessment of individual abilities and interests as they relate to vocational training and/or higher education.

35. Conduct an individualized transition plan meeting in which the student and his/her family identify future goals and steps to those goals in various areas (e.g., independent living, higher education or vocational training, community involvement, leisure/recreation); include agency representatives who can contribute to the planning.

36. Engage the student in a peer-mediated social skills instructional/therapy group targeting antisocial behaviors of the blind or visually

impaired student as well as sighted peers, providing role-playing experiences, verbal feedback, and discussions of socially appropriate responses in different situations that could occur in school, at home, and in the community (see *The Development of Social Skills by Blind and Visually Impaired Students* [Sacks, Kekelis, and Gaylord-Ross]).

37. Organize environments in which the student learns to play and understand the rules of various games and activities with positive prompts from sighted peers (see *The Development of Social Skills by Blind and Visually Impaired Students* [Sacks, Kekelis, and Gaylord-Ross]).

38. Write a behavior contract with the student, targeting more serious or overt social infractions, describing desired behaviors and outcomes, establishing goals with the student, and providing incentives for change (see *The Development of Social Skills by Blind and Visually Impaired Students* [Sacks, Kekelis, and Gaylord-Ross]).

39. Provide guidance and counseling to the student in understanding issues relevant to vision loss or blindness: (1) the implications of vision loss for overall development; (2) society's attitudes and

misconceptions and the
prejudice toward individuals with visual impair-
ments; (3) similarities and
differences in all students;
(4) developing social awareness of self, others, and the
greater community; (5) promoting independence; and
(6) teaching assertiveness
techniques to express
wants, needs, goals, and
frustrations in socially acceptable ways (see *Blind
and Visually Impaired Students: Educational Service
Guidelines* [Pugh and Erin]
and *The Development of
Social Skills by Blind and
Visually Impaired Students*
[Sacks, Kekelis, and
Gaylord-Ross]).

40. Refer the student and family to a mental health professional outside the school
setting with background in
working with blind or visually impaired youth to resolve issues of depression,
anxiety, or anger manage-
ment.

41. Support the parents in their
efforts to encourage their
child in positive ways including accepting his/her
deficits and needs.

42. Provide the parents with information regarding local
support groups and national
organizations (e.g., American Council for the Blind—
Council of Families with
Visual Impairment, the National Federation of the

Blind—National Organization of Parents of Blind Children, and the National Association for Parents of the Visually Impaired.

43. Provide the parents with frequent, routine communication updates on their child's progress, needs, problems, and successes.

44. Hold communication meetings with school staff and the parents every four to six weeks or as needed to discuss needs and successes of the student and to problem solve concerns.

45. As a new school year approaches, hold a staff meeting to pass on to new teachers and staff the documentation regarding the student's strengths, weaknesses, supports, and other salient information to ensure future successes.

—. _____

_____

—. _____

_____

—. _____

_____

WRITTEN EXPRESSION

BEHAVIORAL DEFINITIONS

1. Significantly low achievement in the area of written language.
2. A deficit in revisualization impeding the ability to write spontaneously or from dictation.
3. A deficit in visual-motor integration skills impeding the execution of the handwriting process.
4. Deficits in formulation, syntax, and general language usage in written communication are apparent and significantly discrepant to oral communication.
5. Poor spelling skills.
6. Inadequate attention to, or lack of understanding of, the mechanical rules of written language (e.g., capitalization and punctuation).
7. Limited sophistication of vocabulary in writing tasks in contrast to spoken language.
8. Inability to organize thoughts and ideas into written form in a logical or sequential manner.
9. Difficulties in written language interfere with achievement in other academic areas and/or in daily living activities.

—. _____
   _____

—. _____
   _____

—. _____
   _____

LONG-TERM GOALS

1. Increase overall written expression achievement to a level commensurate with learning potential to meet basic writing needs of daily living.
2. Understand the weaknesses of written language difficulties and work to overcome or significantly improve deficit areas.
3. Improve handwriting skills to the level of potential given any motor disabilities.
4. Learn word-processing skills, technological supports (e.g., spell check), and/or voice-activated technology to gain greater independence with the writing process.
5. Attain spelling skills commensurate with potential and routinely use accommodating interventions as needed to improve the overall quality of spelling in daily work.
6. Acquire accuracy with following the mechanical rules of written language and master competent editing skills.
7. Parents accept the student's achievement deficits and provide supports to improve remedial areas.

—. _____

_____

—. _____

_____

—. _____

_____

SHORT-TERM OBJECTIVES

1. Cooperate with a hearing, vision, and/or medical examination. (1, 2)
2. Participate in a comprehensive psychoeducational evaluation. (3)
3. Participate in an occupational therapy evaluation. (4)
4. Parents participate in an interpretive meeting to discuss test results. (5)
5. Parents take part in an IEP team meeting and agree to

THERAPEUTIC INTERVENTIONS

1. Refer the student for hearing, vision, and/or medical examinations to rule out any physical impairment that could be the cause of his/her deficit in the written expression area.
2. Explore with the family any sensory modality reasons for their child's written expression difficulties (e.g., vision or hearing deficits).
3. Refer the student for a psychoeducational evaluation.

implementation of a written language improvement plan. (6)

6. Demonstrate improved spelling accuracy to a 90 percent level. (7, 8)

7. Increase accurate spelling of phonetic words to a 90 percent level. (9, 10, 11)

8. Increase accurate spelling of nonphonetic words to a 90 percent level. (12, 13, 14)

9. Effectively use spelling accommodations in daily writing tasks. (15, 16, 17)

10. Cooperate with an occupational therapist's instruction in writing skills. (18, 19)

11. Demonstrate greater competency with handwriting skills. (20, 21, 22)

12. Effectively use handwriting alternative accommodations to replace frustrations of handwriting deficits. (23)

13. Consistently demonstrate accurate knowledge and implementation of sentence structure. (24, 25, 26, 27)

14. Increase the frequency of the appropriate use of new words in writing vocabulary. (28, 29, 30, 31, 32)

15. Incorporate prewriting strategies into the writing process. (33, 34, 35, 36, 37)

16. Write an intact paragraph with a topic sentence. (38, 39, 40)

4. Refer the student for an occupational therapy evaluation.

5. School evaluation clinicians meet with the parents to discuss assessment results.

6. Conduct an IEP team meeting with the student's parents present to determine the student's eligibility for special education programs and services or to ascertain a general education plan to address his/her written expression deficits.

7. Use the cued spelling method (e.g., a 10-step process including selection of a word by the student, checking on the correct spelling of the word, reading the word together [student and peer], selecting a cue [rule] that applies to the word, and in the end, the student says the cue and writes the word independently) with the student and a peer or parent tutor to assist him/her in learning the spelling of new words (see "Cued Spelling: A Powerful Technique for Parent and Peer Tutoring" by Topping in *The Reading Teacher* [1995, 48: 374–383]).

8. Engage the student in various games to master words from the weekly spelling list (e.g., the Spelling Fortune Tellers game from *Dyslexia: Research and Resource Guide* [Spafford and Grosser]).

17. Demonstrate skills with recognizing and using correct language usage (e.g., verb tense, plurals, possessives). (41, 42)

18. Identify different purpose types of formal writing and the format for each type, addressing the voice and audience of one's writing. (43)

19. Show skill in developing a good thesis statement. (44)

20. Complete an initial draft of a paper independently and revise it for improvement. (45)

21. Identify and use the mechanical rules of written expression. (46, 47, 48)

22. Show competency with editing skills. (49, 50, 51, 52, 53)

23. Use accommodations for potential mechanical errors on in-class assignments. (54)

24. Independently word process a final draft of a formal writing piece. (55)

25. Show competent writing skills with a variety of writing formats. (56)

26. Parents demonstrate a more accepting attitude and understanding of their child's written expression deficit. (57, 58)

27. Parents report satisfaction with their child's overall school experience and progress. (59)

9. Teach a four-sense modality process whereby the student sees the word, hears the word, traces the word, feels the word, reads the word, and spells the word throughout the process (see *Remedial Techniques in Basic School Subjects* [Fernald]).

10. Provide instruction in a systematic training of sound to symbol correspondence using oral and written spelling formats, dictionary work, and handwriting practice (see *Remedial Training for Children with Specific Disability in Reading, Spelling and Penmanship* [Gillingham and Stillman]).

11. Instruct the student in a word chunking approach to pronounce words (e.g., student reads the word, then says the word one syllable at a time, and finally writes each syllable as he/she says and spells it), using auditory cues where familiar word parts and syllables are emphasized (see *Learning Disabilities: Educational Principles and Practices* [Johnson and Myklebust]).

12. Provide instructional exercises to increase visual recognition and recall (e.g., showing four choices of a word and having the student select the correct spelling).

__. _____
   _____
__. _____
   _____
__. _____
   _____

13. Move the student from partial to total recall in a visual memory spelling task in which he/she is first shown an entire word, studies its configuration and sequence of letters, and then is shown the word again but must fill in omitted letters; at the end of the exercise, the student must spell/write the entire word from recall.

14. Supply the student with a list of the most frequently used nonphonetic words, allowing him/her to refer to the list when completing a writing task.

15. Interject accommodations as needed into daily spelling and writing tasks to prevent the student from being unduly penalized for his/her spelling disability (e.g., using the underlining method—the student underlines every word he/she is uncertain of how to spell on in-class assignments, and thus, is not penalized for inaccuracy).

16. Allow the use of resources (e.g., glossaries, word banks, a poor speller's dictionary) to provide support for the student to be more accurate with spelling.

17. Introduce technological assistance (e.g., electronic spellers and computer spell checks) to enhance the student's spelling proficiency on writing tasks.

18. The occupational therapist instructs the student in the correct grasp of the writing tool, paper position, posture, motor planning skills, directionality, spatial planning, and fine motor movements as part of prewriting and writing skills to be mastered.

19. Reinforce the instructional directions of the occupational therapist as they are carried out by the student in the classroom.

20. Give handwriting instruction using the program from *Handwriting Without Tears* or *Cursive Success* (Olsen) as an alternative approach in teaching manuscript or cursive.

21. Provide models of correct letter formations for the student with revisualization difficulties so a reference is always available.

22. Teach the motor-impaired student only manuscript *or* cursive to avoid frustration.

23. Introduce alternative ways for the student to complete written tasks, including dictating to the teacher, peer, or tape recorder to obtain lecture notes from a competent peer and teaching word-processing skills to the student to use in place of handwriting.

24. Teach the basics of sentence structure (e.g., subject/predicate/noun/verb, etc.) by giv-

ing the student a format to
follow (e.g., answering questions: Which? [my], Who or
what? [dog], Does
or did? [licked], What or
whom? [the mail carrier],
Where? [on the arm]) (see
*Teaching Special Needs
Students in Regular Classrooms* [Morsink]).

25. Use a daily oral language
exercise (e.g., write out a
sentence with intentional
errors to be corrected by the
student who then tells the
teacher how to change the
sentence to eliminate errors
and replace with correc-
tions) as practice to allow
the student to locate sentence structure, spelling,
and mechanical errors.

26. Assist the student with
sentence-building activities
in which words or phrases
are pieced together by the
student to construct competent sentences, or the
teacher gives a sentence
starter and the student
finishes it with correct
structure.

27. Instruct the student in
other elements of accurate
sentence structure (e.g., recognizing run-on sentences,
sentence fragments, and
correct verb tenses).

28. Integrate weekly spelling
words with vocabulary ac-
quisition by extending word
knowledge as part of the
spelling grade require-
ments.

29. Integrate word knowledge with literature or topic in content areas by selecting salient vocabulary from this material to be learned.

30. Teach the student the benefits of using a thesaurus.

31. Have the student keep a vocabulary journal or words learned during the school year to frequently use in his/her writings.

32. Include the student in a group using vocabulary self-collection strategy in which four steps are followed: (1) The group selects words to be learned, (2) defines the words, (3) finalizes the word list, and (4) uses the chosen words in different activities (see "The Vocabulary Self-Collection Strategy: Using Student Interest and Word Knowledge to Enhance Vocabulary Growth" by Haggard in *Journal of Reading* [1986, 29: 634–642]).

33. Engage the student in a group activity involving brainstorming of topics and/or subtopics to write on, tapping into the student's prior knowledge.

34. Give the student time to reflect or think about topic choices and to make a selection (see *Writing for Learning in the Content Areas* [Wolfe and Reising]).

35. Assist the student with gathering information (zero draft) through free writing,

games, discussion, library work, and the Internet to create an outline (see *Writing for Learning in the Content Areas* [Wolfe and Reising]).

36. Teach the student to create a graphic representation of his/her ideas potentially organized in a list, chart, diagram, or web.

37. Brainstorm with the student and have the student research potential energized, colorful vocabulary which could be useful with the writing topic.

38. Teach the student to develop an organized paragraph that is logical and meaningful, and has relevant supporting details and a clearly identifiable topic sentence (e.g., provide a variety of models for the student, have the student complete a paragraph, and then give prompt, detailed feedback on his/her work).

39. As a practice activity, provide writing models in which the student must identify the topic sentence in each paragraph.

40. Provide writing models with missing paragraphs in which the student is assigned to complete the missing pieces.

41. Establish and review language usage rules, frequently using traditional

grammar texts or work-
books.

42. Focus on one language-
usage concept (e.g., plurals)
at a time (e.g., having the
student correct writing
models *only* for accurate use
of plurals).

43. Focus with the student on
different organizational
patterns of writing (e.g.,
pro/con, comparison, con-
trast, process, classification,
definition), providing models of each type for the student.

44. Have the student focus on
identifying the thesis statement in various documents
and instruct him/her as to
how to write a good thesis
statement.

45. Use the peer inquiry
method whereby small
groups of students exchange
ideas discussing potential
changes in their first draft
work (see *Writing for Learning in the Content Areas*
[Wolfe and Reising]).

46. Teach the student punctuation and capitalization (e.g.,
use a traditional grammar
text covering appropriate
lessons on such rules).

47. Give the student adequate
opportunities to practice the
rules of mechanics of written expression by editing
the writing pieces (e.g., in a
Daily Oral Language activity [see Great Source Edu-

cation Group, Wilmington, MA]).

48. Instruct the student in using the grammar check on the computer to correct inaccuracies in mechanics when word processing.

49. Teach a procedural checklist to assist the elementary student with competent proofing/editing: capitalization, organization/overall appearance, punctuation, and spelling/sentence structure (COPS, see "Learning Strategies: An Instructional Alternative for Low Achieving Adolescents" by Deschler and Schumaker in *Exceptional Children* [1986, 52(6): 583–590]).

50. Teach a procedural checklist to assist the middle school student with competent proofing/editing: sentence structure, tenses, organization/order, punctuation, spelling (STOPS, see *Strategies For Success* [Meltzer, Roditi, Haynes, Biddle, Paster, and Taber]).

51. Teach a procedural checklist to assist the high school student with competent proofing/editing: content, sentence structure, capitalization, organization, order and neatness, punctuation, spelling (C.SCOOPS, see *Strategies For Success* [Meltzer, Roditi, Haynes, Biddle, Paster, and Taber]).

52. Give practice to the student with editing skills by doing large group editing of various writing models and by giving detailed feedback to the student on some of his/her completed writing pieces.

53. When completing a first draft, have the student write or word process in a double-spaced manner to give a better visual display in which to analyze his/her own work.

54. On writing assignments completed *in class,* allow the student to make every attempt to use correct capitalization and punctuation, but to use a highlighter to identify marks and capitals he/she is uncertain of in terms of accurate application; thus the student is not penalized for mistakes on highlighted areas.

55. Provide a writing format whereby the student can integrate the skills acquired to create a competently produced final draft of a formal writing piece.

56. Organize opportunities for the student to practice completing job applications, writing creative entries in a spontaneous and/or take-home journal or in a nature journal, completing learning log entries on content subject area experiences, letter writing, and general

activities to allow writing across the curriculum.

57. Communicate with the parents frequently to keep them well informed of their child's learning needs and progress.

58. Assist the parents with seeking out information and support on writing disabilities with organizations (e.g., the International Reading Association.

59. Case manager (learning specialist, resource teacher) gathers information on the strategies and supports that are most effective for the student to share with the teacher(s) prior to the new school year.

___. _____
      _____

___. _____
      _____

___. _____
      _____

Appendix A

BIBLIOTHERAPY FOR PARENTS

Asperger's Disorder

Attwood, T. (1998). *Asperger's Syndrome: A Guide for Parents and Professionals*. Philadelphia, PA: Jessica Kingsley Publications.

Fling, E. (2000). *Eating an Artichoke: A Mother's Perspective on Asperger Syndrome*. London, United Kingdom: Jessica Kingsley Publications.

Hall, K. (2001). *Asperger's Syndrome, The Universe and Everything*. London, United Kingdom: Jessica Kingsley Publications.

Myles, B. S., and J. Southwick (1999). *Asperger Syndrome and Difficult Moments: Practical Solutions for Tantrums, Rage and Meltdowns*. Shawnee Mission, KS: Autism Asperger Publication.

Online Asperger's Syndrome Information and Support (OASIS): www .ude/edu/bkirby/asperger/ education

Tony Attwood's Website on Asperger's Syndrome: www.tonyattwood.com

Willey, L. H. (1999). *Pretending to be Normal: Living with Asperger's Syndrome*. London, United Kingdom: Jessica Kingsley Publications.

Attention-Deficit / Hyperactivity Disorder—Adolescent

Alexander-Roberts, C., and P. T. Elliott (1995). *Adhd and Teens: A Parent's Guide to Making It Through the Tough Years*. Dallas, TX: Taylor Publications.

Guyer, B. P., and E. M. Hallowell (1999). *ADHD (Attention-Deficit Hyperactivity Disorder): Achieving Success in School and in Life*. Needham Heights, MA: Allyn & Bacon.

Zeigler-Dendy, C. A. (1995). *Teenagers with ADD: A Parent's Guide*. Bethesda, MD: Woodbine House.

Attention-Deficit / Hyperactivity Disorder—Child

Barkley, R. A. (1995). *The Complete, Authoritative Guide for Parents.* New York, NY: Guilford Press.

Barkley, R. A., and C. M. Benton (1998). *Your Defiant Child: 8 Steps to Better Behavior.* New York, NY: Guilford Press.

Ingersoll, B. (1988). *Your Hyperactive Child.* New York, NY: Doubleday.

Phelan, T. W. (1996). *All About Attention Deficit Disorders.* Glen Ellyn, IL: Child Management.

Silver, L. B. (1999). *Dr. Larry Silver's Advice to Parents on Attention Deficit Hyperactivity Disorder.* New York, NY: Times Books.

Warren, U., and B. Steinberg (1994). *Helping Your Child: Untying the Knot of Attention Deficit Disorders.* New York, NY: Warner Books.

Autism

Greenspan, S. I., and S. Weider (1998). *The Child with Special Needs.* Reading, PA: Perseus Books.

McClannahan, L. E., and P. J. Krantz (1999). *Activity Schedules for Children with Autism: Teaching Independent Behaviors.* Bethesda, MD: Woodbine House.

Waltz, M. (1999). *Pervasive Developmental Disorder: Finding a Diagnosis and Getting Help.* Sebastopol, CA: O'Reilly.

Basic Reading Skills

Baumer, B. H. (1998). *How to Teach Your Dyslexic Child to Read: A Proven Method for Parents and Teachers.* Secaucus, NJ: Citadel Press.

Huford, D. M. (1998). *To Read or Not to Read: Answers to All Your Questions About Dyslexia.* New York, NY: Scribner.

Behaviorally / Emotionally Disabled—Adolescent

Forgatch, M., and G. R. Patterson (1990). *Parents and Adolescents Living Together.* Eugene, OR: Castalia.

Goleman, D. (1995). *Emotional Intelligence.* New York, NY: Bantam Books.

Phelan, T. W. (1993). *Surviving Your Adolescents: How to Manage and Let Go of Your 13 to 18 Year Olds.* Glen Ellyn, IL: Child Management.

Behaviorally / Emotionally Disabled—Child

Barkley, R. A., and C. M. Benton (1998). *Your Defiant Child: 8 Steps to Better Behavior.* New York, NY: Guilford Press.

Bloomquist, M. L. (1996). *Skills Training for Children with Behavior Disorders: A Parent and Therapist Guidebook.* New York, NY: Guilford Press.

Goleman, D. (1995). *Emotional Intelligence.* New York, NY: Bantam Books.

Greene, R. W. (1998). *The Explosive Child.* New York, NY: HarperCollins.

Greenspan, S. (1995). *The Challenging Child.* Reading, MA: Perseus Books.

Hallowell, E. M. (1997). *When You Worry About the Child You Love: Emotional and Learning Problems in Children.* New York, NY: Fireside.

McCauley, C. S., and R. Schachter (1988). *When Your Child is Afraid.* New York, NY: Simon and Schuster.

Miller, J. A. (1998). *The Childhood Depression Sourcebook.* Lincolnwood, IL: Lowell House.

Phelan, T. (1995). *1-2-3 Magic: Training Your Preschoolers and Preteens to Do What You Want.* Glen Ellyn, IL: Child Management.

Chronically Health Impaired

Freeman, J. M., E. Vining, and D. J. Pillas (1997). *Seizures and Epilepsy in Childhood: A Guide for Parents.* Baltimore, MD: The John Hopkins University Press.

Loving, G. (1993). *Parenting a Child with Diabetes.* Lincolnwood, IL: Lowell House.

General Learning Disabilities—Adolescent

Boyles, N. S., and D. Contadino (1997). *The Learning Differences Sourcebook.* Lincolnwood, IL: Lowell House.

General Learning Disabilities—Child

McNamara, F. J. (1995). *Keys to Parenting a Child with a Learning Disability.* Hauppauge, NY: Barrons Educational Series.

Rimm, S. (1996). *Dr. Sylvia Rimm's Parenting for Today: How to Parent So Children Will Learn.* New York, NY: Random Books.

Silver, L. B. (1998). *The Misunderstood Child: Understanding and Coping with Your Child's Learning Disabilities.* New York, NY: Times Books.

Smith, S. L. (1995). *No Easy Answers: The Learning Disabled Child at Home and School.* New York, NY: Bantam Books.

Hearing Impaired and Deaf

Morgan-Candlish, P. (1996). *Not Deaf Enough: Raising a Child Who is Hard of Hearing With Hugs and Humor.* Washington, DC: Alexander Graham Bell Association for the Deaf.

Ogden, P. W. (1996). *The Silent Garden: Raising Your Deaf Child.* Washington, DC: Gallaudet University Press.

Schwartz, S. (Ed.). (1996). *Choices in Deafness: A Parent's Guide to Communication Options.* Bethesda, MD: Woodbine House.

Spradley, T. S., and J. P. Spradley (1987). *Deaf Like Me.* Washington, DC: Gallaudet University Press.

Listening Comprehension

Hamaguchi, P. (1995). *Childhood Speech, Language and Listening Problems—What Every Parent Should Know.* New York, NY: John Wiley & Sons.

Mathematics Calculation

Spann, M. B. (1999). *25 Instant and Irresistible Math Board Games: Reproducible Games That Teach Essential Math Skills Including Multiplication, Fractions, Time, Money, and More.* New York, NY: Scholastic Prof Book Div.

Mathematics Reasoning

Freedman, S. D. (1997). *25 Activities Connecting Writing and Math.* New York, NY: Scholastic Trade.

Glasthal, J. B. (1997). *American History Math: 50 Problem-Solving Activities That Link Math to Key Events in U.S. History.* New York, NY: Scholastic Trade.

Mild Mentally Impaired—Adolescent

Smith, R. E., and E. Kennedy Shriver (1993). *Children with Mental Retardation: A Parent's Guide.* Bethesda, MD: Woodbine House.

Mild Mentally Impaired—Child

Pueschel, S. M. (1995). *A Parent's Guide to Down Syndrome.* Baltimore, MD: Paul H. Brookes Publishing.

Oral Expression / Language

Hamaguchi, P. (1995). *Childhood Speech, Language and Listening Problems: What Every Parent Should Know.* New York, NY: John Wiley & Sons.

Physically Health Impaired

Kent, D., and K. A. Quinlan (1997). *Extraordinary People With Disabilities.* Dansbury, CT: Children's Press.
Lutkenhoff, M. (Ed.). (1999). *Children with Spina Bifida.* Bethesda, MD: Woodbine House.

Preschool Children with Developmental Delays

Cipani, E. (1991). *A Guide to Developing Language Competencies in Preschool Children with Severe and Moderate Handicaps.* Springfield, IL: Charles C. Thomas.
Greenspan, S. I., and S. Weider (1998). *The Child with Special Needs: Encouraging Intellectual and Emotional Growth.* Boulder, CO: Perseus Press.
Newman, S. (1999). *Small Steps Forward: Using Games and Activities to Help Your Pre-School Child with Special Needs.* Philadelphia, PA: Jessica Kingsley Publications.
Schwartz, S., and J. Miller (1996). *The New Language of Toys: Teaching Communication Skills to Special-Needs Children.* Bethesda, MD: Woodbine House.

Reading Comprehension

Harvey, S., and A. Goudvis (2000). *Strategies That Work: Teaching Comprehension to Enhance Understanding*. Portland, ME: Stenhouse Publications.

Severely Multiply Impaired

Fitton, P. (1994). *Listen to Me: Communicating the Needs of People with Profound and Multiple Disabilities*. Philadephia, PA: Jessica Kingsley Publications.

Speech Disorders

Hamaguchi, P. (1995). *Childhood Speech, Language and Listening Problems: What Every Parent Should Know*. New York, NY: John Wiley & Sons.

Tourette's Disorder

Haerle, T. (1992). *Children with Tourette Syndrome: A Parent's Guide*. Bethesda, MD: Woodbine House.
Murphy, J. (1995). *Tourette's and Attention Deficit Hyperactivity Disorder: Toughing It Out at Home and at School*. Baton Rouge, LA: The Baton Rouge Tourette's Support Group.

Trainable Mentally Impaired—Adolescent

Bierne-Smith, M., R. Ittenbach, and J. R. Patton (Eds.). (1998). *Mental Retardation*. Columbus, OH: Merrill.
Trainer, M., and H. Featherstone (1991). *Differences in Common: Straight Talk on Mental Retardation, Down Syndrome, and Your Life*. Bethesda, MD: Woodbine House.

Trainable Mentally Impaired—Child

Brill, M. T. (1993). *Keys to Parenting a Child with Down Syndrome*. Hauppauge, NY: Barrons Educational Series.

Johansson, I. (1994). *Language Development in Children with Special Needs: Performative Communication.* Philadelphia, PA: Jessica Kingsley Publications.

Traumatic Brain Injury

Gronwall, D. M. A., P. Wrightson, and P. Waddell (1998). *Head Injury: The Facts: A Guide for Families and Care-Givers.* Oxford: Oxford University Press.

Winslade, W. J., and J. S. Brady (1999). *Confronting Traumatic Brain Injury: Devastation, Hope and Healing.* New Haven, CT: Yale University Press.

Violent and Dangerous

Goleman, D. (1995). *Emotional Intelligence.* New York, NY: Bantam Books.

Magid, K., and C. A. McKelvey (1989). *High Risk: Children Without a Conscience.* New York, NY: Bantam Books.

Papolos, D., and J. Papolos (1999). *The Bipolar Child.* New York, NY: Broadway Books.

Visually Impaired and Blind

Harrison, F., and M. Crow (1993). *Living and Learning with Blind Children.* Toronto: University of Toronto Press.

Holbrook, M. C. (Ed.). (1996). *Children with Visual Impairments: A Parents' Guide.* Bethesda, MD: Woodbine House.

Written Expression

Bradley-Johnson, S., and J. Lucas Lesiak (1989). *Problems in Written Expression.* New York, NY: Guilford Press.

Appendix B

BIBLIOGRAPHY FOR PROFESSIONALS

Asperger's Disorder

Cumine, V., J. Leach, and G. Stevenson (1998). *Asperger Syndrome: A Practical Guide for Teachers.* London: David Fulton Publishers.

Ehlers, S., C. Gillberg, and L. Wing (1999). "A Screening Questionnaire for Asperger Syndrome and Other High-Functioning Autism Spectrum Disorders in School Age Children." *Journal of Autism and Developmental Disorders,* 29(2): 129–141.

Fullerton, A., J. Stratton, P. Coyne, and C. Gray (1996). *High Functioning Adolescents and Young Adults with Autism.* Austin, TX: ProEd.

Klin, A., F. R. Volkmar, and S. S. Sparrow (2000). *Asperger Syndrome.* New York, NY: Guilford Press.

Mark, S. U., C. Schrader, M. Levine, C. Hagie, T. Longaker, M. Morales, and I. Peters (1999). "Social Skills for Social Ills: Supporting the Social Skills Development of Adolescents with Asperger's Syndrome." *The Council for Exceptional Children,* (Nov./Dec.: 56–61).

Rinaldi, W. (1992). *The Social Use of Language.* Windsor: NFER-Nelson.

Schopler, E., G. B. Mesibov, and L. J. Kunce (1998). *Asperger Syndrome or High-Functioning Autism?* New York, NY: Plenum Press.

Attention-Deficit / Hyperactivity Disorder—Adolescent

Barkley, R. A. (1998). *Attention-Deficit Hyperactivity Disorder: A Handbook for Diagnosis and Treatment.* New York, NY: Guilford Press.

Barkley, R. A., G. H. Edwards, and A. L. Robin (1999). *Defiant Teens: A Clinician's Manual for Assessment and Family Intervention.* New York, NY: Guilford Press.

Bender, W. N. (1997). *Understanding ADHD: A Practical Guide for Teachers and Parents.* Upper Saddle River, NJ: Prentice Hall.

DuPaul, G. J., and G. Stoner (1994). *ADHD in the Schools: Assessment and Intervention Strategies.* New York, NY: Guilford Press.

Flink, G. L. (2000). *Managing Teens with ADHD*. West Nyack, NY: The Center For Applied Research in Education.

Huggins, P., and D. Huggins (1993). *Helping Kids Handle Anger: A Validated Washington State Innovative Education Program*. Longmont, CO: Sopris West.

Huggins, P., D. W. Manion, and L. Moen (1993). *Teaching Friendship Skills, An Intermediate Version*. Longmont, CO: Sopris West.

Robin, A. L., and R. A. Barkley (1998). *Adhd in Adolescents: Diagnosis and Treatment*. New York, NY: Guilford Press.

Attention-Deficit / Hyperactivity Disorder—Child

Barkley, R. A. (1987). *Defiant Children: A Clinician's Manual for Parent Training*. New York, NY: Guilford Press.

Camp, B., and M. Bash (1981). *Think Aloud*. Champaign, IL: Research Press.

Goldstein, A. (1999). *The Prepare Curriculum: Teaching Prosocial Competencies*. Champaign, IL: Research Press.

Goldstein, S., and M. Goldstein (1992). *Hyperactivity—Why Won't My Child Pay Attention?* New York, NY: John Wiley & Sons.

Hinshaw, S. P. (1994). *Attention Deficits and Hyperactivity in Children*. Thousand Oaks, CA: Sage.

Paniagua, F. A., P. B. Morrison, and S. A. Black (1988). "Clinical Effects of Correspondence Training in the Management of Hyperactive Children." *Behavioral and Residential Treatment*, 3: 19–40.

Phelan, T. (1996). *All About Attention Deficit Disorders*. Glen Ellyn, IL: Child Management.

Autism

Earles, T. L., J. K. Carlson, and S. J. Bock (1998). Instructional Strategies to Facilitate Successful Learning Outcomes for Students with Autism. In R. L. Simpson and B. Smith Myles (Eds.), *Educating Children and Youth with Autism*. Austin, TX: ProEd.

Fullerton, A., J. Stratton, P. Coyne, and C. Gray (1996). *Higher Functioning Adolescents and Young Adults with Autism*. Austin, TX: ProEd.

Gerlach, E. K. (1993). *Autism Treatment Guide*. Arlington, TX: Future Horizons.

Gray, C. (2000). *The New Social Stories: Illustrated Edition*. Arlington, TX: Future Horizons.

Hodgdon, L. A. (1996). *Visual Strategies for Improving Communication.* Troy, MI: Quirk Roberts Publishing.

Koegel, R. L., and L. K. Koegel (1995). *Teaching Children with Autism.* Baltimore, MD: Paul H. Brookes Publishing.

McClannahan, L. E., and P. J. Krantz (1999). *Activity Schedules for Children with Autism: Teaching Independent Behavior.* Bethesda, MD: Woodbine House.

Mesibov, G. B., L. W. Adams, and L. G. Klinger. (1997). *Autism—Understanding the Disorder.* New York, NY: Plenum Press.

Olsen, J. Z. (1998). *Handwriting Without Tears.* Potomac, MD.

Penning, M. (1992). *A Language/Communication Curriculum for Students with Autism and Other Language Impairments.* Lansing, MI: Citizens Alliance to Uphold Special Education.

Quill, K. A. (1995). *Teaching Children with Autism.* New York, NY: Delmar Publishers.

Richard, G. L. (1997). *The Source for Autism.* East Moline, IL: Lingui Systems.

Sigman, M., and L. Capps (1997). *Children with Autism: A Developmental Perspective.* Cambridge, MA: Harvard University Press.

Simpson, R. L., and B. Smith Myles (1998). *Educating Children and Youth with Autism.* Austin, TX: ProEd.

Basic Reading Skills

Adams, M. J., B. R. Foorman, I. Lundberg, and T. Beeler (1998). *Phonemic Awareness in Young Children—A Classroom Curriculum.* Baltimore, MD: Paul H. Brookes Publishing.

Clay, M. M. (1988). *The Early Detection of Reading Difficulties.* Auckland, New Zealand: Heinemann Educational Books.

Council for Exceptional Children—Division for Learning Disabilities, 1920 Association Dr., Reston, VA 22091.

Fernald, G. M. (L. Idol, Ed.). (1988). *Remedial Techniques in Basic School Subjects.* Austin, TX: ProEd.

Gillingham, A., and B. W. Stillman (1966). *Remedial Training For Children With Specific Disability in Reading, Spelling and Penmanship.* Cambridge, MA: Educators Publishing.

Glass, G. G., and E. W. Glass (1994). *Glass Analysis for Decoding Only.* Garden City, NY.

Honert, D. V. D. (1985). *Reading From Scratch/RFS.* Cambridge, MA: Educators Publishing.

International Reading Association, P.O. Box 8139, Newark, DE 19711.

Jenkins, J. R., B. Matlock, and T. A. Slocum (1989). "Two Approaches to Vocabulary Instruction: The Teaching of Individual Word Meanings and Practice in Deriving Word Meaning from Context." *Reading Research Quarterly,* 24: 215–235.

Layton, L., K. Deeny, and G. Upton (1998). *Sound Practice: Phonological Awareness in the Classroom.* London: David Fulton Publishers.

Lindamood, C. H., and P. C. Lindamood (1975). *The Lindamood Auditory Discrimination In-Depth Program.* Higham, MA: Teaching Resources.

Manzo, A. V., and U. C. Manzo (1993). *Literacy Disorders: Holistic Diagnosis and Remediation.* New York, NY: Harcourt Brace Jovanovich.

Meltzer, L. J., B. N. Roditi, D. P. Haynes, K. R. Biddle, M. Paster, and S. E. Taber (1996). *Strategies For Success.* Austin, TX: ProEd.

Slingerland, B. H. (1976). *A Multi-Sensory Approach to Language Arts for Specific Language Disability Children: A Guide for Primary Teachers.* Cambridge, MA: Educators Publishing.

Spafford, C. S., and G. S. Grosser (1996). *Dyslexia: Research and Resource Guide.* Needham, MA: Allyn & Bacon.

Spaulding, R. B., and W. T. Spaulding (1990). *The Writing Road to Reading.*

Taba, H. (1967). *Teacher's Handbook for Elementary Social Studies.* Reading, MA: Addison Wesley.

Behaviorally / Emotionally Impaired—Adolescent

Brooks, B. L., and D. A. Sabatino (Eds.). (1996). *Personal Perspectives on Emotional Disturbance/Behavioral Disorders.* Austin, TX: ProEd.

Clarizio, H. F. (1980). *Toward Positive Classroom Discipline.* New York, NY: John Wiley & Sons.

Federation of Families for Children's Mental Health, Alexandria, VA 22314, (703) 684-7710.

Goldstein, A. P., B. Glick, and J. C. Gibbs (1998). *Aggression Replacement Training—A Comprehensive Intervention for Aggressive Youth.* Champaign, IL: Research Press.

Goldstein, A. P., and E. McGinnis (1997). *Skillstreaming the Adolescent: New Strategies and Perspectives for Teaching Prosocial Skills.* Champaign, IL: Research Press.

Lobitz, W. C. (1974). "A Simple Stimulus Cue for Controlling Disruptive Classroom Behavior." *Journal of Abnormal Child Psychology,* 2: 143–152.

Meichenbaum, D. H. (1977). *Cognitive-Behavior Modification.* New York, NY: Plenum Press.

Michigan Department of Education—Office of Special Education and Early Intervention Services. (2000). *Positive Behavior Support for*

ALL Michigan Students: Creating Environments That Assure Learning. Charlotte, MI: Eaton Intermediate School District.

National Alliance for the Mentally Ill, 200 North Glebe Rd., Suite 1015, Arlington, VA 22203, (800) 950-6264 Youth Family Outreach.

Ninness, H. A., S. S. Glenn, and J. Ellis (1993). *Assessment and Treatment of Emotional or Behavioral Disorders.* Westport, CT: Praeger.

Pauk, W. (1984). *How to Study in College.* Boston, MA: Houghton Mifflin.

Robinson, F. P. (1970). *Effective Study.* New York, NY: Harper and Row.

Salend, S. J., N. R. Jantzen, and K. Giek. (1992). "Using a Peer Confrontation System in a Group Setting." *Behavior Disorders,* 17: 211–218.

Walker, H. M., B. Todis, D. Holmes, and G. Horton (1987). *The ACCESS Program: Adolescent Curriculum for Communication and Effective Social Skills.* Austin, TX: ProEd.

Young, K. R., R. P. West, D. J. Smith, and D. P. Morgan (2000). *Teaching Self-Management Strategies to Adolescents.* Longmont, CO: Sopris West.

Zimmerman, B. F. (2000). *On Our Best Behavior: Positive Behavior-Management Strategies for the Classroom.* Horsham, PA: LRP Publications.

Behaviorally / Emotionally Impaired—Child

Barkley, R. A. (1987). *Defiant Children: A Clinician's Manual for Parent Training.* New York, NY: Guilford Press.

Bloomquist, M. L. (1996). *Skills Training for Children with Behavior Disorders: A Parent and Therapist Guidebook.* New York, NY: Guilford Press.

Burton, J. E., and L. A. Rasmussen (1998). *Treating Children with Sexually Abusive Behavior Problems.* Binghamton, NY: The Haworth Press.

Camp, B., and M. Bash (1981). *Think Aloud.* Champaign, IL: Research Press.

Clarizio, H. F. (1980). *Toward Positive Classroom Discipline.* New York, NY: John Wiley & Sons.

Federation of Families for Children's Mental Health, Alexandria, VA 22314, (703) 684-7710.

Goldstein, A. (1999). *The Prepare Curriculum: Teaching Prosocial Competencies.* Champaign, IL: Research Press.

Jongsma, A. E., L. M. Peterson, and W. P. McInnis (2000). *The Child Psychotherapy Treatment Planner, Second Edition.* New York, NY: John Wiley & Sons.

Lennox, D. (1991). *See Me After School: Understanding and Helping Children with Emotional and Behavioral Difficulties.* London: David Fulton Publishers.

McNamara, S., and G. Moreton (1995). *Changing Behaviour: Teaching Children with Emotional and Behavioral Difficulties in Primary and Secondary Classrooms.* London: David Fulton Publishers.

Michigan Department of Education—Office of Special Education and Early Intervention Services (2000). *Positive Behavior Support for ALL Michigan Students: Creating Environments That Assure Learning.* Charlotte, MI: Eaton Intermediate School District.

Morgan, S. R., and J. A. Reinhart (1991). *Interventions for Students with Emotional Disorders.* Austin, TX: ProEd.

Newcomer, P. L. (1980). *Understanding and Teaching Emotionally Disturbed Children.* Boston, MA: Allyn & Bacon.

Ninness, H. A., S. S. Glenn, and J. Ellis (1993). *Assessment and Treatment of Emotional or Behavioral Disorders.* Westport, CT: Praeger.

Rhode, G., W. R. Jenson, and H. K. Reavis (1992). *The Tough Kid Book, Practical Classroom Management Strategies.* Longmont, CO: Sopris West.

Robinson, F. P. (1970). *Effective Study.* New York, NY: Harper and Row.

Salend, S. J., N. R. Jantzen, and K. Giek (1992). "Using a Peer Confrontation System in a Group Setting." *Behavior Disorders,* 17: 211–218.

Shelton, T., A. Anastopoulous, and J. Linden (1985). "An Attribution Training Program with Learning Disabled Children." *Journal of Learning Disabilities,* 18(5): 261–265.

Sheridan, S. (1995). *The Tough Kid Social Skills Book.* Longmont, CO: Sopris West.

Walker, H. M., and N. K. Buckley (1972). "Programming Generalization and Maintenance of Treatment Effects Across Time and Across Settings." *Journal of Applied Behavior Analysis,* 5: 209–224.

Zimmerman, B. F. (2000). *On Our Best Behavior: Positive Behavior-Management Strategies for the Classroom.* Horsham, PA: LRP Publications.

Chronically Health Impaired

Mesec, A. L., and C. H. Fraser (1997). *Serious Illness in the Classroom.* Englewood, CO: Teacher Ideas Press.

Michael, R. J. (1995). *The Educator's Guide to Students with Epilepsy.* Springfield, IL: Charles C. Thomas.

Perske, R., and M. Perske (1988). *Circle of Friends.* Nashville, TN: Abingdon Press.

Synoground, S. G., and M. C. Kelsey (1990). *Health Care Problems in the Classroom.* Springfield, IL: Charles C. Thomas.

Tompkins, W. W., and T. P. Shannon (1993). *Student Health Problems: An Educator's References.* Albany, NY: Delmar Publishers.

Wishnietsky, D. B., and D. H. Wishnietsky (1996). *Managing Chronic Illness in the Classroom.* Bloomington, IN: Phi Delta Kappa Educational Foundation.

General Learning Disabilities—Adolescent

Learning Disabilities Association of America, Pittsburgh, PA.

Lenz, B. K. (1996). *Teaching Learning Strategies to Adolescents and Adults with Learning Disabilities.* Austin, TX: ProEd.

Lenz, B. K., F. C. Clark, D. D. Deshler, J. B. Schumaker, and J. A. Rademacher (Eds.). (1990). *SIM Training Library: The Strategies Instructional Approach.* Lawrence, KS: University of Kansas Center for Research on Learning.

Lenz, B. K., E. S. Ellis, and D. Scanlon (1996). *Teaching Learning Strategies to Adolescents and Adults with Learning Disabilities.* Austin, TX: ProEd.

McNamara, B. E. (1998). *Learning Disabilities—Appropriate Practices for a Diverse Population.* Albany, NY: State University of New York Press.

Meichenbaum, D. (1985). Teaching Thinking: A Cognitive-Behavioral Perspective. In S. F. Chipman, J. W. Segal, and R. Glaser (Eds.), *Thinking and Learning Skills: Vol. 2: Research and Open Questions.* Hillsdale, NJ: Erlbaum.

Meltzer, L. J. (1993). *Strategy Assessment and Instruction for Students with Learning Disabilities.* Austin, TX: ProEd.

Mercer, Cecil D. (1997). *Students with Learning Disabilities, Fifth Edition.* Upper Saddle River, NJ: Prentice Hall.

National Center for Learning Disabilities, New York, NY.

Patton, J. R., and G. Blalock (1996). *Transition and Students with Learning Disabilities.* Austin, TX: ProEd.

Pauk, W. (1984). *How to Study in College.* Boston, MA: Houghton Mifflin.

Robinson, F. P. (1970). *Effective Study.* New York, NY: Harper and Row.

Sabornie, E. J., and L. U. deBettencourt (1997). *Teaching Students with Mild Disabilities at the Secondary Level.* Upper Saddle River, NJ: Merrill.

Varnhagen, C. K., and S. R. Goldman (1986). "Improving Comprehension: Causal Relations Instruction for Learning Handicapped Learners." *The Reading Teacher,* 39: 896–904.

General Learning Disabilities—Child

Duffy, G., L. R. Roehler, and D. Reinsmoen (1981). *Two Styles of Direct Instruction in Teaching Second-Grade Reading and Language Arts: A Descriptive Study.* East Lansing, MI: Institute for Research on Teaching, Michigan State University.

Ingersoll, B. D., and S. Goldstein (1993). *Attention Deficit Disorder and Learning Disabilities—Realities, Myths, and Controversial Treatments.* New York, NY: Doubleday.

Learning Disabilities Association of America, Pittsburgh, PA.

McNamara, B. E. (1998). *Learning Disabilities—Appropriate Practices for a Diverse Population.* Albany, NY: State University of New York Press.

Meltzer, L. J., B. N. Roditi, D. P. Haynes, K. R. Biddle, M. Paster, and S. E. Taber (1996). *Strategies For Success.* Austin, TX: ProEd.

National Center for Learning Disabilities, New York, NY.

Palinscar, A. S., and D. A. Brown (1984). "Reciprocal Teaching of Comprehension-Fostering and Comprehension-Monitoring Activities." *Cognition and Instruction,* 1: 117–175.

Robinson, F. P. (1970). *Effective Study.* New York, NY: Harper and Row.

Shelton, T., A. Anastopoulous, and J. Linden (1985). "An Attribution Training Program with Learning Disabled Children." *Journal of Learning Disabilities,* 18(5): 261–265.

Winebrenner, S. (1996). *Teaching Kids with Learning Difficulties in the Regular Classroom.* Minneapolis, MN: Free Spirit Publishing.

Wong, B. (1982). *Metacognition and Learning Disabilities.* Gaithersburg, MD: Aspen Systems.

Hearing Impaired and Deaf

Alexander Graham Bell Association for the Deaf, 3417 Volta Place N.W., Washington, DC 20007-2778.

American Speech, Language and Hearing Association, 10801 Rockville Pike, Rockville, MD 20852-3279.

Beazley, S., and M. Moore (1995). *Deaf Children, Their Families and Professionals.* London: David Fulton Publishers.

Bigge, J. (1988). *Curriculum Based Instruction for Special Education Students.* Mountain View, CA: Mayfield Publishing.

Dodd, B. (1995). *Differential Diagnosis and Treatment of Children with Speech Disorders.* San Diego, CA: Singular Publishing Group.

Johnson, D., and P. Pearson (1984). *Teaching Reading Vocabulary.* New York, NY: Holt, Rinehart and Winston.

Jones, B., J. Pierce, and B. Hunter (1989). "Teaching Students to Construct Graphic Representations." *Educational Leadership,* 46(4): 20–26.

Luetke-Stahlman, B., and J. Luchner. (1990). *Effectively Educating Students with Hearing Impairments.* White Plains, NY: Longman Publishing.

Nevins, M. E., and P. M. Chute (1996). *Children with Cochlear Implants in Educational Settings.* San Diego, CA: Singular Publishing Group.

Palmer, L. (1988). "Speechreading as Communication." *Volta Review,* 90(50): 33–44.

Plante, E., and P. M. Beeson (1999). *Communication and Communication Disorders.* Needham Heights, MA: Allyn & Bacon.

Listening Comprehension

Chamberlain, C. E., and R. M. Strode (1999). *The Source for Down Syndrome.* East Moline, IL: Lingui Systems.

Paul, R. (1995). *Language Disorders from Infancy through Adolescence: Assessment and Intervention.* St. Louis, MO: Mosby-Year Book.

Stauffer, R. G. (1975). *Directing the Reading-Thinking Process.* New York, NY: Harper and Row.

Tompkins, G. E., and K. Hoskisson (1991). *Language Arts—Content and Teaching Strategies.* New York, NY: Macmillan Publishing.

Watson, L. R., E. Crais, and T. L. Layton (2000). *Handbook of Early Language Impairment in Children: Assessment and Treatment.* Albany, NY: Delmar Publishers.

White, G. (1998). *Listening.* Oxford: Oxford University Press.

Mathematics Calculation

Bley, N. S., and C. A. Thornton (1989). *Teaching Mathematics to the Learning Disabled, Second Edition.* Austin, TX: ProEd.

Bullock, J., S. Pierce, and L. McClellan (1989). *Touch Math.* Colorado Springs, CO: Innovative Learning Concepts.

Cawley, J. F., A. M. Fitzmaurice-Hayes, and R. A. Shaw (1988). *Mathematics for the Mildly Handicapped: A Guide to Curriculum and Instruction.* Newton, MA: Allyn & Bacon.

Conquering Math Series, MECC, 6160 Summit Drive North, Minneapolis, MN.

Davidson, J. (1996). *Mega Math Blaster.* Torrance, CA: Davidson & Associates.

Enright, B. C. (1983). *Enright Diagnostic Inventory of Basic Arithmetic Skills*. North Billerica, MA: Curriculum Associates.

Language Master, Eiki International, Lake Forest, CA.

Meltzer, L. J., B. N. Roditi, D. P. Haynes, K. R. Biddle, M. Paster, and S. E. Taber (1996). *Strategies For Success: Classroom Teaching Techniques for Students with Learning Problems*. Austin, TX: ProEd.

Mathematics Reasoning

Bley, N. S., and C. A. Thornton (1989). *Teaching Mathematics to the Learning Disabled, Second Edition*. Austin, TX: ProEd.

Bos, C. S., and S. Vaughn (1991). *Strategies for Teaching Students with Learning and Behavior Problems, Second Edition*. Needham Heights, MA: Allyn & Bacon.

Exploring Measurement, Time and Money by IBM Special Needs Information Referral Center, P.O. Box 2150, Atlanta, GA.

Forgan, H. W., and C. T. Mangrum (1989). *Teaching Content Area Reading Skills*. Columbus, OH: Merrill.

Meltzer, L. J., B. N. Roditi, D. P. Haynes, K. R. Biddle, M. Paster, and S. E. Taber (1996). *Strategies For Success*. Austin, TX: ProEd.

Midkiff, R. B., and R. D. Thomasson (1993). *A Practical Approach to Using Learning Styles in Math Instruction*. Springfield, IL: Charles C. Thomas.

Montague, M., and C. S. Bos (1986). "The Eight Steps in the Verbal Math Problem Solving Strategy." *Journal of Learning Disabilities,* 19: 27–28.

Polya, G. (1945). *How To Solve It*. Princeton, NJ: Princeton University Press.

Reyes, B. J. (1986). Teaching Computational Estimation: Concepts and Strategies. In H. L. Schoen and M. J. Zweng (Eds.), *National Estimation and Mental Computation: 1986 Yearbook*. Reston, VA: National Council of Teachers of Mathematics.

Spafford, C. S., and G. S. Grosser (1996). *Dyslexia: Research and Resource Guide*. Needham Heights, MA: Allyn & Bacon.

Stiff, L. V., and F. R. Curcio (1999). *Developing Mathematical Reasoning in Grades K–12: 1999 Yearbook*. Reston, VA: National Council of Teachers of Mathematics.

Survival Math by Wings for Learning/Sunburst Communications, 1600 Green Hill Road, P.O. Box 66002, Scotts Valley, CA.

Mild Mentally Impaired—Adolescent

Brolin, D. E. (1989). *Life-Centered Career Education: A Competency Based Approach.* Reston, VA: The Council for Exceptional Children.

Deschler, D. D., and J. B. Schumaker (1986). "Learning Strategies: An Instructional Alternative for Low Achieving Adolescents." *Exceptional Children,* 52(6): 583–590.

Englemann, S., W. Becker, S. Hanner, and G. Johnson (1980). *Corrective Reading Program.* Chicago: Science Research.

Fernald, G. M. (1988). *Remedial Techniques in Basic School Subjects: Methods for Teaching Dyslexics and Other Learning Disabled.* Austin, TX: ProEd.

Frederick, M. M., R. D. Postman, S. J. Leinwand, and L. R. Wantuck (1989). *Practical Mathematics: Consumer Applications.* Austin, TX: Holt, Rinehart and Winston.

Graham, S., and K. R. Harris (1987). "Improving Composition Skills of Inefficient Learners with Self-Instructional Strategy Training." *Topics in Language Disorders,* 7: 66–77.

Hickson, L., L. S. Blackman, and E. M. Reis. (1995). *Mental Retardation: Foundations of Educational Programming.* Needham Heights, MA: Allyn & Bacon.

McDonnell, J., B. Wilcox and M. L. Hardman (1991). *Secondary Programs for Students with Developmental Disabilities.* Needham Heights, MA: Allyn & Bacon.

McIntosh, R., S. Vaugh, and D. Bennerson (1995). "Fast Social Skills with a Slam and a Rap: Providing Social Skills Training for Students with Learning Disabilities." *Teaching Exceptional Children,* 28: 37–41.

Morsink, C. V. (1987). *Teaching Special Needs Students in the Regular Classroom.* New York, NY: Harper Collins College.

Palinscar, A. S., and A. L. Brown (1984). "Reciprocal Teaching of Comprehension-Fostering and Comprehension-Monitoring Activities." *Cognition and Instruction,* 1: 117–175.

Sabornie, E. J., and L. U. deBettencourt (1997). *Teaching Students with Mild Disabilities at the Secondary Level.* Upper Saddle River, NJ: Prentice Hall.

Schumaker, J. B., P. H. Denton, and D. D. Deschler (1984). *Learning Strategies Curriculum: The Paraphrasing Strategy.* Lawrence, KS: University of Kansas.

Schumaker, J. B., and J. Sheldon (1985). *Learning Strategies Curriculum: The Sentence Writing Strategy.* Lawrence, KS: University of Kansas.

Thomas, E. G. (1996). *Teaching Students with Mental Retardation: A Life Goal Curriculum Planning Approach.* Englewood, NJ: Prentice Hall.

Wehman, P. (1981). *Competitive Employment.* Baltimore, MD: Brookes.

Will, M. C. (1984). *OSERS Programming for the Transition of Youth with Disabilities: Bridges from School to Working Life.* Washington, DC: Office of Special Education and Rehabilitation Services, U.S. Department of Education.

Mild Mentally Impaired—Child

Barr, R., and B. Johnson (1991). *Teaching Reading in the Elementary School.* New York, NY: Longman Publishing.

Bullock, J., S. Pierce, and L. McClelland (1989). *Touch Math.* Innovative Learning Concepts.

Cawley, J., J. Miller, and S. Carr (1989). In G. A. Robinson, J. R. Patton, E. A. Polloway, and L. R. Sargent (Eds.), *Best Practices in Mild Mental Disabilities* (pp. 67–85). Reston, VA: The Division on Mental Retardation of the Council for Exceptional Children.

Chaffin, J., and B. Maxwell (1982). *Academic Skill Builders in Math.* Allen, TX: Developmental Learning Materials.

Fernald, G. M. (1988). *Remedial Techniques in Basic School Subjects: Methods for Teaching Dyslexics and Other Learning Disabled.* Austin, TX: ProEd.

Glass, G. G., and E. W. Glass (1994). *Glass Analysis for Decoding Only.* Garden City, NY.

Heckelman, R. G. (1969). "A Neurological-Impress Method of Remedial-Reading Instruction." *Academic Therapy,* 4: 277–282.

Hickson, L., L. S. Blackman, and E. M. Reis (1995). *Mental Retardation—Foundations of Educational Programming.* Needham Heights, MA: Allyn & Bacon.

Leon, J., and H. Pepe (1983). "Self-Instruction Training: Cognitive Behavior Modification for Remediating Arithmetic Deficits." *Exceptional Children,* 50(1): 54–60.

McIntosh, R., S. Vaugh, and D. Bennerson (1995). "Fast Social Skills with a Slam and a Rap: Providing Social Skills Training for Students with Learning Disabilities." *Teaching Exceptional Children,* 28: 37–41.

Orelove, F. P., and D. Sobsey (1987). *Educating Children with Multiple Disabilities.* Baltimore, MD: Brookes.

Quigley, S. P., C. M. King, P. L. McAnally, and S. Rose (1991). *Reading Milestones.* Austin, TX: ProEd.

Taylor, G. R. (1998). *Curriculum Strategies for Teaching Social Skills to the Disabled.* Springfield, IL: Charles C. Thomas.

Thomas, G. E. (1996). *Teaching Students with Mental Retardation.* Englewood Cliffs, NJ: Prentice Hall.

Oral Expression / Language

American Speech-Language-Hearing Association, 10801 Rockville Pike, Rockville, MD 20852.

Bernstein, D. K., and E. Tiegerman (1993). *Language and Communication Disorders in Children.* New York, NY: Macmillan Publishing.

Chamberlain, C. E., and R. M. Strode (1999). *The Source for Down Syndrome.* East Moline, IL: Lingui Systems.

Downing, J. (1987). "Conversational Skills Training: Teaching Adolescents with Mental Retardation to be Verbally Assertive." *Mental Retardation,* 25: 147–155.

German, D. J. (1992). "Word-Finding Interventions for Children and Adolescents." *Topics in Language Disorders,* 13(1): 33–50.

Lloyd, P., E. Baker, and J. Dunn (1984). Children's Awareness of Communication. In C. Garvey, L. Feagans, and R. Golinhoff (Eds.), *The Origins and Growth of Communication* (pp. 281–296). Norwood, NJ: Ablex.

Mercer, C. D. (1997). *Students with Learning Disabilities.* Upper Saddle River, NJ: Prentice Hall.

Nagy, W. E., R. C. Anderson, and P. A. Herman (1987). "Learning Word Meanings From Context During Normal Reading." *American Educational Research Journal,* 24: 237–270.

Nelson, C. D. (1991). *Practical Procedures for Children with Language Disorders.* Austin, TX: ProEd.

Nelson, N. W. (1998). *Childhood Language Disorders in Context.* Needham Heights, MA: Allyn & Bacon.

Owens, R. E. (1991). *Language Disorders.* Needham Heights, MA: Allyn & Bacon.

Pressley, M., J. R. Levin, and G. E. Miller (1981). "How Does the Keyword Method Affect Vocabulary Comprehension and Usage?" *Reading Research Quarterly,* 16: 213–225.

Taba, H. (1967). *Teacher's Handbook for Elementary Social Studies.* Reading, MA: Addison Wesley.

Watson, L. R., E. Crais, and T. L. Layton (2000). *Handbook of Early Language Impairment in Children: Assessment and Treatment.* Albany, NY: Delmar Publishers.

Physically Health Impaired

Bigge, J. L. (1991). *Teaching Individuals with Physical and Multiple Disabilities.* New York, NY: Merrill/Macmillan Publishing.

Brolin, D. E. (1989). *Life-Centered Career Education: A Competency-Based Approach.* Reston, VA: The Council for Exceptional Children.

Halliday, P. (1989). *Special Needs in Ordinary Schools: Children with Physical Disabilities.* London: Cassell Educational Limited.

Hill, J. L. (1999). *Meeting the Needs of Students with Special Physical and Health Care Needs.* Upper Saddle River, NJ: Merrill/Prentice Hall.

Koppenhaver, D. A., and D. Yoder (1989). "A Spelling Study Strategy for Physically Disabled Augmentative Communication Users." *Communication Outlook,* 10(3): 10–12.

Ross, A. O. (1964). *The Exceptional Child in the Family.* New York, NY: Grune & Stratton.

Rowley-Kelly, F. L., and D. H. Riegel (1993). *Teaching the Student with Spina Bifida.* Baltimore, MD: Paul H. Brookes Publishing.

Sowers, J., and L. Powers (1991). *Vocational Preparation and Employment of Students with Physical and Multiple Disabilities.* Baltimore, MD: Paul H. Brookes Publishing.

Synoground, S. G., and J. C. Kelsey (1990). *Health Care Problems in the Classroom.* Springfield, IL: Charles C. Thomas.

Wallace, G., and J. M. Kauffman (1986). *Teaching Children with Learning and Behavior Problems.* Columbus, OH: Merrill.

Preschool Children with Developmental Delays

Allen, K. E. (1992). *The Exceptional Child: Mainstreaming in Early Childhood Education.* Albany, NY: Delmar Publishers.

Bailey, D. B., and M. Wolery-Allegheny (1992). *Teaching Infants and Preschoolers with Disabilities.* Upper Saddle River, NJ: Merrill.

Bondurant-Utz, J. A., and L. B. Luciano (1994). *A Practical Guide to Infant and Preschool Assessment in Special Education.* Needham Heights, MA: Allyn & Bacon.

Cavallaro, C. C., and M. Haney (1999). *Preschool Inclusion.* Baltimore, MD: Paul H. Brookes Publishing.

Cook, R. E., A. Tessier, and M. D. Klein (1992). *Adapting Early Childhood Curricula for Children with Special Needs.* New York, NY: Macmillan Publishing.

Davis, M. D., J. L. Kilgo, and M. Gamel-McCormick (1998). *Young Children with Special Needs: A Developmentally Appropriate Approach.* Needham Heights, MA: Allyn & Bacon.

Division for Early Childhood of the Council for Exceptional Children, 1920 Association Drive, Reston, VA 20191-1589.

Exceptional Parent (a subscription journal) P.O. Box 3000, Department EP, Denville, NJ 07834 (877) 372-7368.

Federation for Children with Special Needs, 95 Berkley St., Suite 104, Boston, MA 02116, (617) 482-2915.

Howard, V. F., B. F. Williams, P. D. Port, and C. Lepper (1997). *Very Young Children with Special Needs: A Formative Approach for the Twenty-First Century.* Upper Saddle River, NJ: Prentice Hall.

Odom, S. L., and M. E. McLean (1996). *Early Intervention/Early Childhood Special Education: Recommended Practices.* Austin, TX: ProEd.

Peck, C. A., S. L. Odom, and D. D. Bricker (1993). *Integrating Young Children with Disabilities into Community Programs.* Baltimore, MD: Paul H. Brookes Publishing.

Wilson, R. A. (1998). *Special Educational Needs in the Early Years.* New York, NY: Routledge.

Reading Comprehension

Bigman-Skidell, M., and S. G. Becker (1998). *Main Idea, The: Reading to Learn.* Needham Heights, MA: Allyn & Bacon.

Cooper, J. D. (1999). *Literacy: Helping Children Construct Meaning.* Boston, MA: Houghton Mifflin College.

Council for Exceptional Children—Division for Learning Disabilities, 1920 Association Dr., Reston, VA 22091.

Heckelman, R. G. (1969). "A Neurological-Impress Method of Remedial-Reading Instruction." *Academic Therapy,* 4: 277–282.

International Reading Association, P.O. Box 8139, Newark, DE 19711.

Lazarus, B. D. (1991). "Guided Notes, Review and Achievement of Learning Disabled Adolescents in Secondary Mainstream Settings." *Education and Treatment of Children,* 14: 112–128.

Mandler, J. M. (1984). *Stories, Scripts and Scenes: Aspects of a Schema Theory.* Hilldale, NJ: Erlbaum.

Reutzel, R. D. (1985). "Story Maps Improve Comprehension." *The Reading Teacher,* 38: 400–405.

Robb, L. (1999). *Easy Mini-Lessons for Building Vocabulary: Practical Strategies That Boost Word Knowledge and Reading Comprehension.* New York, NY: Scholastic Paperbacks.

Simpson, M. L., C. G. Hayes, N. Stahl, R. T. Connor, and D. Weaver (1988). "An Initial Validation of a Study Strategy System." *Journal of Reading Behavior,* 20: 149–180.

Taylor, B. M., M. F. Graves, and P. Van Den Broek (2000). *Reading for Meaning—Fostering Comprehension in the Middle Grades*. New York, NY: Teachers College Press.

Tonjes, M., R. Wolpow, and M. Zintz (1999). *Integrated Content Literacy*. Boston, MA: McGraw-Hill College.

Tovani, C., and E. O. Keene (2000). *I Read It, But I Don't Get It: Comprehension Strategies for Adolescent Readers*. Portland, ME: Stenhouse Publications.

Varnhagen, C. K., and S. R. Goldman (1986). "Improving Comprehension: Causal Relations Instruction for Learning Handicapped Learners." *The Reading Teacher,* 39: 896–904.

Wallace, G., S. C. Larsen, and L. K. Elksnin (1992). *Educational Assessment of Learning Problems: Testing for Teaching*. Boston, MA: Allyn & Bacon.

Severely Multiply Impaired

Bigge, J. L. (1991). *Teaching Individuals with Physical and Multiple Disabilities*. New York, NY: Macmillan Publishing.

Brimer, R. W. (1990). *Students with Severe Disabilities: Current Responses and Practices*. Mountain View, CA: Mayfield Publishing.

Cipani, E. C., and F. Spooner (1994). *Curricular and Instructional Approaches for Persons with Severe Disabilities*. Needham Heights, MA: Allyn & Bacon.

Orelove, F. P., and D. Sobsey (1996). *Educating Children with Multiple Disabilities: A Transdisciplinary Approach*. Baltimore, MD: Paul H. Brookes Publishing.

Romski, M. A., and R. A. Sevcik (1996). *Breaking the Speech Barrier: Language Development Through Augmented Means*. Baltimore, MD: Paul H. Brookes Publishing.

Sowers, J., and L. Powers (1991). *Vocational Preparation and Employment of Students with Physical and Multiple Disabilities*. Baltimore, MD: Paul H. Brookes Publishing.

Wehman, P. (1981). *Competitive Employment*. Baltimore, MD: Paul H. Brookes Publishing.

Wehman, P., and S. Schleien (1980a). "Assessment and Selection of Leisure Skills for Severely and Profoundly Handicapped Persons." *Education and Training of the Mentally Retarded,* 14: 50–58.

Wehman, P., and S. Schleien (1980b). Leisure Skills Programming for Severely Handicapped Children. In G. Cartlege and S. Cartwright (Eds.), *Teaching Social Skills to Exceptional Children*. New York, NY: Pergamon Press.

Speech Disorders

Adams, M. J., B. R. Foorman, I. Lundberg, and T. Beeler (1998). *Phonemic Awareness in Young Children—A Classroom Curriculum*. Baltimore, MD: Paul H. Brookes Publishing.

American Speech-Language-Hearing Association, 10801 Rockville Pike, Rock-ville, MD 20852.

Caruso, A. J., and E. A. Strand (1999). *Clinical Management of Motor Speech Disorders in Children*. New York, NY: Theime.

Chamberlain, C. E., and R. M. Strode (1999). *The Source for Down Syndrome*. East Moline, IL: Lingui Systems.

Layton, L., K. Deeny, and G. Upton (1998). *Sound Practice: Phonological Awareness in the Classroom*. London: David Fulton Publishers.

Nelson, N. W. (1998). *Childhood Language Disorders in Context*. Needham Heights, MA: Allyn & Bacon.

Owens, R. E. (1995). *Language Disorders*. Needham Heights, MA: Allyn & Bacon.

Peters, T. J., and B. Guitar (1991). *Stuttering: An Integrated Approach to Its Nature and Treatment*. Baltimore, MD: Williams and Wilkins.

Plante, E., and P. M. Beeson (1999). *Communication and Communication Disorders: A Clinical Introduction*. Needham Heights, MA: Allyn & Bacon.

Silverman, F. H. (1992). *Stuttering and Other Fluency Disorders*. Englewood Cliffs, NJ: Prentice Hall.

Van Riper, C. (1973). *The Treatment of Stuttering*. Englewood Cliffs, NJ: Prentice Hall.

Young, E. C. (1983). "A Language Approach to Treatment of Phonological Process Problems." *Language, Speech, and Hearing Services in Schools,* 14: 47–53.

Tourette's Disorder

Berecz, J. M. (1992). *Understanding Tourette Syndrome, Obsessive Compulsive Disorder and Related Problems: A Developmental and Catastophe Theory Perspective*. New York, NY: Springer Publishing.

Leckman, J. F. (1998). *Tourette's Syndrome—Tics, Obsessions, Compulsions: Developmental Psychopathology and Clinical Care*. New York, NY: John Wiley & Sons.

Robertson, M., and S. Baren-Cohen (1998). *Tourette Syndrome: The Facts*. London: Oxford University Press.

Trainable Mentally Impaired—Adolescent

Brimer, R. W. (1990). *Students with Severe Disabilities: Current Perspectives and Practices.* Mountain View, CA: Mayfield Publishing.

Browder, D. M. (1991). *Assessment of Individuals with Severe Disabilities.* Baltimore, MD: Paul H. Brookes Publishing.

Cipani, E. C., and F. Spooner (1994). *Curricular and Instructional Approaches for Persons with Severe Disabilities.* Needham Heights, MA: Allyn & Bacon.

Fredericks, H. D., S. Hanks, L. Makohon, C. Fruin, W. Moore, T. Piazza-Templeman, L. Blair, B. Dalke, P. Hawkins, M. Coen, S. Renfroe-Burton, C. Bunse, T. Farnes, C. Moses, J. Toews, A. M. McGuckin, B. Moore, C. Riggs, V. Baldwin, R. Anderson, V. Ashbacker, V. Carter, M. A. Gage, G. Rogers, and B. Samples (1980a). *The Teaching Research Curriculum for Moderately and Severely Handicapped: Gross and Fine Motor.* Springfield, IL: Charles C. Thomas.

Fredericks, H. D., L. Makohon, C. Fruin, W. Moore, T. Piazza-Templeman, L. Blair, B. Dalke, P. Hawkins, M. Coen, S. Renfroe-Burton, C. Bunse, T. Farnes, C. Moses, J. Toews, A. M. McGuchin, B. Moore, C. Riggs, V. Baldwin, R. Anderson, V. Ashbacker, V. Carter, M. A. Gage, G. Rogers, and B. Samples (1980b). *The Teaching Research Curriculum for Moderately and Severely Handicapped: Self-Help and Cognitive.* Springfield, IL: Charles C. Thomas.

Haugen, J. (1993). *Safety Skills: Learning to Be Careful.* San Antonio, TX: PCI.

Neel, R. S., and F. F. Billingsley (1989). *IMPACT: A Functional Curriculum Handbook for Students with Moderate to Severe Disabilities.* Baltimore, MD: Paul H. Brookes Publishing.

Olsen, J. Z. (1999). *Cursive Success.* Potomac, MD.

Slaggert, K. H., and A. E. Jongsma (2000). *The Mental Retardation and Developmental Disability Treatment Planner.* New York, NY: John Wiley & Sons.

Spellman, C. R., T. DeBriere, D. Jarboe, S. Campbell, and C. Harris (1978). Pictorial Instruction: Training Daily Living Skills. In M. E. Snell (Ed.), *Systematic Instruction of the Moderately and Severely Handicapped* (pp. 391–411). Columbus, OH: C. E. Merrill.

Wehman, P. (1981). *Competitive Employment.* Baltimore, MD: Paul H. Brookes Publishing.

Wehman, P., and S. Schleien (1980a). "Assessment and Selection of Leisure Skills for Severely and Profoundly Handicapped Persons." *Education and Training of the Mentally Retarded,* 14: 50–58.

Wehman, P., and S. Schleien (1980b). Leisure Skills Programming for Severely Handicapped Children. In G. Cartlege and S. Cartwright

(Eds.), *Teaching Social Skills to Exceptional Children.* New York, NY: Pergamon Press.

Will, M. C. (1984). *OSERS Programming for the Transition of Youth with Disabilities: Bridges from School to Working Life.* Washington, DC: Office of Special Education and Rehabilitation Services, U.S. Department of Education.

Trainable Mentally Impaired—Child

Brimer, R. W. (1990). *Students with Severe Disabilities: Current Perspectives and Practices.* Mountain View, CA: Mayfield Publishing.

Cipani, E., and F. Spooner (1994). *Curricular and Instructional Approaches for Persons with Severe Disabilities.* Needham Heights, MA: Allyn & Bacon.

Olsen, J. Z. (1999). *Handwriting Without Tears/Cursive Success.* Potomac, MD.

Quigley, S. P., C. M. King, P. L. McAnally, and S. Rose (1991). *Reading Milestones.* Austin, TX: ProEd.

Spellman, C. R., T. DeBriere, D. Jarboe, S. Campbell, and C. Harris (1978). Pictorial Instruction: Training Daily Living Skills. In M. E. Snell (Ed.), *Systematic Instruction of the Moderately and Severely Handicapped* (pp. 391–411). Columbus, OH: C. E. Merrill.

Taylor, G. R. (1998). *Curriculum Strategies for Teaching Social Skills to the Disabled.* Springfield, IL: Charles C. Thomas.

Traumatic Brain Injury

Clark, E. (1996). "Children and Adolescents with Traumatic Brain Injury: Reintegration Challenges in Educational Settings." *Journal of Learning Disabilities,* 29(6): 633–642.

Glang, A., G. Singer, and B. Todis (1997). *Students with Acquired Brain Injury: The School's Response.* Baltimore, MD: Paul H. Brookes Publishing.

Glang, A., B. Todis, E. Coolery, J. Wells, and J. Voss (1997). "Building Social Networks for Children and Adolescents with Traumatic Brain Injury: A School-Based Intervention." *Journal of Head Trauma Rehabilitation,* 12(2): 32–47.

Goldberg, A. L. (1996). *Acquired Brain Injury in Childhood and Adolescence: A Team and Family Guide to Educational Program Development and Implementation.* Springfield, IL: Charles C. Thomas.

Shelton, T., A. Anastopoulous, and J. Linden (1985). "An Attribution Training Program with Learning Disabled Children." *Journal of Learning Disabilities,* 18(5): 261–265.

Singer, G. S., A. Glang, and J. M. Williams (Eds.). (1996). *Children with Acquired Brain Injury: Educating and Supporting Families.* Baltimore, MD: Paul H. Brookes Publishing.

Violent and Dangerous

Bemak, F., and S. Keys (2000). *Violent and Aggressive Youth: Intervention and Prevention Strategies for Changing Times.* Thousand Oaks, CA: Corwin Press.

Caraulia, A. G., and L. Steiger (1997). *Nonviolent Crisis Intervention.* Brookfield, WI: Crisis Prevention Publishing.

Curwin, R. L., and A. N. Mendler (1997). *As Tough As Necessary: Countering Violence, Aggression, and Hostility in Our Schools.* Alexandria, VA: Association for Supervision and Curriculum Development.

Curwin, R. L., and A. N. Mendler (1988). *Discipline With Dignity.* Alexandria, VA: Association for Supervision and Curriculum Development.

Eggert, L. (1995). *Anger Management for Youth: Stemming Aggression and Violence.* Bloomington, IN: National Educational Service.

Ford, E. E. (1997). *Discipline for Home and School, Book One.* Scottsdale, AZ: Brandt Publishing.

Ford, E. E. (1999). *Discipline for Home and School, Book Two.* New York, NY: Mass Market Paperback.

Forehand, R. L., and R. J. McMahon (1981). *Helping the Noncompliant Child: A Clinician's Guide to Parent Training.* New York, NY: Guilford Press.

Goldstein, A. (1999). *The Prepare Curriculum: Teaching Prosocial Competence.* Champaign, IL: Research Press.

Goldstein, A. P., B. Glick, and J. C. Gibbs (1998). *Aggression Replacement Training—A Comprehensive Intervention for Aggressive Youth.* Champaign, IL: Research Press.

Goldstein, A. P., and E. McGinnis (1997). *Skillstreaming the Adolescent: New Strategies and Perspectives for Teaching Prosocial Skills.* Champaign, IL: Research Press.

Horne, A. M., and T. V. Sayger (1990). *Treating Conduct and Oppositional Defiant Disorders in Children.* New York, NY: Pergamon Press.

Johns, B. H., and V. G. Carr (1995). *Techniques for Managing Verbally and Physically Aggressive Students.* Denver, CO: Love Publishing.

Lochman, J. E., S. E. Dunn, and S. Klimes-Dougan (1993). "An Intervention and Consultation Model from a Social Cognitive Perspective: A Description of the Anger Coping Program." *School Psychology Review,* 22(3): 458–471.

Lochman, J. E., L. B. Lampion, T. C. Gemmer, and S. R. Harris (1987). Anger Coping Intervention with Aggressive Children: A Guide to Implementation in School Settings. In P. A. Keller and S. R. Heyman (Eds.), *Innovations in Clinical Practice: A Source Book* (Vol. 6, pp. 339–356). Sarasota, FL: Professional Resource Exchange.

Marlowe, H., J. B. Reid, G. R. Patterson, M. R. Weinrott, and L. Bank (1988). *A Comparative Evaluation of Parent Training for Families of Chronic Delinquents.* Manuscript submitted for publication.

Michigan Department of Education—Office of Special Education and Early Intervention Services (2000). *Positive Behavior Support for ALL Michigan Students: Creating Environments That Assure Learning.* Charlotte, MI: Eaton Intermediate School District.

Nelson, R. O. (1988). "Relationships Between Assessment and Treatment Within a Behavioral Perspective." *Journal of Psychopathology and Behavioral Assessment,* 10: 155–170.

Patterson, G. R., J. B. Reid, R. R. Jones, and R. W. Conger (1975). *A Social Learning Approach to Family Intervention* (Vol. 1). Eugene, OR: Castalia.

Schneider, M., and A. Robin (1976). The Turtle Technique: A Method for the Self-Control of Impulsive Behavior. In J. Krumboltz and C. Thoreson (Eds.), *Counseling Methods* (pp. 157–162). New York, NY: Holt, Rinehart and Winston.

Webster-Stratton, C. (1993). "Strategies for Helping Early School-Aged Children with Oppositional Defiant and Conduct Disorders: The Importance of Home-School Partnerships." *School Psychology Review,* 22(3): 437–457.

Webster-Stratton, C. (1994). *Troubled Families—Problem Children: Working with Parents—A Collaborative Process.* New York, NY: John Wiley & Sons.

Visually Impaired and Blind

American Council for the Blind—Council of Families with Visual Impairment, 1515 15th St., N.W., Suite 720, Washington, DC 20005, (800) 424-8666.

Best, A. B. (1992). *Teaching Children with Visual Impairments.* Bristol, PA: Open University Press.

Bishop, V. E. (1971). *Teaching the Visually Limited Child.* Springfield, IL: Charles C. Thomas.

Etheridge, D., and H. Mason (1994). *The Visually Impaired: Curricular Access and Entitlement in Further Education.* London: David Fulton Publishers.

Millar, S. (1997). *Reading by Touch.* New York, NY: Routledge.

National Association for Parents of the Visually Impaired, Inc., P.O. Box 317, Watertown, MA 02272-0317, (800) 562-6265.

National Federation of the Blind—National Organization of Parents of Blind Children, 1800 Johnson St., Baltimore, MD 21230, (410) 659-9314.

Pogrund, R. L., D. L. Fazzi, and J. S. Lampert (1992). *Early Focus: Working with Young Blind and Visually Impaired Children and Their Families.* New York, NY: American Foundation for the Blind.

Pugh, G. S., and J. Erin (Eds.). (1999). *Blind and Visually Impaired Students: Educational Service Guidelines.* Watertown, MA: Perkins School for the Blind.

Sacks, S. Z., L. S. Kekelis, and R. J. Gaylord-Ross (1992). *The Development of Social Skills by Blind and Visually Impaired Students.* New York, NY: American Foundation for the Blind.

Trief, E. (Ed.). (1992). *Working with Visually Impaired Young Students: A Curriculum Guide for Birth–3 Year Olds.* Springfield, IL: Charles C. Thomas.

Webster, A., and J. Roe (1998). *Children with Visual Impairments.* New York, NY: Routledge.

Written Expression

Daily Oral Language, Daily Oral Math, Daily Oral Geography. Wilmington, MA: Great Source Education Group.

Deschler, D. D., and J. B. Schumaker (1986). "Learning Strategies: An Instructional Alternative for Low Achieving Adolescents." *Exceptional Children,* 52(6): 583–590.

Fernald, G. M. (1988). *Remedial Techniques in Basic School Subjects: Methods for Teaching Dyslexics and Other Learning Disabled.* Austin, TX: ProEd.

Gillingham, A., and B. W. Stillman (1966). *Remedial Training for Children with Specific Disability in Reading, Spelling and Penmanship.* Cambridge, MA: Educators Publishing.

Haggard, M. R. (1986b). "The Vocabulary Self-Collection Strategy: Using Student Interest and Word Knowledge to Enhance Vocabulary Growth." *Journal of Reading,* 29: 634–642.

Hubbard, R. S., and K. Ernst (1996). *New Entries: Learning By Writing and Drawing.* Portsmouth, NH: Heinemann.

International Reading Association, P.O. Box 8139, Newark, DE 19714.

Johnson, D. J., and H. R. Myklebust (1967). *Learning Disabilities: Educational Principles and Practices.* New York, NY: Grune & Stratton.

Meltzer, L. J., B. N. Roditi, D. P. Haynes, K. R. Biddle, M. Paster, and S. E. Taber (1996). *Strategies For Success.* Austin, TX: ProEd.

Morsink, C. V. (1987). *Teaching Special Needs Students in Regular Classrooms.* New York, NY: Harper Collins College.

Olsen, J. Z. (1999). *Handwriting Without Tears Curriculum.* Potomac, MD:

Ruddell, M. R. (1993). *Teaching Content Reading and Writing.* Needham Heights, MA: Allyn & Bacon.

Ryder, R. J., and M. F. Graves (1994). *Reading and Learning in Content Areas.* New York, NY: Macmillan College Publishing.

Spafford, C. S., and G. S. Grosser (1996). *Dyslexia: Research and Resource Guide.* Needham Heights, MA: Allyn & Bacon.

Topping, K. J. (1995). "Cued Spelling: A Powerful Technique for Parent and Peer Tutoring." *The Reading Teacher,* 48: 374–383.

Wolfe, D., and R. Reising (1983). *Writing for Learning in the Content Areas.* Portland, ME: J. Weston Walch.